LEISURE AND CLASS IN VICTORIAN ENGLAND

STUDIES IN SOCIAL HISTORY

Editor: HAROLD PERKIN

Professor of Social History, University of Lancaster

Assistant Editor: ERIC J. EVANS

Lecturer in History, University of Lancaster

For a list of books in the series see back endpaper

LEISURE AND CLASS IN VICTORIAN ENGLAND

Rational recreation and the contest for control,
1830–1885

Peter Bailey

Department of History
University of Manitoba

LONDON: Routledge & Kegan Paul
TORONTO AND BUFFALO: University of Toronto Press

First published in 1978
in Great Britain
by Routledge & Kegan Paul Ltd
and in Canada and the United States of America by
University of Toronto Press
Toronto and Buffalo
Printed in Great Britain by
Redwood Burn Limited
Trowbridge & Esher
Copyright © Peter Bailey 1978

British Library Cataloguing in Publication Data

Bailey, Peter, b. 1937
Leisure and class in Victorian England – (Studies
in social history).
1. Recreation – Great Britain History –
19th century
I. Title   II. Series

301.5'7'0941   GV75   78-40390

RKP ISBN 0 7100 8849 3
UTP ISBN 0 8020 2258 8

In memory of Cec

Contents

Acknowledgments

The writing of this book has been a protracted and mostly solitary endeavour. Though I may have unwittingly rubbed shoulders with the greats in the anonymous intimacy of the British Museum Reading Room and the various waterholes in its vicinity, I have had no readily available group of fellow social historians of the period to use as a sounding board for my work, no intellectual kitchen cabinet to expedite the painful process whereby the tyro's half-baked ideas cohere into a sufficiently substantial dish to set before a wider public. But if therefore my errors be legion, my acknowledgments are few.

I do owe a considerable debt to the often dauntingly high quality work of many of the scholars who have pioneered the social history of the period, in this and complementary fields, and my gratitude on this account is particularised in the notes. I am also grateful to Dr John Norris for his sympathetic and effective supervision of my 1974 University of British Columbia thesis which provided the basis for this book. For various other forms of encouragement, kindness and assistance I would like to thank Eric Sager, Jim Winter, Ed Hundert, Raphael Samuel, Margaret Elsworth, Mrs Zena Ward, the editors of this series, and John 'The Throat' Blackwell. I have also to thank 'Victorian Studies' and the Trustees of Indiana University for their permission to reproduce in chapters 3 and 4 material which formed a substantial part of my article of autumn 1977, 'A mingled mass of perfectly legitimate pleasures': the Victorian middle class and the problem of leisure. I am further indebted to the Canada Council and the University of Manitoba Research Board for the generous financial assistance without which this study could have been neither undertaken nor brought to conclusion. Canada in general has been good to me.

My greatest debt is to my wife Bonnie, who has shared

much of the burden of this enterprise; in addition to her
considerable secretarial skills she has provided just the
right mix of psychological support and petticoat government to keep the self-doubting writer at his task. We
look forward to savouring some leisure of our own.

Winnipeg   P.C.B.
1978

Introduction

Leisure is widely recognised as an increasingly significant component of life in modern Western society and has
for some time been given serious attention by sociologists
and a variety of social commentators and planners, yet it
is an area which until recently has been greatly neglected
by historians. In the latters' conventional hierarchy of
human activities, leisure has most often been a mere ap-
pendix, an unexplored and scarcely acknowledged minor
tributary to the mainstream of history. The subject has
been left to the amateur student of manners, the antiquarian or the folklorist, whose enthusiasms and industry
have rarely been matched by any regard for historical perspective or social context. Within the last few years,
however, the increasing range and confidence of the modern
social historian (a pullulating breed) have brought several aspects of the field under scholarly examination. In
the new canon of studies, leisure time and its activities
are acknowledged as a significant element of social experience, whose history is of particular importance in the
broader exercise of reconstructing the kind of life lived
by the ordinary people of the past. To this end, the main
focus of recent attention has been on popular rather than
élitist recreations, though the best of the new work has
been concerned to understand them not only in the context
of their own culture but in relation to the structure of
society as a whole and the wider patterns of social
change. From such endeavours in modern British studies
some kind of intelligible and coherent map of the field
is emerging.
    It is obvious from early reconnaissance that the
nineteenth century saw great changes in popular leisure
patterns in Britain as part of a fundamental transformation in the culture of an industrial working class.
According to Briggs and Hobsbawm, the 1830s and 1840s

1

were the 'dark age' of working-class culture (a phrase
which echoes the diagnosis of the Hammonds - honourable
exceptions to the rule of previous scholarly neglect).
In these decades an older, pre-industrial culture broke
up, leaving amid its wreckage many of the people's traditional recreations. Another culture formed, better
adapted to the milieu of a modern urban industrial
society, and by the last quarter of the century the
British working class were settled into a new way of life
which boasted a distinctive new range of popular recreations - music halls, association football, seaside holidays and the like - recreations which, as Hobsbawm points
out, have become so familiar to us that they have in turn
come to be regarded as 'traditional'. In the 1890s, it is
suggested, a cluster of new techniques in communications
and the complementary development of modern advertising
and consumer capitalism signalled a further phase in the
history of leisure, when a virtual leisure industry
emerged to shape and service the mass culture of the
twentieth century. (1)

This elementary schema is gradually being filled out.
In particular, our knowledge of the world of traditional
or pre-industrial leisure has been enhanced by Robert
Malcolmson's account of English popular recreations in the
eighteenth and early nineteenth centuries. Here we learn
of a robust and ritualistic popular culture rooted in the
tightly knit, inward-looking world of the country village,
its calendar generously studded with festivals and holidays that derived their warranty and meaning from an intimate connexion with the seasonal rhythms of the agricultural year and the working life of the community. In
common with other pre-industrial societies there was no
clear-cut division between labour and leisure and the
daily round was seasoned with a good deal of complementary
sociability. The material apparatus of recreation was
rudimentary and for the most part freely available from
the common resources of the community. With little discrimination between generation or sex the people made
their own amusement, though itinerant professional entertainers often contributed to the excitement of local fairs
and wakes. Popular leisure was public and gregarious, and
both its great and small occasions were heavily bound by
the prescriptive ties of communal custom reinforced by a
powerful oral tradition. The general good humour of the
common people at play was punctuated at fairly regular
intervals by the rituals of violence and excess: cruelty
to animals and other kinds of brutality were commonplace
as entertainment, and certain major holidays evoked the
ancient licence of carnival when all social restraints on

ch, intro

the human appetite were lifted and eating, drinking,
fighting and love-making were celebrated in orgiastic
fashion. On such occasions, too, the authority structure
of village society could be temporarily inverted in the
time-honoured ceremonies of saturnalia - the common man
was king for the day and the world was turned upside down,
as villagers thumbed their noses (and worse) at their
betters. Far from taking offence, the governing classes
tolerated and often patronised these and other popular
festivities; as Malcomson and others show, their goodwill
was in part a reflection of their own membership of the
village community, in part a recognition of the utility of
such rites in dissipating popular frustrations and thus
reinforcing the authority of the rural oligarchy. Though
we have no similar account for London and the big towns
where social life was obviously more diverse and volatile,
it seems clear enough that popular recreations there displayed many of the same characteristics. Work and leisure
intermingled in the life of the workshop where traditional
craft practices laid down the ritual patterns of celebration and good fellowship. The symbiosis of town and
country in this era meant that the seasonal flux of urban
leisure carried a strong echo of the cyclical rhythms of
the agricultural year. Certainly many of the town
worker's recreations were bucolic in form and inspiration
and displayed a similar zest for the brutal and the carni-
valesque; this also was likely to be indulged by an urban
ruling class which recognised the stabilising effect of
intervals of licence. (2)
    We are dealing with the institutions of a predominantly
stable and conservative society, but as Malcolmson shows,
the complex of powerful social changes that overtook
English society in the eighteenth century undermined the
material and cultural base of the traditional way of life
and began the breakdown of the old pattern of popular
recreations. The Enclosure movement, the growth of
cities, the rise of evangelicalism and the rigorous disciplining of labour under the new industrial capitalism destroyed the old community of interest and generated a new
temper among the ruling class; thus their paternalist
tolerance now gave way to a sour impatience with plebeian
culture as morally offensive, socially subversive, and a
general impediment to progress. From the middle of the
eighteenth century folk recreations came under direct
attack from a new puritanism and Malcomson describes the
growing momentum of class hostility that hastened their
demise amid the general dislocation of traditional
culture. Though the area lies outside his chosen brief,
he alludes to the even greater severity of the crisis in

the big towns and cities. Thus we are back again in the
dark or bleak age of the second quarter of the nineteenth
century, on the brink of that reconstruction of popular
leisure which takes place after 1850 and the closing of
Malcolmson's enquiry.

Though some significant contributions are beginning to
appear and a small army of researchers are beavering away
off-stage, we have nothing like a comprehensive account of
this next phase. What we do have, however, from historians as well as sociologists, is a sharper awareness of the
proposition that leisure took on a fundamentally new form
and meaning in this era. The demands of mechanised
factory production and the accelerated growth of big
cities led to a radical restructuring of the temporal and
spatial patterns of economic and social life. 'During the
industrial revolution', observes de Grazia, 'leisure
disappeared under an avalanche of work.' When it re-
emerged it had not only been reduced but relocated in the
life-space, forming a separate and self-contained sector
in an increasingly compartmentalised way of life. Work
and leisure were no longer intertwined in the continuum
of shared activities that characterised the daily and
yearly round within the closed world of the small and
homogeneous traditional community. In the populous and
extensive industrial city, leisure was time clearly marked
off from work, to be pursued elsewhere than in the
workplace and its environs, and undertaken in company no
longer in the nature of things comprised predominantly of
workmates. Moreover, the activities of this leisure time
were no longer regulated as a whole by the tight mores and
collective obligations of traditional social life. Thus
the characteristic recreations of the second half of the
nineteenth century were radically different from their
predecessors: not only were they in many cases the
products of a new technology and new social groupings, but
they now took place within the unique circumstances of
modern leisure, a condition of individual free choice specific to industrial society and a qualitatively new di-
mension in the experience of the masses. When a man
walked out of the factory gates in the big industrial city
he was in a sense freer than in any previous age. (3)

In this respect then, modern leisure made its début in
Victorian England, the first mature industrial society.
Of course, it was not all so cut and dried: the creature
of custom that was the homo ludens of traditional culture
was not transformed overnight into the free agent of an
atomistic modern world. Traditional modes and mentalities
persisted, community norms in one way or another were
maintained, and severe material constraints often made a

mockery of leisure's putative freedoms. We are dealing in
what might be called the sophisticated crudity of an ideal
typology that needs elaborating, qualifying and, above
all, humanising. Yet by the second half of the century
leisure was to a significant degree an area of relative
autonomy in the everyday life of all classes - 'a sort of
neutral ground which we may fairly call our own', as one
Victorian cleric observed neatly in the 1870s. (4)
    It was, however, precisely this feature of leisure which
made its growth a source of considerable tension as well
as gratification, for this fluid and open territory
threatened to outstrip the reach of existing systems of
social control. The middle class, as the most substantial
beneficiaries of the new bonus, were themselves uneasy
about the potentially corrupting effect of leisure on the
internal disciplines of their own class; all the more so
then were they apprehensive about the effects of leisure
and its freedoms on a working class with a traditional
taste for wantonness and an uncertain allegiance to the
authority of its betters. Viewed from above, leisure
constituted a problem whose solution required the building
of a new social conformity - a play discipline to complement the work discipline that was the principal means of
social control in an industrial capitalist society. In
contrast to the harsh offensive of the earlier period of
industrialisation, however, this policy was now to be
pursued through the reform of popular recreations rather
than their repression; but this more liberal disposition
did not ensure it an easy passage in a society with a
recent history of severe class conflict, for working
people evinced a determination to make their own leisure
in ways which resisted assimilation to middle-class ideology. In trying to respectabilise popular leisure,
reformers also met with hostility and competition from
powerful vested interests in working-class life - most
notably the licensed trade, for whom the traditional ap-
purtenances of popular recreation, most notably strong
drink, represented both a basic livelihood and a chance
to exploit fat new commercial opportunities. Leisure was
one of the major frontiers of social change in the
nineteenth century, and like most frontiers it was dis-
puted territory.
    This book examines the contest and interaction between
these social forces and the part they played in creating
the new leisure world of Victorian England during the
fifty years or so of cultural reconstruction from the
1830s to the 1880s. It describes the indigenous process
of renewal in popular culture, and the ways in which the
working class realised the freedoms of modern leisure amid

the unique complex of opportunities and constraints that
defined an urban industrial society;   attention is given
here to themes of continuity as well as change, and the
climacteric of the 'dark age' is looked at for evidence
of growth as well as destruction.   In turn the book in-
vestigates the role of the middle-class activists who
sought to shape working-class choice by providing an alternative world of reformed recreations which would immu-
nise workers against the alleged degenerations of their
own culture and counter the more corrupt appeals of an
embryonic leisure industry;   here I have considered the
reform ideal in relation to the changing experience and
significance of leisure in the lives of the middle class
in general.   After examining the cultural politics of
three specific areas of development in popular recreation,
the Working Men's Club movement, the new athleticism and
the music hall, the book concludes with a consideration of
the significance of leisure for the broader questions of
class relationships and consciousness in Victorian society.
    If at times I have talked of leisure in a loose and
common-sense fashion as man's general pursuit of enjoyment
or some such readily identifiable social phenomenon I have
none the less had in mind throughout this book the soci-
ologist's more specific usage of the term.   Defining
leisure in this company can be a complex and controversial
exercise, but leaving aside the idealism of the neo-
classicists and the more obvious ambiguities the arguments
seem to reduce to two main propositions: modern leisure
is a certain kind of time spent in a certain kind of way.
The time is that which lies outside the demands of work,
direct social obligations and the routine activities of
personal and domestic maintenance;   the use of this time,
though socially determined, is characterised by a high
degree of personal freedom and choice. (5)   The Victorians
talked less about leisure than recreation (in itself a
significant preference) and this term also carries a
specialised meaning for some of today's writers.   I have
explained at certain points in the text the particular
sense in which Victorians could use the word, but in
general I have simply taken recreation or its plural to
denote those activities and interests that form the typical occupations of leisure time.
    The campaign for improved recreation - rational recre-
ation - was a piecemeal operation which was part of a
broader front comprising the more clearly defined and
institutionalised movements for temperance and educational
reform.   Abstinence and edification were common prescriptions of rational recreation, but I have paid more

attention to reform schemes which were sensitive to the
popular need for recreation in entertainment, play and
relaxation. Source material for this kind of study is
abundant but diffuse. The state of popular recreation
was a perennial topic of public comment but its discussion
was often incidental to that of other issues. Certain
reform schemes generated their own literature and particular sports and entertainments were often served by a
specialist press, but there is no single major corpus of
documents. I have had, therefore, to track chronicle and
debate over a wide area, through an extensive sampling of
press and periodicals, reports of government committees,
sermons and pamphlet literature, works of social commentary, memoirs, novels and ephemera. To a considerable
extent I have let the Victorians speak for themselves,
attempting to catch the authentic voice from below as well
as that of the official or dominant culture. This book is
not meant to be a comprehensive leisure history of the
period (such a work is a long way off), but I have tried
to capture the essentials of the common experience of
leisure in urban and metropolitan England in these years,
while providing a modest running case study in local
history in the references to Bolton, Lancashire as a typical new industrial town. I should add, too, that I have
left quantification to others - as an individual and a
historian I am by temperament and talent a craft worker
not a technician.

1

Popular Recreation in the Early Victorian Town

The early historians of England as an urban industrial
society have left us with an overall picture of popular
recreation which is cramped and joyless - the Hammonds,
for example, concluded that 'the new towns were built for
a race that was allowed no leisure.... recreation was
waste' - yet, while it must be recognised that the town
worker suffered from lack of time and space for recreation, and that the amusements of the poor were still
under frequent attack from the superior classes, what is
just as remarkable is the vitality and adaptability displayed by popular recreation under these siege conditions.
(1)

I

In seeking first to demonstrate the vitality of popular
recreation in this period, one must allow that the evidence for this does in part help to confirm the Hammonds'
picture of gross deprivation. Foreigners had frequently
been alarmed at the exuberance of the Englishman at play -
a Frenchman who witnessed a football game in Derby in 1829
was moved to remark that, if Englishmen called this
playing, it would be impossible to say what they would
call fighting - but it becomes clear enough that such occasions were often now formless and convulsive compensations for the strains of a coercive industrial society,
rather than the ritualised exercises of a traditional
popular hedonism. The new industrial wage-earner was
still in a minority in the workforce, but the unprecedented regularity and intensity that characterised his
working hours were gradually being demanded of all
sections of the labouring population and, in general, the
pattern of tension and release in working life had become

tauter. Contemplating Manchester in 1844 another
Frenchman, Léon Faucher, was much disturbed at the im-
moderation in all things which characterised the new industrial Englishman. He thought that overworking was a
malady which Lancashire had inflicted on the whole
country; it was balanced only by another extreme, the
incontinence of the Englishman's recreation. 'They cannot
partake of anything in moderation; they must partake of
it to repletion.' Francis Place, recalling the grinding
demands placed on his early working life, remembered how
he would tear himself away from his work and rush out to
some park or open space in the city for a brief respite
before 'returning to his vomit'. Given such experience,
he professed himself well able to understand the reactions
of the 'uninformed man', and the latter's urgent need 'to
procure the excitement which MUST be procured'. Looking
back at the improvement in manners from the vantage point
of 1867, two students of working-class life recalled the
pattern of the 1830s as one of 'noisy, drunken riot ...
alternated with sullen, silent work'. (2)

Noise and drink were common accompaniments of popular
recreation - in some minds no doubt their dual presence
thereby constituted a riot - but they did not always or
necessarily indicate a simple reflex action of despair to
the grinding tedium of work. Mention of them should,
however, remind us that working-class leisure was for the
most part public and gregarious, and that its principal
everyday setting was that of the public house. As an old
workingman pointed out in recalling conditions in industrial Yorkshire in the 1830s: (3)

> There were only two places to go in spending spare time
> away from one's own house - church, chapel or alehouse;
> the former were seldom open, while the latter was
> seldom closed. The first was not attractive, the
> second was made attractive.

Among the attractions of the pub were a great variety of
recreations which brought enrichment as well as escape to
the life of the town worker.

Reports in Bolton's local press reveal how diverse and
extensive were the activities held in the pub or its
gardens: bowling, quoiting, glee clubs and free and
easies, amateur and professional dramatics, fruit and
vegetable shows, flower shows, sweepstake clubs and the
meetings of trades' and friendly societies. (4) The
latter occasions combined business with pleasure, and
serve as an example of how the pull of the public house as
the institutional hub of working-class recreation was
reinforced by the wide range of social and economic
services which it offered. The pub served as a labour ex-

change, a pay station and a port of call for the tramping
artisan. Initiation into particular trades and other
customs of the workplace still often demanded the treating
of workmates, which tied men further to the credit of the
local pub. For the single man in lodgings the pub was the
closest thing to a home - here he would take his meals and
read the newspapers. And always there was beer - 'the
friendly mug of beer' - which, as Charles Booth later
remarked, 'was the primordial cell of British social
life'. Thus in an age of social dislocation the pub
remained a centre of warmth, light and sociability for
the urban poor, a haven from the filth and meanness of
inadequate and congested housing, a magnet for the disori-
ented newcomer and the disgruntled regular alike. 'There
is plenty of gas and company to keep us alive', explained
the customers who were quizzed by an enquiring cleric;
'there is always society in the pubs, and the men there
are so very agreeable.' (5)
     The most prominent among the many clubs and associ-
ations which met on pub premises were the friendly societies. Their activities were well reported in Bolton where
membership grew during the 1830s and 1840s despite
frequent hard times, and in 1850 there were over 200
lodges of the various societies in the town. Sociability
and entertainment were among the prime functions of these
fraternities of working people and the 'Grand Lodge Circular' of the Bolton Oddfellows records the recitations and
songs with which members regaled one another throughout
the year, but the annual feasts were the great occasions.
As many as thirty or forty might be held on a single
night, with the lodge banners decorated with evergreens
flying from the pub windows. Foot races and dancing were
held in the street, but it was the inner man (and woman)
who came first, for it was food and drink in abundance
which marked the successful anniversary. (6) The staples
of roast beef and strong ale were not merely customary -
they were part of the birthright of the freeborn
Englishman; 'a mechanic at a feast', noted a contemporary, 'thinks himself scurvily used if he is supplied with
less than a gallon of strong ale.' (7)
     But as the previous inventory of activities demon-
strates, pub life was not all cakes and ale, and there
was enough 'rationality' in popular recreation inside and
outside the pub, to secure the acknowledgement of middle-
class contemporaries alert to such qualities. In Nottingham, reported James Hudson, in his survey of adult education written in 1851, 'there are several Working Men's
libraries HELD IN PUBLIC HOUSES' (the emphasis seems more
intended to counter the incredulity of the reader than to

underline the exceptional). 'At two of these houses',
Hudson continued, 'political discussions are also held
under judicious regulations.' A churchman in Bolton recorded how two workingmen explained their absence from a
Sunday lecture at chapel – they were attending a discussion at their local pub on the existence of God. From
Manchester, Faucher reported that Handel and Haydn were
'as household words' in the manufacturing districts of
Lancashire; there was no difficulty in raising choirs
among the factory operatives. (8) The popularity of clubs
and choirs confirms the continuing communal nature of
working-class recreation, but one must note here too the
already familiar exception of the working-class solitary:
Job Legh, the weaver botanist, in Mrs Gaskell's 'Mary
Barton'; Joseph Gutteridge, a weaver from real life who
studied natural history in the fields around Coventry;
Charles Manby Smith, a journeyman printer from London, who
painted water-colours and studied the pianoforte. (9) In
these and certain other interests individual workingmen
found a private freedom of expression in their leisure
time. Thus literate and intellectual interests coexisted
with the more boisterous traditional recreations among a
working class whose culture had been as much stimulated as
disrupted by economic upheaval and social conflict. Whatever the partisan emphasis, Samuel Bamford's pride in
listing the accomplishments of his Lancashire workmates in
1844 seems well justified: (10)

they are the greatest readers; can show the greatest
number of good writers; the greatest number of sensible and considerate public speakers. They can show a
greater number of botanists; a greater number of
horticulturists, a greater number who are acquainted
with the abstruse sciences; the greatest number of
poets, and a greater number of good musicians, whether
choral or instrumental.

II

Together with this resilient and diverse vitality, popular
recreation displayed the further strength of adaptibility,
as revealed in the response to those constraints noted by
the Hammonds: the curtailment of time and space, and the
hostility of the superior classes.
    Conditions of regular employment in the manufacturing
towns appeared to allow only the merest scrapings of free
time. In the previous century normal working hours had
been long enough – ten hours was the traditional day's
labour – and in many trades the week had culminated in a

feverish climax of activity to catch market deadlines, but
the rhythm of work had been largely self-imposed and often
leisurely, weekends had been elastic and holidays numerous. The stricter work discipline of capitalist production had severely curtailed such liberalities. (11)
In 1840 the prominent factory inspector, Leonard Horner,
found that the twelve-hour working day that was now normal
in textile mills left the worker 'utterly unfit for anything like mental improvement ... and not very fit for
much social enjoyment with his family'. John Fielden, the
reforming manufacturer, was greatly struck by the testimony of a youngster in one of the mills that there was
'never any time to play'; another millowner admitted that
the time left for recreation and improvement after the
average working day was scarcely two hours. (12) Sunday
was the only day commonly free from work, but for the
working wife it was the one day available for the washing
and other accumulated domestic tasks; for the rest of the
family the propensity to stay in bed on a Sunday was no
doubt less a matter of choice than a necessary recruitment
of strength. (13) By 1834 there were only eight statutory
half-holidays in England, and the traditional calendar of
religious feast days and the celebrations of seasonal
tasks or particular trades had been considerably pruned,
both by the employers and the Church. (14)
    But the working classes stretched the meagre allowance
of free time. Sunday's leisure, for example, could still
be extended through the largesse of 'St Monday', who continued to claim many devotees. Disraeli recorded the
popularity of the extended weekend in describing the industrial town of Wodgate in 'Sybil, or the Two Nations',
his novel on the 'Condition of England' in the 1840s: (15)
    The social system is not an unvarying course of infi-
    nite toil. The plan is to work hard, but not always.
    The men seldom exceed four days of labour in the week.
    On Sunday the master workmen begin to drink; for the
    apprentices there is dog-fighting without stint. On
    Monday and Tuesday the whole population is drunk. Here
    is relaxation, excitement.
It was in the 1840s too that the factory commissioners
reported frequent occasions when extra holidays were conceded. 'It was', they remarked, 'not due to liberality on
the part of the masters, but to custom.' In one area of
Lancashire it was averred that the workers enjoyed a
fortnight's break at Christmas, a full week at Whitsun,
'three or four days at Ringley Wakes, about the same at
Ratcliff Races, and at odd times besides'. Often it was
sport as much as drink that was irresistible. Thus the
exploits of Ben Hart, Bolton's pedestrian champion of

these years, drew crowds which left the local mills half-
empty. From the Warwickshire pits a witness reported:
(16)

> When there is such a matter of universal interest as a
> prize fight most go to see it, and it is a day's play.
> Upon the average there may be five or six such oc-
> casions in the course of a summer.

Elections also occasioned impromptu holidays – when an MP
complained of a certain bill in 1828 which proposed to
limit the duration of elections, that 'it abridged the
constitutional enjoyments of the people', he was not referring to their rights of suffrage; similarly, 'The
Times' noted that the great reform demonstration in
Birmingham in 1833 had 'the appearance of a great fair ...
the excuse for making holyday'. (17) Also relevant here,
of course, is the measure of what might be called involun-
tary leisure in working-class life, when the work schedule
was interrupted by structural breakdowns in production,
seasonal drops in particular trades or periods of general
business depression. Though they rued the economic consequences, men habituated to such fluctuations must have developed some capacity for improvising casual diversions in
these breaks. In any case, enough has been said to nod in
agreement with one experienced contemporary who concluded
that the workingman 'possesses more facilities for getting
holidays than is generally supposed'. (18)

The practice of such time-honoured delinquencies as St
Monday obviously varied according to the economic setting.
In Disraeli's Wodgate (modelled on the lockmaking town of
Willenhall in Staffordshire) small workshops rather than
factories provided the typical work situation, and there
masters and men shared a common indulgence. Domestic
outworkers were less confined than factory hands – in
Bury in the 1830s the handloom weavers would drop their
work whenever the hounds passed by and join in the chase.
(19) Men in relatively minor trades, on the other hand,
might lack the numbers necessary to outface their employers – we learn from the 'Bolton Chronicle' for 9
August 1834 that five apprentice combmakers 'who seemed
to consider that they had a prescriptive right to a holiday on the Horse Fair Day' were successfully prosecuted
for absenteeism. Among factory workers, for whom industrial discipline was tightest, the claims of St Monday
and other unscheduled and illicit breaks were far from
extinguished, but here labour's principal response to the
new rigorism was that of organised protest rather than the
sporadic reaffirmation of traditional rights. The
northern textile workers' struggle for the Ten Hours Bill
(passed into law in 1847) was in a sense conservative, for

it sought a return to the traditional measure of a normal day's work, but its logic was modern and forward-looking. The movement implicitly acknowledged the separation of work and leisure into exclusive domains while trying to negotiate a more humane balance between the two; in principle labour was now prepared to accept the austere regimen of factory production in return for the guaranteed regularity of a fair level of leisure time.   The simultaneous demand for a Saturday half-holiday reflected the same philosophy and was supported by a substantial minority of employers who appreciated that such a concession on their part might not only win better attendance and punctuality in working hours, but might also effectively stabilise the workers' leisure within the fixed limits of a mutually defined weekend.   The 'short Saturday' written into the 1847 act was still eight hours long, but a further measure in 1850 obliged textile mills to cease work at 2 p.m. on Saturday and in Manchester the new hours soon became standard for most other trades.   Elsewhere these gains were still to be won, but in the north-west the modern English weekend was clearly taking shape. (20)

Restrictions on space were severe in the industrial town, and were more difficult to overcome.   Open space vanished before the march of bricks and mortar: in Coventry, the mayor complained of the enclosure of the town's open park which had deprived the young men of 'much active exercise' and driven them into the public house;   in Bolton, the gardeners' club, which had been formed to encourage workingmen's allotments, had become the preserve of gentlemen's gardeners from the suburbs as the patches of old cottage gardens disappeared from the town itself. (21)   One common resort, the pub garden, was vulnerable to the pressure on building space, rising ground rents and neighbours' complaints of the crowd nuisance.   In London, the somewhat more ambitious pleasure gardens, often descendants of eighteenth-century institutions, had long since lost their fashionable clientèle, and were similarly prone to complaints from the respectables. (22)   It is commonly suggested that even in the 1850s and 1860s few towns or cities were so large that the countryside was more than a few minutes' walk away.   It should be pointed out, however, that, on the evidence of Bolton, it seems that such an apparently simple excursion could be extremely hazardous where it meant negotiating the often hostile streets beyond one's immediate neighbourhood.   In any case, access to the countryside was further limited by the denial of footpath rights by the landowners. (23)

The most obvious escape from confinement was the mass breakout such as Dickens described in the Londoners'

'spring rush' to Greenwich Fair. Bolton held major fairs
in its market square at New Year and Whitsuntide, but
equally popular were the wakes, a succession of fairs
celebrated in late summer in the villages and townships
surrounding the borough. At Whitsun the country cousins
came to town and their awe at beholding the big city gave
the break its local title of 'Gaping Sunday'; in August
and September the flow was reversed and the town workers
burst out into the villages. (24) Race meetings were
other great occasions in the popular calendar. The
progress of the London crowds from the metropolis to
Epsom Downs on Derby Day was advertised by the huge
swirling cloud of dust which hung over their route. On
race days Mancunians debouched to Kersal Moor, the 'mons
sacer' of the cotton towns as Engels called it. Belle Vue
pleasure gardens (the scene of early brass band contests)
also provided an important outlet for Manchester. (25)
Trains and steamboats increased the range of the excursionist: a depressed Gravesend was revivified by
boatloads of London pleasure-seekers; hitherto remote
country race meetings, such as Goodwood, were inundated
with townspeople; the wakes at the Cheshire villages of
Hale and Tranmere were transformed into major proletarian
festivals by the regular descent of the Liverpool working
class from across the Mersey. From Bolton Henry Ashworth
reported on the excursion travels of his workpeople:
'They will go to Ireland, or London, or Scotland, wherever
the coach or the steamboat will carry them, and spend
their time rationally.' (26)
     Such occasions, however, provided only temporary
relief, and the problem of open space for everyday recreation and exercise remained chronic. As footpaths, public
gardens and common land were swallowed up or subjected to
a more exclusive interpretation of property rights, the
street alone was left as the new commons of the industrial
poor. Street life in the Victorian town and city was much
enlivened by the diversion and entertainment of its many
professional habitués: Punch and Judy men, buskers,
ballad hawkers (the 'flying stationers'), street
preachers, stump orators and patent medicine salesmen.
The street also provided an informal meeting place for
gossiping neighbours, and a seasonal promenade for the
young and flirtatious. In some cases traditional recreations were adjusted to suit its particular dimensions -
thus the processional Whit walks in northern England can
be seen as linear expressions of the round dances of the
village green. But traffic and pollution limited its
amenity, and the street was at best a constricted and
unsalutary playground. (27)

It was not just a problem of open space but of adequate
indoor facilities as well; moreover, as a corollary,
there was the problem of the increasing pressure of sheer
numbers. A London tradesman appearing before a parliamentary inquiry into drunkenness in 1834 made the point
that all the pubs seemed much fuller than ever he could
recall. When asked where the new customers came from he
replied simply enough: 'I think they came from the
current in the streets.' (28) Thus the pub was the
natural resting place for this increase in human traffic.
The pub changed to accommodate the increasing volume of
callers. Many old pubs were little more than the parlours
or kitchens of private houses, presided over by an ex-
butler or the like (when the Sedleys' business collapsed
in 'Vanity Fair' the butler, 'with the infatuation of his
profession', set up a pub); new pubs built in the 1830s -
the so-called gin palaces - were entirely different in
scale, in lay-out, in style and in management. They
solved the problem of space by doing away with seats;
this also discouraged dawdling, which in turn meant a more
rapid turnover in customers. Any feeling of congestion
among the new generation of 'perpendicular drinkers' was
relieved by an upward spaciousness provided by higher
ceilings and the illusion of roominess contrived by the
generous use of mirrors and plate glass. The huge gas
lamps (a feature which impressed itself so greatly on
contemporaries) hung outside as well as inside, and extended the territory of the pub into the street at all
hours of the night. A bar counter separated the customers
from the liquor and its dispensers, indicative of a more
businesslike approach by the proprietors, some of whom
were alleged to spend more time in the counting house than
waiting on their customers. That function was increasingly taken over by barmaids, who constituted as much of an
attraction as the elaborate fittings, and in some cases
were just as garish. The domesticity of the old pub had
given way to the commercialised glamour of new people's
palaces, gaudy compensations for the meanness of everyday
life. They were, as Dickens noted, 'invariably numerous
and splendid in precise proportion to the dirt and poverty
of the surrounding neighbourhood'. But in that they were
vast as well as spectacular they offered some solution to
the problem of the spatial as well as the social limitations of town life. (29)
Drinking, the simple company of the pub - these could
be a recreation in themselves; but the working population
demanded entertainment too. This was provided by the
'free and easy', an informal and predominantly amateur
sing-song of longstanding popularity in the history of the

pub, which was developed into a more formalised and frequent kind of tavern concert. Here again, new space was created by the more economical use of existing space: inn yards, billiard rooms, skittle alleys, even the publican's own sleeping quarters, were converted into 'singing saloons', the prototype music halls. (30)   At a London licensing session in 1834, a sympathetic magistrate passed the following comment on the new phenomenon: (31)

> He rejoiced in seeing so many applications for music licenses, as they proved the growing desire on the part of the public for intellectual and rational amusements. At the same time, he regretted the number of applications, as they proved that a power had too long been exercised to abridge popular recreations.

Such a remark brings us to a consideration of those who discerned little or no intellectual or rational content in the amusements of the people; their hostility constituted the other major constraint upon popular recreation.

III

The concern to police the amusements of the poor had a long history in English life but, as has been noted, it took on a new severity from the middle of the eighteenth century, and this preoccupation had scarcely lessened by the early Victorian period. Among its principal agents were the factory employers. In their drive for greater economy and efficiency they extended working hours, outlawed the traditional workshop pranks and diversions of the old craft culture - particularly those involving drink - and curtailed the number of local holidays. Some of the more single-minded of them used their considerable local influence to extend their surveillance beyond the factory and maintain a formidable discipline over their employees outside working hours. (32) More pervasive was the increasing influence of evangelicalism which by the 1830s had found support among clergy of all denominations and taken firm root in the middle classes. Its teachings stressed the need to strengthen personal and social standards of morality and evinced a deep suspicion of all worldly pleasures. In the Nonconformist churches its sentiments reinforced a long-standing hostility to traditional recreations, and the Methodists in particular were credited with some remarkable reforms of popular behaviour. (33) The Established Church, on the other hand, though it too had censured popular recreations in its time, had also traditionally been their patron - the northern wakes, for example, were originally parish

feasts, and the old holiday calendar was as much ecclesiastical as agrarian in inspiration. But during the
eighteenth century the Anglican clergy had increasingly
distanced themselves from plebeian culture and withdrawn
their patronage from its traditional festivities. Under
the influence of evangelicalism estrangement was converted
into an active hostility. In the 1820s this was accentu-
ated by leading churchmen anxious to exorcise the surviving image of the traditional sporting parson with his
love of field sports and country dancing. (Sidney Smith
parodied the new commandments against clerical worldliness
thus: 'Hunt not, fish not, shoot not, dance not, fiddle
not, flute not.') (34) So church and chapel, as the old
Yorkshireman had remarked, provided little for the
workingman's recreation and indeed condemned such that he
had. This greater censoriousness was noted in a snatch of
popular verse from Peacock:
   The poor man's delight
   Is a sore in the sight
   And a stench in the nose of piety.
   By the 1830s there were several active reform movements
- predominantly evangelical in inspiration and middle
class in membership - whose campaigns against certain
abuses in public life threatened the form and content of
much popular recreation. Principal targets were animal
cruelty, sabbath-breaking and intemperance. The Royal
Society for the Prevention of Cruelty to Animals included
in its brief the suppression of all blood sports, and its
inspectors were zealous in reporting infringements of the
act of 1835 which had made the sports illegal. The society played a prominent role in suppressing the traditional bull-running at Stamford in Lincolnshire in the
late 1830s, though many smaller-scale blood sports continued to flourish clandestinely. (35) The sabbatarians,
operating principally through the Lord's Day Observance
Society, offered a greater threat to popular recreation,
for they sought to close all institutions (including the
pub) which required the employment of labour on a Sunday,
or otherwise distracted the populace from attending
church. Sunday, as noted previously, was sanctified to
the working classes in other ways - it was generally the
one day a week which was regularly free for recreation and
domestic tasks. The cause was not popular in Parliament
and its proposals were often greeted with ridicule or
disdain, not least because its spokesman in the Commons,
Sir Andrew Agnew, had a peevish and almost inaudible
voice; in the street his bills were known as Agony Bills
which, according to vulgar wit, forbade even the working
of Epsom salts on a Sunday. But the sabbatarians were

well enough organised as a lobby and their flourish of
petitions ('greater than on any subject other than those
against West Indian slavery') earned them some deference
from succeeding administrations – they won select committees in 1831, 1847 and 1851, successfully postponed the
opening of the British Museum on a Sunday for over fifteen
years, and secured the passage of some important restrictive legislation in the mid-1850s. (36) The Temperance movement comprised many local and several national
organisations, but there was a common trend in the mid-
1830s away from general appeals for moderation in drink-
taking to an insistence upon complete abstention or tee-
totalism. The movement was split as to how this could
best be achieved, but its hostility to drink and its
purveyors cut at the roots of much popular recreation.
Its early champions in Parliament were received as de-
risively as Agnew, but out of doors the local organisations proved formidable in petitioning the magistracy
for the restriction of drink licences. (37) Temperance
reformers often formed a common front with sabbatarians
in opposing the Sunday opening of the pub.

It is clear that local authorities often played a major
part in abridging popular recreations, either on their own
initiative, or as servants (reluctant or otherwise) of the
reform interests. In Bolton, for example, the magistracy
proved amenable to a campaign by local clergy against the
leading singing saloon in the town, the Star Museum and
Concert Hall. In 1843 the proprietor, William Sharples,
was frustrated in his bid for a theatre licence for his
expensively remodelled premises by petitioners to the
bench led by Bolton's vicar, who complained of the degeneracy of the concert room. The following year the same
lobby secured a magistrate's order prohibiting Sunday performances at the Star. But the local millhands voted with
their feet and the Star's popularity continued to grow.
When the Star burnt down in 1852 church and chapel took
the lead in forming an anti-singing saloon association
pledged to prevent its resurrection, and successfully
petitioned at the annual brewster sessions for the sus-
pension of Sharples's licence. But the magistrates'
action is not necessarily evidence of a single-minded
concern for public morality, for a revealing commentary
in the 'Era', the national trade paper of the licensed
victuallers, claimed that the bench discriminated against
Sharples for political and commercial reasons: as Liberals, the magistrates were anxious to retain the chapel
vote in a forthcoming municipal election; as landlords
of other public houses in town, they were securing their
own tenants against the powerful competition of the Star.

(38) Elsewhere, as we have seen in the remarks of the
London JP quoted above, magistrates were actively sympathetic towards popular recreation - several who appeared
before the select committee on licensing in the early
1850s clearly recognised the adequate social controls
built into the singing saloons and were prepared to defend
them. On other occasions magistrates were respectful of
popular traditions; some invoked the Stuart 'Book of
Sports' in defence of Sunday sport and evinced great distaste for actions brought on the evidence of common informers, a frequent device of the sabbatarians. (39) Thus
there was obviously great local and individual variation
in the attitudes of the magistracy, though on balance they
were probably more repressive than benevolent.

     Other local bodies were frequently hostile to tra-
ditional amusements. In London, the Common Council in the
City (largely under the prompting of its Methodist con-
tingent, so we are told) strangled the historic
Bartholomew Fair by degrees. During the 1840s it raised
the rents for stall-holders, limited the duration of the
fair and succeeded in forcing it to use another, less convenient site. Thus 'old Bartlemy' was dead by 1854,
following the fate of several other London fairs (some
dispatched by private bills). (40) Robert Slaney, an MP
greatly concerned with the contraction of popular recreation, accused local authorities of allowing nuisances at
fairs to go unchecked in order to build up a case for
their complete suppression. (41) Municipal incorporation
in the mid-1830s gave office to a generation of council-
lors preoccupied with retrenchment, often at the expense
of traditional festivities - certainly the fat geese
roasted to celebrate success at Michaelmas elections
disappeared in most boroughs. Other administrative
rationalisations could trim away time-honoured local
recreations - W.E.Adams recalled how the introduction
of the new Poor Law in Cheltenham in the 1840s put an end
to the agreeable annual ritual of 'beating the bounds',
for it discontinued the subsidy which, under the old law,
had paid for the wagonloads of drink. Incorporation could
produce an officious local bureaucracy - in Bolton, the
new inspector of nuisances was indefatigable in his
campaign to exterminate pigeon-flying, already a popular
working-class sport. (42)

     The officers who had the greatest impact upon popular
recreations were the officers of the new police. They
were organised in both town and countryside during these
decades, following the model of Peel's reform of the
metropolitan police in 1829. Constables were soon a
prominent feature of the fairground and race track:

intercepting the Swell Mob, flushing out the pickpockets
and other small fry, and harassing the itinerant
showpeople whom they regarded as a cover for the criminal
nuisance. The police enforced the law against blood
sports. In Spitalfields in London, for example, they put
an end to the bull-running on Easter Monday, an occasion
which the old specials had been powerless to control. The
bobbies were also effective in curtailing other wild
sports, such as the Shrove Tuesday football game in Derby,
which engulfed the streets with its mob of players, but
which yielded to official limitations in 1846. (43)

There was considerable opposition to the introduction
of the new police from all levels of society, and there
is some indication that they were initially cautious in
interfering with popular pleasures; eventually, however,
it was only by conspicuous zeal in such matters that they
could justify their existence to the more cantankerous and
influential among the ratepayers. 'Where are the new
police?' became a common cry in letters to the Bolton
press in the 1840s - why did the officers of this offensive new institution (maintained at great local expense) do nothing about the young men playing pitch and
toss in Great Moor Street, about the boys playing 'piggy'
(a Lancashire game of tip-cat) behind Walmsley's
Warehouse, about the crowds of louts who gathered to
cheer on pedestrian races and obstructed rights of way?
(44) The list of cases before the local courts show that
the police did indeed come to bear down heavily upon these
'nuisances'; the players and spectators of street games
were prosecuted for obstruction, trespass, breaches of the
peace, vagrancy and desecration of the sabbath. Thus the
police invaded the daily occasions for recreation as well
as the popular festivals of the fair and race meeting. In
clearing the streets, they not only threatened to deprive
the working class of its last resort of public assembly,
but also cut off many of its diversions by moving on the
street performers. (45)

The hostility of the reform associations and local
authorities was only the most forceful expression of a
general middle-class impatience with the intractable
crudities and excess of so much of popular recreation.
The respectable citizens of Bolton who demanded police
action against street games were not just concerned to
criticise the efficiency of a distasteful new service,
but were generally affronted by what they saw and heard
of. In an age of progress and rationality it was frankly
incomprehensible that people should amuse themselves by
eating scalding porridge with their fingers or stripping
the wicks from a pound of candles with their teeth, all

for the sake of a wager and the applause of an audience of
like-minded boobies. These folk pleasures were popular
contests at the yearly Halshaw Wakes held near Bolton, but
similar feats took place all the year round - eight pounds
of treacle consumed in twenty minutes by a butcher's assistant (the commonest of participants) provides a ready
example. (46) Such displays were generally attended by a
great deal of drinking and gambling. The gentry and the
respectable middle classes recoiled from such uncouth
congenialities and, like the clergy, no longer appeared as
patrons of the local fairs and feasts.

One persistent defence of the aberrations witnessed at
the annual festivals - that they provided a safety valve
for the discontents and frustrations of a hard-driven
working people - found no support among the middle
classes, particularly since this traditional licence
encouraged recrudescences of saturnalia which they found
offensive to their sense of station and social order. (47)
In Lancashire at Eastertime the ancient practice of
begging for eggs or 'pace-egging' provided sanction for
gangs of youths to dress in outlandish garb and march in
procession from pub to pub, blowing trumpets and banging
on the tables till free drink was brought. Respectable
passers-by were badgered into contributing drink money,
and Henry Richard recorded an occasion when 'a rabble
sort' stormed the Commercial Room of his hotel in search
of tribute. At Ashton in Cheshire, revellers demanded
beer money for the Black Knight, who was paraded in effigy
at the annual fair - missiles hurled at the Knight had a
way of breaking windows or spattering the better-dressed
bystanders. (48) In many of these cases the full flourish
of the traditional ritual had been pared away, but this
attrition seems to have given the celebrations a sharper
retaliatory edge - a popular retort to the studied neglect, compounded by official harassment, which characterised the attitudes of the superior classes to the workingman's amusements.

Before turning to consider the general response of the
lower orders, it should be noted that there were some
great popular festivals which significantly resisted curtailment, though castigated as morally degenerate. Race
meetings head this category. Racing had long been a
target for the reformers of manners - an early sign of
Wilberforce's conversion had been his pointed refusal of
the stewardship of York races in 1790 - but the aristocracy and its county allies were successful in protecting the
sport from its enemies. A committee of the House of Lords
considered that the traditional arguments for the defence
still held good in the 1840s:

The Committee think it desirable that this amusement
should be upheld, because it is in accordance with a
long-established national taste, because it serves to
bring together for a common object, vast bodies of
people in different parts of the country, and to promote intercourse between different classes of society.
The committee went on to recall how Manchester races had
been allowed to take place immediately after the Peterloo
massacre; despite official misgivings, the meeting had
not provided a new rallying ground for the disaffected,
but had afforded a three-day armistice. The sport could
also be defended as necessary for maintaining the good
quality of English blood-stock. There were problems of
public order on the Turf, but the Jockey Club, the aristocratic governing body, went some way to putting its own
house in order during the 1840s and 1850s. (49) So the
race meeting remained a stronghold of aristocratic patronage and life-style, trading on the patriotic claims and
status associations of equestrianism; its broad and
harmonious social mix received its apotheosis in Frith's
classic picture, 'Derby Day', painted in 1858.

Racing increased in popularity with the working class
in this period, and certain big city meetings became
almost exclusively proletarian occasions. This was true
at Manchester, Newcastle and at Doncaster, where by 1850
it was a matter of comment that 'the family carriage has
been superseded by the bus'. The spread of excursion
traffic and the continuing lure of a day in the open
account for some of the growth, but an additional attraction was quite obviously the betting market. There
was an immense increase of on-course betting for individu-
ally small sums, and the editor of 'Bell's Life in
London', the leading sporting paper, concluded: 'The
great majority of betters are persons from the manufacturing towns.' As a betting medium, racing was also popular
away from the track: off-course betting shops were numerous (some as lavishly appointed as the gin palace),
carrier pigeons relayed the results from the meetings and
avid punters hung over bridges to catch the name of the
big race winner from the fireman as the express train
flashed through. (50) Gambling was a familiar vice among
English workmen and it was well within living memory that
such enthusiasms had been encouraged by a state-run
national lottery; by the mid-century, however, the common
man as gamester appeared as a threat to property in
government eyes, for it was feared that gambling debts
would lead the workman to theft, and the shopman to
plunder his master's till. The remedy was the 1853 act
for suppressing betting shops, which also outlawed the

promotion of betting lists in the pubs. The legislation
was meant to eliminate excessive betting from the towns,
though the gentleman's right to wager was protected by
significant loopholes in the new law (Lord Palmerston was
supposedly responsible for cutting out some of the bill's
more drastic proposals in the committee stage). The act
was never a very watertight measure and, in any case,
betting was still permitted at the race meeting itself.
To prohibit betting on the course would have invited
political disaster, but this relative tolerance suggests
that, as a safety valve, the race meeting was regarded by
the authorities as a manageable explosion which could be
left to crackle away in a kind of quarantine on the edges
of towns or beyond. Local opinion could be reconciled to
any disturbances by the extra business brought by the
influx of gentry and excursionists. (51)

The prize ring deserves some attention at this point,
since it displayed a social formula similar to that of the
Turf. It had a long history of aristocratic patronage,
but all classes and callings were found among its follow-
ers, giving the sport its dominant feeling of social
equality. In the mythology of the Ring, the fist was
England's national weapon and the skilful and courageous
wielding of it in public kept alive the spirit of
Waterloo. Prize matches were generally fought in the
countryside, and the style of the sport was heavily
rustic; 'on the whole', observed Dickens, 'the associations entwined with the pugilistic art are much in the
manner of Izaak Walton.' As with the Turf, there was much
gambling, considerable piecemeal commercialisation, and a
pronounced criminal fringe. The Ring was also very popular with the working class. The champion fighters were
great popular heroes who often provided a focus for fierce
local loyalties, and news of the big matches brought excitement to the slums. As the costermongers told Mayhew,
fighting was considered a necessary part of any boy's education, and the rather portly muscularity and rubicund
complexion of the pugilist embodied popular ideals of
physical health. A successful career in the Ring for a
working-class professional could mean substantial enrichment and the company of nobility - at least it generally meant enough money to open a pub. (52)

But the prize fight was a bloody and unruly affair, and
it came under heavy attack from humanitarians and reforming magistrates. Publicans who promoted fights were
prosecuted for breaches of the peace, or were unable to
renew their liquor licence at the next brewster sessions;
on the not infrequent occasions when a pugilist was
slugged to death, his adversary was charged with homicide.

The coming of the new police increased the odds against
the sport's survival, but a few hardy promoters continued
to trade upon such intelligence as that 'the Constables
and Justices slept more soundly in Cambridgeshire than in
Essex', and the Ring survived in a somewhat attenuated but
largely unreformed state. (53)   In 1860 the great international match between Sayers and Heenan provided the
final climax for pugilism and revealed the subterfuges to
which its supporters had had to resort.   A special train
left London before dawn, bound for a secret rendezvous
beyond the reach of mounted police patrols;   the con-
tenders had gone before, in disguise.   The press generally
treated the event as a brutal anachronism, but assertions
of the traditional warranty for the sport were still
heard: in the Commons, Palmerston (who was accused of
conniving at the outwitting of the authorities) made plain
his personal approval of the Ring as a manly exercise in
self-defence. (54)   The lordly patronage of prize-fighting
had by then greatly declined, but on such occasions, and
in their continuing presence on the Turf, the aristocracy
showed themselves the custodians of certain of the great
myths of the English at play - the egalitarian bonhomie of
the sporting fraternity, and the necessary role of the
fist fight in building a sturdy national character.   As an
apologia for two heavily criticised institutions these
sentiments provided some protection for popular participation.

IV

Generally, however, the working classes could count on
little protection for their amusements from their betters;
how, then, did they react to the campaigns against popular
recreation?   Reformers often met with harassment: parish
officers attempting to enforce Sunday closing were sere-
naded with 'rough music' and the clanging of dustmen's
bells;   racegoers and fairground crowds man-handled religious fanatics who harangued them on their sinfulness.
(55)   There were also occasions of fiercer and more sustained resistance.   The new police were ambushed and
stoned and a two-day mêlée ensued when they attempted to
disperse the gambling tables at Lancaster races in 1840.
Attempts to suppress bull-baiting in West Bromwich provoked extensive rioting, and such was the defiance of the
crowds at the annual bull-running at Stamford in Lincolnshire that the dragoons had finally to be called in to
assist the police in its suppression. (56)   A similar
though comparatively minor incident in Berkshire is a

reminder that these occasions were not only sporting
events but expressions of community, and defended as such:
in Wokingham, a local alderman donated the bull, and the
proceeds from the sale of the dead animal (whose meat was
allegedly improved by baiting) went to charity, together
with the hide, which made shoes for the poor. (57) In a
small country town such an occasion would dominate the
calendar. In the cluster of manufacturing towns and industrial villages in Lancashire there were so many feasts
and wakes that some succumbed to reform pressures without
arousing any recorded popular protest - in Bolton and
district, Horwich races, the Cross Keys Fair and Tonge
Fold Fair disappeared quietly within a few years of each
other in the late 1840s, at the apparently uncontested
promptings of 'moralists' and 'influential gentlemen'.
(58) What excited determined resistance in the big towns
were measures which threatened the more commonplace occasions of recreation and sociability. In Bolton in 1853,
the working-class secularist society successfully organised mass protest meetings against sabbatarian proposals
to close the pubs on Sunday. Two years later there were
serious riots in London against similar measures; in this
case not only recreation but domestic habit was threatened, for Parliament was proposing to stop all trading in
the city on Sunday. (59) Such campaigns were interpreted
as an attack upon the whole fabric of working-class life.
    The language of resistance shows that workingmen often
saw these confrontations as part of a broader social and
political conflict. There is, for instance, a story (its
origins as yet still obscure) of how the Chartists took up
the case of the proprietor of a London saloon theatre who
was prosecuted for playing the drama, at a time when
dramatic licences were still restricted to the patent
theatres. The Chartists picketed Westminster carrying
placards with the following legends: 'Freedom for the
People's Amusements'; 'Workers Want Theatres'; 'One Law
for the Rich, Another for the Poor'. (60) A more reliable
example is provided by the Bolton protesters against
sabbatarianism, whose leaders were veterans of the radical
politics of the 1840s; the latter repeated a long and
well-rehearsed catalogue of grievances against the local
clergy - how they had sabotaged the Peel Park scheme, obstructed Sunday excursions, vetoed the Mechanics' Institute, and neglected the welfare of the people in the hard
times of previous years. In Newcastle-upon-Tyne in the
same year a workman warned his mates against the
shopkeepers and clergymen of a local anti-race committee
in words which carry the authentic note of class hostility: (61)

They promise nought to replace this workman's holiday
.... They would legislate for our morals.... in their
desire to deny us recreation and amusement they only
add another to the many proofs they have already given
us of their utter ignorance of human nature.... They
are very fond of indulging in invectives against the
publican, but the most casual observer among them
cannot fail to have perceived that this body furnishes
the only instances of providing amusements which,
judging from the patronage they have received, appear
to be most in demand.... They only speak of workmen's
intelligence on rare occasions and display concern for
their welfare when they want to use us to promote a
scheme of their own.... I would say to you then, my
fellow working men, be up and stirring in this matter;
you, more than either the publican or the brewer, are
interested in it, as it is only the prelude to a series
of attempts to prevent, if possible, all recreation and
amusement - it is the thin edge of the wedge which they
will use all their efforts to drive home.

Given these examples of defiance it is difficult to
explain away the apparently uncontested truncations of
popular festivals in terms of working-class indifference.
In an open letter to the Prime Minister in 1856 attacking
the cessation of Sunday band concerts in London parks
under pressure from the bishops, the radical, G.J.Holy-
oake, was anxious to counter this impression. 'It is', he
said, 'a farce to talk of, and a wrong to assume, the
"indifference of the people" from their silence - even on
questions vital to them.' It was, however, in Holyoake's
experience, difficult to marshal popular opposition, and
thus many abridgments of popular recreation seemed to pass
without offence, until accumulated resentment finally ex-
ploded in riot, as in the case of the Sunday trading riots
in London in the previous year. (62) Holyoake's contentions are sound, but it seems likely too that the
workingman was better able to accept and overcome many of
the undoubted losses of these years because of the
emergence of a new urban popular culture whose recreations
were more appropriate to the environment of the modern industrial town.

In moving on to consider the singing saloons as one of
the more prominent and, in middle-class eyes, more disturbing manifestations of the new popular culture, we meet
up with the most formidable vested interest in popular
recreation - the publican. The primacy of the publican
derived in large part from his dominating position in the
food and drink trade, and the traditional social skills he
displayed in his stewardship of the pub. He sang in the

pub harmonic society and presided over the Derby
sweepstakes; he provided the prizes for the clubs which
met on his premises; he played host and stakeholder to
the various sporting fraternities, and gave cover to
'listmen', the early bookmakers; he put up the leg of
mutton or the new chemise for which contestants danced or
ran at the local fair. He also sold the refreshments for
the fair, like Jack Entwhistle of the Falcon and Four
Factories at Cross Keys Fair in Bolton, 'better known as
Happy Jack - there in all his glory, surrounded by beer
barrels and beer buyers'. (63) This was the 'genial Boniface', the people's friendly major-domo. Moreover, his
central position in popular recreation, as the workingman
from Newcastle had indicated, was reinforced by the with-
drawal of such erstwhile patrons as the clergy and other
local worthies.

   The publican had to defend his commanding position
against the reformers, particularly the Temperance
movement. His free beer fuelled many of the working-class
demonstrations noted above, and publicans (or licensed
victuallers as they increasingly preferred to be known)
formed trade protection societies whose function included
propaganda in which the publican stood for the very ideal
in good living, as we may learn from a report of the
Manchester licensed victuallers' annual dinner in 1850:
'Here were jolly faces, healthful countenances and athletic men, whose thews showed the strength that roast
beef, plum pudding and John Barleycorn create.' The
glowing image was contrasted with that of Temperance
diners picking at their food - 'as pale, decayed and thin
a set of human beings as ever scowled on humanity'. In
his defence the publican also laid claim to a unique professional expertise. 'Public amusements', argued the
'Era', 'is a trade and a mystery and requires to be
learned like any other trade.... no amateur ever ventured
into it without damaging its character, and injuring its
professors.' (64)

   This retort was made in criticism of a particular
attempt by clergymen to provide amusements which would
counter the attractions of the pub, but the publican was
more threatened during this era by competition from within
his own bailiwick. The Beershop Act of 1830 had thrown
open the retail trade in beer, allowing any ratepayer to
brew and sell beer on his premises; licences were available from the local excise officer, and the beershop proprietor did not, like the publican, have to present
sureties of solvency and good character, or submit to the
magistrates for the annual renewal of his licence. Beershops proliferated. The publican was also likely to find

himself in competition with his own kind, for the conditions of entry into public house proprietorship had also
become easier under the influence of the free licensing
movement. (65)   Publicans made shift to outface their
rivals – as one of them explained to a government committee in 1831, the search for extra attractions had led
him and his fellows to resort to 'very great show and
ornament'.   Hence the elaborations of the gin palace and
the regular entertainment of the singing saloon, which
show the publican on the defensive as much as on the make.
Given the burgeoning 'current in the streets', the situation was almost certainly never as bad as the trade made
out – one witness who knew the business from the inside
maintained that some London publicans had increased their
profits so substantially in the 1830s that they were di-
versifying into steamboat excursions. (66)   But many of
them were worried about hanging on to their share of the
drinking public;   as rival leisure attractions multiplied
in the following decades, publicans came to conform less
to the popular image of a genial Boniface than to
Dickens's picture of the proprietor of a Liverpool singing
saloon: 'Mr Licensed Victualler ... a sharp and watchful
man, with tight lips and a complete edition of Cocker's
arithmetic in each eye.' (67)

The commercial operation of the singing saloons reveals
also that despite growth there were significant economic
and social limitations to the leisure market of the
period.   Revenue came from the sale of food and drink,
particularly the latter.   Admission to the saloons was by
purchase of a refreshment check, a bronze or copper disc
bearing the name of the pub and the value of the refreshments for which it was exchangeable inside the hall
(in some areas this practice relieved the publican of the
need to hold a music licence, and also obviated an old law
forbidding the taking of money for admission on Sundays,
often a popular night at the saloons). (68)   The publican
tried to sell more drink than that provided on the refreshment check – he had to cover rising rents and increased overheads.   The chairman, who conducted the entertainment, was therefore required to ensure frequent breaks
for ordering drinks, setting a personal example by his own
readiness to accept a glass from the audience.   His duties
were graphically described by a Lancashire magistrate:
    there were diverting pleasant fellows who had what is
    called 'the run of their teeth';   that is, they were
    allowed to eat and drink, and they were employed by the
    publicans to sing songs and tell stories, and badger
    any country fellow who came till they made him drink.
The waiters, too, kept up the pressure, as another witness

recorded: '[Visitors] are soon made to understand by the
waiter coming to them that they must order drink or leave
the place.... they are compelled to order drink as the
condition of remaining to witness the performance.' (69)
These practices demonstrate that however numerous popular
demand might have been, it was not very effective in terms
of spending power - a full singing saloon did not auto-
matically guarantee a full till. The refreshment ticket
and the importunities of the saloon staff were necessary
devices to prise revenue from the meagre competences of a
working-class public with no established habit of direct
payment for entertainment, particularly not for entertainment as familiar and largely self-generated as the
free and easy. The singing saloons were called into being
by the working classes, and the working classes asserted a
remarkable degree of popular control over them. Not until
the 1850s did certain of the more enterprising publican
entrepreneurs devise a new and more remunerative market
formula.

In the meantime the saloons flourished as a popular
institution. The new tavern concerts were most numerous
in London and the north. Between 1829 and 1849 applications for music and dancing licences to the Middlesex
bench increased eightfold, and an increasing proportion
of these were granted. By the 1840s London had a substantial body of professionals working the singing
saloons; they had their own benevolent society and used
the Hope Tavern off Drury Lane as a clearing house for
engagements. (70) Here was evidence of a growing commercialisation and regularity. There were thriving music
rooms in Manchester by 1834, there being six to one street
in Ancoats alone. 'Many of them', reported one observer
alert to the conspicuous consumption of the poor, 'have an
organ, or a pianoforte, or a musical clock worth one
hundred and fifty guineas.' From Preston in 1851, James
Hudson reported: 'Singing-rooms are numerous, prosperous
and constantly well-attended.' At first the music had
only been provided in the winter months, but by the 1840s
concerts were being held throughout the year, and the
entertainment and appointments were on a grander scale.
William Dodd has left us a good picture of a thriving
singing saloon in his description of The Jolly Hatters in
Stockport in 1842, where a large extension had just been
opened. This annexe, the 'Thespian Gallery and Temple of
the Muses', was 'beautifully painted and well furnished',
and could accommodate 400 to 500 customers for its nightly
performances. (71)

A good example of the rise of the singing saloon to a
dominating local position in working-class recreation is

provided by the Star in Bolton. Opened in 1840 by Thomas
Sharples, a prominent publican of the town, the Star had
gradually expanded under his son's management to incorporate a picture gallery, a museum and a menagerie. The
museum held historical relics such as the axe reputed to
have been used at Derby's execution, geological specimens,
stuffed birds, a photographic studio and a ship's mainmast
complete with rigging. Lectures on these various exhibits
and topical subjects such as emigration were held in the
Star, as well as the music and dancing associated with
saloon entertainment. 'The principle of the concert
room', explained George Gray, the manager, 'is to combine
social enjoyment with wholesome instruction.' Referring
to disappointing experiments in popular education, he
championed the saloons as 'the only engines for public
instruction now existing in society'. Gray's formula was
certainly attractive to the Bolton working class. The
Star could hold over 1,000 folk, and at weekends in particular it was bursting at the seams with the influx of
excursion crowds from surrounding towns. A score of minor
rivals operated in its shadow, but in 1852 it accounted
for the biggest share of the estimated nightly attendance
of 3,000 to 4,000 at Bolton's singing saloons. Though
family groups were reported among the audience, the Star
was particularly attractive to the young of both sexes,
who used it for their courting; most of them were unat-
tended by their parents. Sharples's account books provide
several examples of the headaches of management, but they
show too, amid the confusions of his own personal style of
accounting, that the Star yielded a handsome and regular
profit. (72)
    The entertainment set before the saloon audiences was
diverse in its materials, illustrating the wide resources
of popular culture; the songs, dances and tricks were
derived from the travelling show and popular theatre, the
village green and the street, the drawing room and the
church, and the recently imported nigger-minstrel shows.
The style was boisterous, vulgar and irreverent - Dodd, in
his 1842 description of The Jolly Hatters at Stockport,
noted a satirical song entitled 'The Parson and his Pigs',
a young woman 'in a stylish undress' and 'an indecent
mongrel kind of dance'. The saloon audience also had a
taste for spectacle (tableaux of battle scenes and repro-
ductions of great historic events) but essential to all
performances was the chorus singing, in which the audience
came into its own. The fierce enthusiasm of their participation is described here by a member of the 'improving' press, who records with some amazement the lèse-
majesté visited upon some of his own favourite songs:

By name, they are often the same as we see in music-
sellers' windows and on our own drawing-room tables;
but they are garbled and interpolated here in a manner
to defy description. They are sung, or rather roared,
with a vehemence that is stunning, and accompanied with
spoken passages of the most outrageous character. At
the end of every verse the audience takes up the chorus
with a zest and vigour which speaks volumes - they
sing, they roar, they yell, they scream, they get on
their legs and waving dirty hands and ragged hats
bellow again till their voices crack. When the song is
ended, and the singer withdraws, they encore him with a
peal that seems enough to bring the rotting roof on
their heads.

Whatever the abandon, by the 1850s the procedure was well
formalised in some of the halls: 'programme books thick
as a magazine are laid upon the tables for our acceptance,
and as the song is announced by the chairman, he refers
you to the number in the volume, beneath which you may
find the words.' (73)

The singing saloons in particular emphasise the continuing strengths of popular recreation - the vitality and
capacity for adaptation. Their success represents a
victory over the constrictions and impersonality of the
new towns. They utilised and stretched existing resources
to accommodate the increasing numbers from the street who
were hungry for company and diversion. As with the gin
palace (often one and the same set of premises with the
saloon) the gas light and other advances in technology
were pressed into service to allow for greatly enlarged
assemblies, yet the gregarious intimacy of saloon entertainment retained an essentially human and personal
pattern of contact within the new scale of things: the
logistics were such that the audience could perambulate
and intermingle at will; the performers - despite an
incipient professionalism - were not yet irrecoverably
distanced from their public; and the chorus singing was
a compelling ritual that reaffirmed the common identity of
its celebrants. It is significant too that despite the
incessant clatter of bonhomie good order prevailed among
the singing saloon crowds. In his tour of Lancashire in
1842, the journalist and historian Cooke Taylor recorded:
'I have gone into some of the concert-rooms attached to
favoured public houses which they (the operatives of
Manchester) frequent, and I have never been in a more
orderly and better behaved company.' Some ten years later
a spokesman for a Manchester association for the reform of
public houses found no need to demand any alteration in
the hours which the singing saloons kept because he

allowed: 'The people regulate the hours - all the working
people leave by 9:30.' The same witness also acknowledged
that there was very little drunkenness among saloon audiences, and Sharples's accounts testify that ginger beer or
'pop' sold as well as the stronger stuff. (74) With
emphasis on the north-west again, it seems plain that a
substantial section of the working class was by now dis-
tributing its leisure time and energies to a more disciplined pattern, in closer correspondence than before with
the parameters of a standardised industrial working week.
If the nature of the experience was therefore modified,
the satisfactions still appear real enough.

The Star in Bolton, with its wide range of attractions,
shows how the saloon could meet the popular thirst for
instruction as well as entertainment. From Bolton too,
there is evidence of how the saloons could fight off the
attacks of the reformers, for Sharples eventually defeated
the designs of the local anti-singing saloon association
and rebuilt the Star after the 1852 fire. On its reopen-
ing, the Bolton dialect paper recorded the cheers of
popular satisfaction: 'We're so fain to see the Star
oppen ogen, that we're just gettin' shut of a bit of eawr
surplus emoshun.... nearly every chops had a grin on it.'
In a more reflective manner, another local correspondent
drew the following conclusion from the controversy over
the Star: 'The Singing Saloons, or Singing Halls, are the
best guarantee for recreation, and approach nearer to the
inclinations and customs of the working classes than any
other institution of the present age.' (75)

These proletarian 'maisons de culture' advertised their
success with a clamant assault upon the senses, for they
were certainly more obtrusive than their more humble forerunners. With their powerful lighting, their enlarged
capacity and the prevailing enthusiasm for chorus singing,
they were a phenomenon of which few can have remained
unaware. The saloons were blazing arcades of light.
Customers crowded outside on the pavement waiting to get
in, while the sounds of popular music-making were roared
abroad - on Sunday nights such favourites as the Doxology
and the Hallelujah Chorus dominated the repertoire. To
Faucher's translator, a middle-class Mancunian, the inclusion of hymns was a sign of an improved taste among the
working classes, but to other respectable citizens passing
by on the other side the saloons afforded fleeting peep-
shows of degeneracy, confirming the evidence of prison
chaplains whose younger charges seemed ever ready to
oblige with testimonies to the corrupting influences of
such places. (76)

The saloons were particularly disturbing to the

reformers. (77) They saw the brutality and crudeness of
the older traditional amusements as the excrescences of a
folk or rustic barbarism - noxious enough, but ultimately
incapable of withstanding the moral advances of a modern
society; they were now confronted with a thriving institution that was the direct product of a modern urban
society, and which so fitted the tastes and conventions
of a large section of the members of that society, that
it threatened to engross all their leisure time. It was
this marked capacity for autonomous renewal in popular
recreation which demanded of reformers that their counter-
attack be constructive rather than merely repressive.

2

‹◇◇◇›

Rational Recreation: Voices of Improvement

‹◇◇◇›

In the 1830s and 1840s English society faced appalling
problems of social order and public health which provoked
a wide-ranging debate on the 'Condition of England'. One
strand in the debate concerned popular recreations and the
desirability of promoting their reform in such a way as to
make a constructive contribution to the general drive for
social amelioration or 'improvement'. In this scenario
improved recreations were an important instrument for educating the working classes in the social values of middle-
class orthodoxy. Rational recreation, as the new prescription was styled, commended itself to a variety of
reform interests and attracted increasing public attention
as the mid-century approached. By then the history of
several schemes launched in its name had revealed the
considerable problems of putting its rationale of social
control into practice. (1)

I

Rational recreation proceeded from a basic humanitarian
sympathy with the plight of the urban masses. Expressions
of regret at the persecution and neglect of their
amusements multiplied during the early Victorian era.
'The very essence of our laws', acknowledged Edward Bulwer
Lytton, the novelist, 'has been against the social
meetings of the humble, which have been called idleness,
and against the amusements of the poor, which have been
stigmatised as disorder.' (2) Such confessions became
calls for action. In the Commons, Robert Slaney, a
country gentleman with a utilitarian interest in the
health of towns, argued that those who abolished the
amusements of the poor were bound to find a substitute.
There were, he maintained, 'great arrears to make up in

this respect towards these neglected classes'. The
concern to humanise life in the towns was reinforced by
practical considerations of social stability. If relief
was not forthcoming, warned Slaney, 'the working classes
will fly to demagogues and dangerous causes'; it was, he
claimed, 'alike wise and benevolent to provide, in regulated amusement for the many, safety valves for their
eager energies'. (3) Chartism was the dangerous cause
uppermost in middle-class minds. Edwin Chadwick was moved
to argue for the provision of improved recreational amenities from the example of one occasion in Manchester, when
potential demonstrators flocked to the zoo and museum
(opened specially at the instigation of the police chief)
rather than a Chartist meeting. A witness to the commission on the health of towns reminded its members that
open spaces and sports were essential for diverting the
lower orders from political disaffection. In particular,
it was the unnerving spectacle of the Chartist agitation
in 1842 which alerted a Manchester banker, Benjamin
Heywood, to the alienation of the working class, and
prompted him to reform the Manchester Lyceums; within
these new recreational centres he hoped to create a
'community of enjoyment' which would engender 'reciprocal
feelings' between employer and employee. Though the
threat of Chartism receded, there still remained the
problem of containing the 'dangerous classes', that inde-
terminate but volatile menace that lurked in the rookeries
of the big cities. (4)
     But rational recreation was not an old-fashioned exer-
cise in placating the mob; Slaney talked of safety
valves, but qualified the image by talking of the need for
'regulated amusement'. Existing popular recreations which
served to dissipate tensions within society were generally
dismissed. While middle-class reformers acknowledged examples of working-class improvement at play and derived
considerable encouragement from them, they stood dismayed
at the prodigality of much working-class leisure with its
determined exploration of the limits of the human appetite
to the point of repletion or collapse. Contemplating the
Staffordshire miners in 1850, Hugh Tremenheere, a factory
inspector of much experience, noted despondently: 'The
half-savage manners of the last generation have been ex-
changed for a deep and almost universally pervading sensuality.' (5) Drunkenness was the most frequently indicated
'sensual' pleasure; feasting, brawling and (less directly
stated) fornication were other regrettable indulgences.
The reformers meant to cut back these excesses by providing alternative recreations which stimulated and restored the mind rather than merely debilitated the body,

yet the new proposals also placed limits on the exercise
of mental energies for there was the fear that these too
could be misplaced if they were lured into the vigorous
radical culture of popular social movements such as
Chartism, where much that was undeniably recreational
(and often enough well disciplined) was none the less
socially subversive. Cooke Taylor, the journalist and
historian met with previously in his tour of Lancashire
in the early 1840s, concluded: (6)

There must be safety valves for the mind; that is,
there must be means for its pleasurable, profitable,
and healthful exertion. These means it is in our power
to render safe and innocent: these means in too many
instances have been rendered dangerous and guilty.

Those who gave the question serious attention in these
years were coming to the realisation that its solution
required more than an immediate rescue and repair operation; even if political tensions were reduced, there
remained the continuing problem of ensuring a socially
tractable working class in a fluid and anonymous urban
society. Any realistic strategy of social control - or
'moral education' as contemporary usage had it - would
have to devise techniques for legitimating its authority
other than those of direct and coercive impressment. To
most social reformers in the early Victorian period,
formal education appeared as the single great lever with
which the working classes could be moved into the light.
Education, in the words of Dr Kay-Shuttleworth, its chief
government policy-maker in the 1840s, was meant not only
to teach occupational skills, but also 'the nature of his
[the artisan's] domestic and social relations ... his political position in society, and the moral and religious
duties appropriate to it'. (7) But, as Cooke Taylor
pointed out: 'The lectures of the schoolroom will be
utterly ineffective when they are counteracted by the
practical lessons of the playground.' 'It was', he asserted, 'the great but neglected truth, that moral education, in spite of all the labours of direct instructors,
is really acquired in hours of recreation.' Some such
dictum has no doubt appeared in the conventional wisdom of
many previous eras, but in this age it carried a new significance, for reformers were being forced to recognise
that the more effective control of popular leisure was an
urgent and difficult undertaking demanding a particular
sensitivity to the changing pattern of life in a modern
world. The problems involved were thus considerable, but
the task also had its exhilarations, for it offered the
opportunity to contribute to what contemporaries conceived
as a general remaking of society. Contemplating the state

of popular recreation and the travails of modern life in
1838, William Howitt concluded that both had reached a
turning point: (8)

There appears to have been a pause in that important
portion of human life, amusement, so far as the common
people are concerned; but it has been in appearance
only. One of the greatest changes that ever took place
in human society has been in this interval maturing:
the change from the last stage of worn out feudalism to
the commencement of the era of social regeneration.

II

How was rational recreation to assist in this regeneration? How was it to be implemented? Reformers were
generally agreed upon the need to provide more recreational amenities in the manufacturing towns as a basic improvement. This was one of the 'immediate remedies' proposed by the select committee on drunkenness in 1834,
which indicated the range and balance required of such
provisions. The committee recommended: (9)

The establishment by the joint aid of Government and
the local authorities and residents on the spot, of
public walks, and gardens, or open spaces for healthy
and athletic exercises in the open air, in the immediate vicinity of every town, of an extent and character
adapted to its population; and of district and parish
libraries, museums and reading rooms, accessible at the
lowest rate of charge; so as to admit of one or the
other being visited in any weather, and at any time.

But governments and local authorities were generally
dilatory in meeting such requests, despite the lobbying
of men like Slaney who regularly promoted bills to secure
public walks and playgrounds. In 1837 Joseph Hume, another Radical interested in the amusements of the poor,
was successful in passing a motion in the Commons which
instructed the enclosure commissioners to ensure that each
enclosure left an open space 'sufficient for the purposes
of exercise and recreation of the neighbouring population'. Two years later, after an inspection of the
breviates of enclosure bills, an interested member reported back that 'the laudable object had been laxly
looked after'. Members for the new towns in the reformed
House recognised the problem but were sceptical of any
municipal improvement which required an increase in the
rates - 'There is', said Fielden to a select committee on
public walks, 'an extraordinary jealousy in that respect.'
In 1840 Parliament voted money to assist local authorities

in providing parks, and in 1845 Peel made a personal
example by a gift of £1,000 towards the establishment of
Peel Park in Manchester; but the boroughs were slow in
response - in Bolton the proposal for a Peel Park was
first made in 1850 and was not brought to fruition till
sixteen years later. (10) Official parsimony effectively
restricted the improvement of mental as well as physical
recreation. William Ewart, a Liberal backbencher,
successfully introduced a bill in 1850 which enabled local
authorities to provide public libraries out of the rates.
It was, said one of his supporters, 'the cheapest police
that could possibly be established'. The Libraries Act
enabled town councils to levy a small rate which paid for
housing and servicing the libraries, but not for buying
books; the select committee on libraries had maintained
that 'donation will abundantly supply the books'. (11)
Once the authorities had grudgingly primed the pump, philanthropy was meant to complete the operation.

Thus recreational reform failed to command any real
priority with the legislators. The Commons seemed happy
enough to debate the issue of the amusements of the poor
as a diversion - the image of Merrie England was freely
invoked as members deplored the puritan zeal of certain
magistrates who prosecuted sabbath-breaking cricket
players, or applied the vagrancy laws to street singers -
but members deprecated direct control as a means of improving the manners of the people. In its inquiry into
the licensing of places of entertainment in the early
1850s, the Commons' select committee obviously preferred
education as an agent of improvement to any extension of
the magistrate's powers. Improvement outside the field of
education, as one MP reminded the House, would come from
'the influence of an increased morality, diffused downward
from the upper class'. This was the current orthodoxy:
'Opinions travel upwards, manners downwards.' No government action, whether through limiting the number of
theatres, legislating for the better observance of the
sabbath or imposing sumptuary laws, was any substitute for
the operation of this mysterious and respected process.
(12)

While reformers would not allow laissez-faire arguments
to excuse the official neglect of amenities, they did
accept the need for example-setting by the superior
classes. Setting an example was, in any case, a salutary
exercise for the superior classes, but it was hoped that
their presence in recreation would engender a mutual moral
vigilance in the community at large. Thus would be
created the police of public opinion - 'mores sans legibus', rather than 'legibus sans mores', as the Lord

Chancellor had put it in a debate on sabbath observance.
In rational recreation the community restraints would be
reinforced by imprinting the values of the superior example on the working-class mind, making them self-acting
imperatives. 'SELF-ACTION FOR SELF-IMPROVEMENT', proclaimed the 'Bolton Chronicle', drawing a moral from the
Factory Operatives Bazaar, 'was the only sure ground for
hope of progress.' (13)

But if the working class needed an example to follow,
exactly who among the rest of society was to provide it?
The patronage of the nobility could be far from appropriate - commenting on the spectacle of the gentry going down
to Newmarket on what had become a regular Easter Sunday
procession, Bishop Blomfield of London declared that there
was 'nothing more likely to unhinge the whole fabric of
civil society than this evil example of the rich'. (14)
Where the moral conduct of the aristocracy had greatly
improved - and this was generally held to be the case -
middle-class commentators suggested that it was the conspicuous rectitude of the middle classes which had shamed
the aristocracy out of its old ways. If, therefore, the
middle classes accepted the aphorism 'opinions travel
upwards, manners downwards', they did so because they saw
themselves as the central point of departure for the diffusion of improvement in both ideas and behaviour. If
aristocracy meant rule by the best, then the English
middle class was beginning to assert its claims to be
better qualified - as Carlyle challenged: 'Not that we
want no aristocracy, but that we want a new one.'

There was considerable apprehension among the middle
class at the persistent attractions of aristocratic
patronage among the workingmen of a nation proverbially
enamoured of a lord. The fear was that aristocratic
paternalism, even when purged of its traditional de-
cadence, would obstruct the diffusion of middle-class
values and stunt the growth of working-class self-help.
Such misgivings quickened in times of political rivalry.
In 1843, Lord John Manners, a supporter of protection and
factory reform and a member of Disraeli's Young England
group, accused the manufacturing interest of 'a utilitarian selfishness which has well nigh banished all unproductive amusements from the land', and demanded extra
holidays for the people and a return of true recreation.
The joys of the maypole and the sports of the village
green were to be restored under the revived alliance of
the nobility and the old High Church: 'Before the
millions are taught to dance and sing, leisure must be
obtained for them and obtained in a way which they shall
be taught thankfully to acknowledge - the way of the

Church Catholic in England.' The following year, with the campaign against the Corn Laws still undecided and Short Time agitation mounting, the Manchester Lyceum (the workingmen's club run by Heywood the banker) asked Manners to be its patron, but was privately warned off such a course by Cobden and the Anti-Corn Law League. (15)

Some working-class reformers were also wary of the insidious grip of the aristocracy and the persistence of habits of deference. Francis Place, for example, was dismayed by the initially strong influence of the aristocracy at Exeter Hall, the London rallying ground for evangelical reformers, for he feared it would seduce middle-class attenders from their duties to workingmen. In a prize essay written for a Leeds Mechanics' Institute in 1850, a workman applauded many of the proposals of Young England for joining the rich with the poor in common pursuit of sports and games, but suspected the group's motives: 'They would', he feared, 're-establish the bond of feudalism.' (16)

The one 'persona non grata' to all reformers was the publican. There were respectable workingmen who defended the 'social glass' and spoke well of the publican and the pub, but the experience of the Temperance Chartists had alienated men like William Lovett who had tried to provide rational recreation for their class. Lovett learnt at first hand of the ruthlessness of the drink interest when he was evicted from his People's Hall in Holborn by the machinations of the publican-entrepreneur Edward Weston, who took over the premises for conversion into a music hall. A Liverpool vicar who ran concerts for his working-class congregation put the reformers' case succinctly: 'The duties of publican and the duties of provider of public amusements for the people are quite incompatible.' (17) Reformers were at least agreed upon the principal figure in their demonology.

Whatever the rivalries over its direction, the general strategy of rational recreation was clear: new amenities would divert the workingman from the pub and provide the proper environment for his exposure to the superior example, whose values would ultimately be internalised. But how was the superior example to be projected to the working classes; was it to be by display or prescription? Slaney provided an example of the former in arguing for public walks: (18)

A man walking out with his family among his neighbours of different ranks, will naturally be desirous to be properly clothed, and that his wife should be also; but this desire duly directed and controlled, is found by experience to be of the most powerful effect in promoting Civilisation and exciting industry.

Family recreation in the company of social superiors would
generate 'a pardonable vanity'. For those reformers untouched by whole-hog sabbatarianism, the 'Continental
Sunday' offered an admirable model. French and Germans of
all classes took their recreation together on their Sunday
promenades; though drink was taken ('a glass of light
beer') the moderation and decorum of these occasions
seemed to prove to English witnesses how effectively the
public parade of bourgeois respectability could impress
the masses. (19) This was also the assumption behind the
tea party or soirée, where the good manners of the middle-
class guests were expected to rub off on the less genteel.
Nature itself - where it plainly bore the mark of man's
assiduous hand - might also set an impressive example:
the 'Bolton Chronicle', 11 September 1852, commended the
local horticultural society's annual show to the 'humbler
classes', confident that, by their inspection of its
awesome batteries of well-drilled fruit and vegetables,
'pleasurable emotions will be engendered and fostered,
lessons of lasting importance will be learned, and high
moral sentiment will be imbibed.' But, as the history of
several schemes for recreational improvement shows,
reformers felt the need to clarify the content of conformity more forcefully, and display and the conventions
of polite social intercourse were generally reinforced and
mostly overtaken by prescription.

III

Samuel Greg's report on the improvements he introduced on
his industrial estate in Cheshire in the late 1830s provides a convenient point at which to begin an examination
of rational recreation in practice, for it reveals
something of the tension which developed between these two
approaches as well as exemplifying a fairly common type of
reform exercise in this field. (20) Greg was a substantial employer who provided a variety of recreations
for his workpeople - music classes, gardens, a playground
for games, and regular tea parties in the winter. He
insisted that other schemes to improve the content of
working-class leisure were often inappropriate - he dismissed the Mechanics' Institutes as offering 'mere intellectual pursuits', maintaining that:

   There are many whose minds are not sufficiently cultivated to avail themselves of these: they have little
   or no taste for them, and yet are quite capable of
   being made very worthy, sensible, respectable, and
   happy men.... By gently leading them, or rather

perhaps by letting them find their own way, from one
step to another, you may at length succeed in making
them what you wish them to be.

Having professed his belief in the perfectibility of
workingmen, he talked of 'letting them find their own
way'; having seen something of the erratic and reluctant
nature of their actual progress towards self-redemption,
he felt the need to expedite the process by 'gently
leading them'. The guiding hand of the reformer was
frequently more impatient and intrusive than the latter
phrase suggests, and Greg himself was more peremptory in
practice than his comments allow; elsewhere in the report
he remarked briskly that he had succeeded in 'breaking
them [his operatives] into my system'.

Greg's schemes were not exceptional among manufacturers
whose operations were confined to an industrial estate or
factory village which constituted a closed community - 'a
little Colony', as Greg put it. Robert Owen's New Lanark
mills had included an annexe comprising a school, museum,
music hall and ballroom. The Ashworth brothers provided
similar facilities at their country mills at Turton, near
Bolton. In the village of Flockton, near Huddersfield,
the firm of Stanfeld and Briggs maintained a clubroom,
choir, playground and gymnasium for their colliers, and
there were several other examples of this kind of welfare
capitalism. (21) The employers were applauded for their
concern to humanise the factory system, and the 'Spectator' commended Greg for providing his work people with
a 'moral' or 'aesthetic' economy to balance the necessary
exigencies of political economy. (22) Though some of them
would have disdained the role and its associations, such
men were readily cast as the new industrial lords of the
manor; they were reaffirming the traditional social bonds
of Merrie England, so the reports went, albeit a Merrie
England bowdlerised by the twopenny pastoralism of the
Victorian press. The ideal inspired Disraeli's picture of
Trafford of Wodgate, the model employer in 'Sybil':

In the midst of this village, surrounded by beautiful
gardens, which gave an impulse to the horticulture of
the community, was the house of Trafford himself, who
comprehended his position too well to withdraw himself
with vulgar exclusiveness from his real dependents, but
recognised the baronial principle, reviving in a new
form, and adapted to the softer manners and more
ingenious circumstances of the times.

It should be noted, however, that the returns of this kind
of paternalism could be disappointing. Greg was very hurt
when his workpeople went on strike in 1847 over the introduction of a new process, especially since they made no

attempts at negotiation with him before abruptly turning
out. At Flockton in 1845 there was a thirteen-week strike
which Tremenheere, the government inspector, regarded as
'an unhappy perverseness of conduct' on the part of employees who were so well provided for. Subsequent reports
from Flockton recorded further disenchantment: 'The
novelty having gone off, the amusements and rational
occupations for leisure hours have fallen into some
neglect.' (23)

It was a common contemporary assertion that such
schemes were only practicable in industries and manufactories located in the countryside; as these centres of
production declined or became absorbed by urban growth,
the factory inspectors tried to encourage some attention
to welfare and recreation on the part of employers in the
towns, where the main thrust of industrial growth now lay.
Welfare capitalism had made but slight progress in this
sector, according to a government report of 1843: (24)

Instances of personal attention on the part of employers to the welfare of their workpeople in general,
and of the younger portion of them in particular can
be regarded only as individual exceptions. It is a
fearful thing to see how exempt the great body of employers hold themselves from moral obligations of every
description towards those from whose industry their own
fortunes spring. Even they who contribute at all to
the education or moral improvement of their workmen do
so in nineteen cases of twenty merely by money, and
without personal pains or superintendence of their own.
These vicarious benevolences are seldom availing.

As the decade progressed, however, the provision of recreational facilities did improve. (25) James Hudson provided one explanation. 'The manufacturer', he claimed,
'finds it PROFITABLE to form schools and factory
libraries, to rear amateur bands of musicians among his
workmen.' A further explanation must be that factory employers in the 1840s felt the need to counter growing
criticism of their class, both in Parliament and out of
doors. Hence the defensive tone to this declamation by
Sir John Potter, manufacturer and mayor of Manchester, on
the occasion of the inauguration of the public library in
the town:

Let it never be said hereafter that the masters, the
employers, the richer classes of Manchester, have no
interest in the improvement and advancement of those
they employ.... Let it never be said that they are not
willing to make sacrifices for the many. Let it not be
said that they seek merely their own advantage: that
they are content with making money for themselves.

Yet where employers offered recreational facilities on the
site the workers' response was often disappointing - John
Bright's brother reported that only a small percentage of
his employees took advantage of the means he offered them
for their improvement. (26)

The demand for public libraries exemplified the need
for more open facilities than those attached to and in-
delibly associated with the workplace; some schemes set
their experiments on more neutral ground and made bids for
a broader clientèle. Heywood's Lyceums offer a good example. The Lyceums were formed in Manchester and Salford
in the late 1830s as auxiliaries to Mechanics' Institutes.
The institutes had generally failed to attract a substantial working-class membership; Heywood recognised
that the formal lectures of the institutes were often too
demanding for the exhausted factory worker, and offered a
lighter regimen of social evenings, sports and excursions.
(27) After the Chartist agitation in 1842 Heywood concentrated his full attention on the Lyceums as an instrument
of community welfare and class reconciliation. He lowered
the subscription and encouraged wives to attend; the
Lyceums were to be a home from home, 'a match for the
public house' and an agreeable meeting ground for masters
and men. Despite the more relaxed and entertaining fare
there was an underlying note of earnestness, as Heywood
revealed: 'Beneath the tempting experience of amusements
and exhibitions, valuable as they are, there must be an
undercurrent of solid instruction to support your progress.' Thus Harriet Martineau's moral tales of political
economy were read aloud while the workingmen took their
coffee.

The Lyceums were a failure according to the criteria of
their promoters. Reporting on the experiment in his
history of adult education, Hudson concluded: 'Their
moral influence has become inoperative against the singing
rooms which have sprung up in the cotton metropolis.'
Heywood found that his efforts to develop a common sociability among employers and employed were vitiated by
social distance. The mechanics' parties were uneasy
parades along the class frontier. The middle-class directors were self-conscious in their bonhomie, and the
workingmen too obviously on their best behaviour to give
these occasions any real conviviality. For the workingmen, trying to be festive in these circumstances must have
been like attempting a clog dance on a tight rope. The
propriety of such occasions disintegrated, as Heywood
mournfully reported to his son in 1851: (28) 'The character of the thing is changed. I am glad you were there,
however, for old sake's sake. It is somewhat humiliating

that the sober speakers should be the stopgaps between the acts.' The danger that amusements might dilute or obliterate instruction was a constant hazard to improvers.

Yet amusements were undeniably important to the appeal of sectional interests no longer assured of a ready flow of working-class recruits. The churches may have turned their backs on traditional recreations, but in the Sunday schools of all denominations they were active in promoting counter-attractions. In Bolton in the 1820s, for example, the Sunday schools had instituted regular tea parties to keep their pupils from defecting on race meeting days. In the early 1840s they began to combine with the junior divisions of the town's Temperance association to dominate the popular holiday ritual of the Whit walks - street processions of witness complete with flags and decorations and marching bands (minus the spiced ale which had been served at Sunday school treats twenty years previously). 'The Half-Holiday Hand-Book', published in Manchester in 1846, was meant 'to assist conductors and superintendents of Sunday schools in selecting a locality for the periodical excursions of their pupils'. It was the Sunday school teachers in Bolton who took the lead in forming the anti-singing saloon association which campaigned against the Star; one teacher pointed out that the best counter to the concert room lay in expanding the schools' recreational programme. (29)

In the schools proper solid instruction predominated, though the policy-makers of education were aware of the didactic potential of recreation. Kay-Shuttleworth acknowledged the importance of the playground as 'a source of moral training', wherein children could be taught to maintain 'mutual good offices ... and propriety of demeanour'. Playgrounds, however, remained scarce. (30) But in the 1840s the education secretary did promote one classroom subject with considerable recreational content. The Education Department gave warm encouragement to the new systems of class instruction in choral music - the Hullah and Tonic Sol-fa methods. Echoing Fletcher of Saltoun, Kay-Shuttleworth declared a people's songs 'an important means of forming an industrious, brave, loyal and religious working class'. 'They might', he ventured, 'inspire cheerful views of industry' and 'associate amusements ... with duties'. A great many schools continued to pay no attention to musical instruction, but the new systems did make an extremely important contribution to popular music-making, particularly in the industrial cities of the north where they reinforced already strong musical traditions. The discipline of the adult choirs and the predominantly sacred content of their programmes

continued to recommend themselves to those concerned with
moral training in the mid-Victorian period. (31)

In the 1840s, however, the single most important agency
of recreational improvement was the rising Temperance
movement. Though most of its injunctions were prohibitive
its founding fathers were not kill-joys. Joseph Livesey
of Preston, for example, in testifying to the 'Drunken
Committee' in 1834, had not objected to either music or
dancing in beershops and pubs, provided there was some
official regulation. Only later did Temperance become
subsumed by the canon of restrictive respectability. Even
then it maintained a constructive concern to defeat the
pub by building up counter-attractions, in the tradition
of James Silk Buckingham's 1834 proposals for parks and
playgrounds, which had been meant 'to draw off by innocent
and pleasurable recreation and instruction, all who can be
weaned from habits of drinking'. (32) The movement showed
considerable energy and imagination in providing counter-
attractions. Though hardly unique to the movement, the
railway excursion became a common Temperance recreation in
the 1840s - Thomas Cook, first Temperance reformer, later
travel magnate, ran his first trip in 1841, to remove
working-class children from the temptations of Leicester
race week. (33) Temperance societies were as prominent as
the Sunday schools in appropriating the popular Whit walks
in the north, and just as keen in proselytising the young
(the two institutions were, of course, frequently maintained under the same religious sponsorship). The enthusiasm of the Temperance youth fife and drum band in
Bolton was such as to condemn it as a public nuisance in
the eyes and ears of some residents. Temperance halls
provided what was often the only facility for large popular assemblies before the great town halls were built:
Bolton's Temperance Hall opened in 1840, its town hall in
1873. The movement developed its own friendly societies
and produced a vast literature which was a recreation in
itself. Though many Temperance meetings were dauntingly
single-minded, the movement was, by the late 1840s,
clearly providing an alternative world of recreation for
the lower middle and working classes. Samuel Smiles made
a note of its progress in 1846:

> Our temperance reformers have been slow to recognise
> the importance of these truths; but they are now
> beginning to act on them. They begin to feel that
> there is no other way to defeat drink but to outrival
> it with attractions of a higher kind - such as music,
> cheap railway excursions, cheap concerts, and cheap
> rural galas.

A few years later, William Howitt concluded: 'The Temperance Associations have approached nearer to the ideal of a

popular festival than any other body yet.... They are
finding out the art to be glad and social, merry and
wise.' (34)

   The appeal of Temperance recreations was, however,
greatly restricted by the strong prejudice against the
movement among the working classes. In a beer culture,
workingmen regarded Temperance itself as a dangerously
unhealthy practice (a point much emphasised in the
counter-propaganda of the publican), and the missionary
zeal of the reformers circumscribed enjoyment of the
recreations. The call for forbearance was too often
translated into unpopular campaigns to close the pubs,
which brought down such recriminations from the working
class as the Bolton and Hyde Park riots in the mid-1850s.
On occasions, Temperance philanthropy was thrown back in
the face of its promoters. In 1844, Thomas Trevaskis, the
'Temperance Father of the West', offered the people of
Padstow in Cornwall a fat bullock to roast for seven
years, to replace the usual revelry of the annual festival
of the Padstow Hobby Horse - when he drove the first
bullock into town, both he and his offering were driven
out by a hail of stones. Temperance reformers were attacked by working-class critics for attributing solely to
intemperance the evils which came from the general squalor
and meanness of the urban environment - evils which could
only be remedied by more comprehensive reforms than restrictions on the availability of drink. The feeling that
the Temperance movement was a fundamental insult to the
capabilities of his class stung Francis Place into a
wholesale attack upon Buckingham's proposals, even though
they recommended a general improvement of amenities. (35)

   Working-class movements of the period spawned their own
schemes of rational recreation, where Temperance was
adopted as one of the necessary disciplines for realising
a broader programme of political and social progress. As
Chartism diversified in the 1840s, its local cells offered
a wide range of activities which nourished recreation as
well as the class cause. William Lovett in his autobiography recalled with distaste the crude amusements of his
youth, and in their antipathy to drink and boorishness the
ground rules that he laid down for his People's Halls
echoed the prescriptions of other similar workers' institutions of the period: 'Let us blend, as far as our means
will enable us, study with recreation, and share in any
rational amusement (unassociated with the means of intoxi-
cation) calculated to soothe our anxieties and alleviate
our toils.' Lovett was an early agitator for the Sunday
opening of art galleries and museums, the epitome of
'study with recreation'. This was all part of his concern

to promote a comprehensively rational life-style for his class. Thus he also emphasised the value of correct diet and proper exercise and encouraged greater attention to personal manners, rejecting in the process the rhetoric of Feargus O'Connor, for whom roughness of speech and bearing was a defiant badge of class. Wrote Lovett: 'Unshorn chins, unwashed faces, and dirty habits will in nowise prepare you for political and social equality with the decent portion of your brethren.'

Lovett displayed something of that puritan streak which appeared in other working-class leaders. Thomas Cooper, for example, another prominent Chartist, extended his strictures on loose entertainment to include all dancing and theatregoing. But, as Lovett's rebuttal of O'Connor indicates, respectability was not an end in itself, but a means to class advancement on a broad front (although the People's Halls were short-lived institutions, Lovett's tactics did pay off, for it was his representations on the part of the working class which did much to secure the favourable report on public libraries). (36) The Owenite movement with its Halls of Science also provided pockets of working-class activists with a meeting place and a regular programme of activities well leavened with recreation. Determinedly teetotal, and earnest and proselytising in tone, the Owenites nevertheless give the lie to any impression that the claims of reason must necessarily extinguish the joy and vigour of the play instinct; their love of music and, more particularly, their love of dancing contributed such an exuberance to their fiercely secular festivals that their clerical enemies were moved to accuse them of veritable orgies of rational recreation. (37) Other reform ventures appear to have achieved a similarly convivial mix of education and entertainment. Christopher Thomson was a lively character who started an Artisans' Improvement Society in Suffolk and revitalised the village feast. One day of the week's celebrations was devoted to 'intellectual training', to balance what he termed the 'beer and pudding business'. (38) But if improvement was not always the dour undertaking it often sounds (a point it is well for us to remember), it is clear enough that a heavy emphasis on discipline and propriety was a necessary policy for those workingmen who sought to make gains for their class within the system.

Only by demonstrating their commitment to the serious duties of recreation could the working class prove their fitness for the shortening of the working day, agitation for which drew increased attention to the question of popular recreation in the mid- and late 1840s. When the chief architect of the Ten Hours Bill, Lord Shaftesbury,

was honoured by a public address in Bolton in 1850, he
took the occasion to warn the working-class audience of
the great responsibility they faced now that the bill had
passed into law; he implored them to turn to good account
the extra free time they had acquired - to ensure that
they did not abuse their additional leisure by 'senseless
and disgusting recreations'. He urged them to see the
bill as a starting point in 'their great career of moral
and social improvement'. (39)

   In this, as in many other matters, the Bolton workingman, like his fellows elsewhere, did not want for good
advice; but he still lacked adequate amenities. The town
had been one of the earliest to take advantage of municipal incorporation and had received its charter in 1838,
but this had done little to stimulate recreational improvement. One impediment had been the political and
sectarian bitterness of the 1840s, which divided public
life in Bolton as in many other towns. The Tories assailed the Liberals as 'political economists' whose re-
trenchments threatened popular amusements in general and
the Cross Keys Fair in particular. The Liberals retorted
by attacking the Tories for celebrating their first
election victory by calling a holiday and squandering
public funds on an inaugural procession to the parish
church, an innovation which gave added offence in its
religious particularism. Bolton's glee club was destroyed
by quarrelling over the Corn Laws and a project for public
baths was delayed by party squabbling. The town's public
library, opened in 1852, was almost the only municipal improvement to recreation. There were enlightened employers
like the Ashworth brothers, but the 'Chronicle' reported
that 'the majority of employers concern themselves only to
see that their operatives do their allotted work, and for
nought beside.' The neglect was still extensive, as the
paper made clear in another lament in the mid-1850s:
'Where is there a town which either in itself, its environment, or its public institutions, offers such scanty
means of either physical or mental recreation to the
workingman?' (40)

IV

The wider evidence suggests that Bolton was far from being
as exceptional as the local editor believed, for the
overall gains in recreational improvement in the 1830s and
1840s were slender. In the first place, the number of
schemes for rational recreation, whatever their provenance, were relatively few in number. As we have seen,

various factors help explain this basic paucity: govern-
mental lack of interest, reinforced by the arguments of
laissez-faire; the financial tightness of the new municipal authorities; the presence of other, infinitely more
threatening problems, which tended to absorb both public
and private reform energies. Education was the great
social panacea - recreation, where its importance was
recognised, was still regarded mostly as an accessory,
and the philanthropy which was expected to assist in its
improvement may have been curtailed by the uneven performance of the economy.
    Schemes that were introduced were often disappointing
to promoters and participants - why was this so? One
common feature which undoubtedly affected working-class
attendance was the insistence upon certain prerequisites
of conduct and appearance. At Flockton, admission to the
company clubroom and playgrounds was dependent upon 'a
respectable demeanour' and, among the children, evidence
that they had signed a Temperance pledge. At a Liverpool
mill, an annual summer fête was open to those employees
'whose general conduct entitles them to a ticket, upon
their being able to give satisfactory proof of being in
the habit of attending some place of instruction or of
public worship on a Sunday'. Samuel Greg considered that
only about a half of his workforce were eligible for more
than one invitation per year to his parties; these were
'the superior ones - the aristocracy of the place'. Admission to a free exhibition in Bury's new Town Hall was
denied to those wearing clogs. 'The Times' provides another tell-tale example of this kind of discrimination in
reporting on the passage of a private bill of Ewart's
which threw open Regent's Park to the public in 1841.
Here, claimed the paper, was an encouraging move in 'the
redemption of the working class through recreation';
after all, it continued, why should the lower orders not
enjoy 'the liberty of taking a walk in the more plebeian
portions of the park, provided they have a decent coat
on'. Provided they had decent coats on, provided they
were regular attenders at Sunday school, provided they
signed a Temperance pledge - all these conditions reduced
the eligibility of workpeople. There were, moreover, some
friends of improvement who found the working classes manifestly too unscrubbed to make a respectable public début.
To Bishop Blomfield, speaking in the Lords, the way to
social salvation lay through the bath-house: 'it must be
obvious that before the needful recreation of the people
can be attained, before museums and public places could be
made available, habits and cleanliness must be diffused
throughout the whole community.' Cleanliness came before

godliness, but a broad hint of both was needed to gain
entrance to the park or playground. (41)

More central to an explanation of working-class disenchantment is class hostility. Tremenheere discerned this
in the collapse of a lending library scheme in the north-
east, which he attributed to 'the spirit of jealous suspicion with which everything set on foot by the masters is
regarded'. Sporadic benevolences could obviously not
dispel overnight the working-class resentment of the assault on popular amusements which more frequently marked
the interest of the middle class in such matters. Reconciliation may have been difficult where improvement was
too crudely designed as an instrument of work discipline.
'The Times' found this motive distressingly common:

> Popular gatherings and merrymakings seem, really, in
> this utilitarian generation, to be tolerated only as
> stimulants for provoking people to 'industry'.... It
> is entirely reprehensible to celebrate with misplaced
> festivities what is in reality the greatest disgrace
> of all - viz, the necessity of securing the good
> conduct of the poor by artificial and secondary con-
> trivances.

It seems too that the employers' benevolences could carry
a sting in the tail, if we take account of the experience
of one workingman, who here recalls his unease at the
spectacle of the boss ingratiating himself with the men at
the printers' traditional autumn feast: (42)

> Somehow it generally happens that this brief moment of
> relaxation is immediately followed by a tightening of
> the reins of government and a rather rough assertion of
> authority. As if the employer were fearful that his
> previous sentiments of universal brotherhood with which
> the hearts of employers expand convulsively and regu-
> larly once a year should be mistaken for anything more
> than they are meant for - mere flowers of rhetoric -
> next day comes some Draconic enforcement of often obso-
> lete laws. At the heels of the weigh-goose, too, there
> frequently comes 'the bullet' as it is termed, or the
> sudden discharge, which sends a third or a half of the
> hands adrift after a fortnight's notice.

Working-class disillusion in Bolton was fed by the
shabby spectacle of the Peel Park scheme, whose erratic
progress was sabotaged by sectional priorities among the
local middle class. (43) Although the machinery and resources of the municipal government were sufficient to
provide for such a park in 1850, public opinion decided
that such an undertaking had to involve a positive act of
will on the part of the whole town, in deference both to
the memory of Sir Robert and to the virtues of self-help.

A committee was struck to raise a public subscription and
make an appeal to the working classes, who as the main
prospective beneficiaries were expected to give the lead;
once their interest in the scheme had been realised in
hard cash, the middle classes, so it was argued, would
come forward with a subvention. Workshop collections over
the winter of 1850-1 mounted steadily, and the Treasury
weighed in with a grant from the government. In the
meantime the park committee's voice grew fainter, and
workingmen's letters to the 'Chronicle' asked if the committee had disappeared. It had certainly gone to ground,
and surfaced only briefly in the spring of 1852 to an-
nounce the shelving of the park scheme in view of the
inordinate expense of land. In the following recriminations the Radical manufacturer Thomasson accused the
'Tory' committee of bad faith; back came the retort that
Thomasson was one of several employers who had refused to
allow collections among their workpeople, for fear of the
party advantage their opponents might derive from the successful promotion of the scheme.

Thomasson's alleged boycott was, however, less offensive to the popular mind than that of the clergy and
Sunday school teachers. The defenders of the Star against
the anti-singing saloon association raised the charge that
the churches had sunk Peel Park (and other schemes) by
reserving their funds for improvements of their own establishments rather than for projects of general public
benefit - this allegation remained a staple of popular
debate in Bolton for nearly twenty years. (44) Such
charges undoubtedly killed working-class support for any
later subscription scheme; when there was talk of a
Public Institution in 1860, one workingman wrote to the
'Chronicle' explaining that he and his father were both
deaf to such appeals, having each lost half-sovereigns on
a previous project. (45)

Compounding such antipathy was the distinct unease
which characterised the social exchanges between the
classes on occasions when recreation was taken in common.
As we have seen, the traditional social bridges which had
been built by the church, the aristocracy and the gentry
had either fallen into disuse or were maintained for the
occasional rites of an obsolescent sub-culture; the
middle-class employer or professional man had no habit of
easy association with his workpeople, certainly nothing of
the studied yet engaging social style of the eighteenth-
century country grandee or squire that E.P.Thompson has
recently anatomised. 'The great practical education of an
Englishman', so a Commons committee still felt it reasonable to maintain at the end of this period, 'is derived

from the incessant intercourse between master and man in
trade', but the social experience of the workplace was
already becoming too discrete and limited to generate much
common sociability in the more loosely structured milieu
of leisure. A fundamental shortcoming among reformers was
that they had little real knowledge of the actual
substance of working-class leisure and recreation; in an
age of extensive social enquiry, the workingman was more
studied, more understood and more respected in the setting
of his work than of his play. At the end of the working
day master and men parted, and from this fact a Sheffield
MP felt obliged to inform a select committee on public
walks: 'I am scarcely a competent witness to their [the
workingmen's] social habits.' William Sargant, a Birmingham manufacturer, recorded how he had deceived himself
with the facile assumption that the steady habits he saw
in his own workshop were consistently reproduced in life
outside work: (46)

> Most of us know very little about what goes on among
> workmen in the evening. We see them in their places
> during the day, we find them always ready to labour
> when they are called upon, and we set them down as men
> of temperate habits; inferring from their regularity
> that they are not guilty of excesses in their leisure
> hours. It is sometimes startling to find that we are
> entirely mistaken.

Plebeian recreation was, therefore, an alien world, and
the middle-class interloper was least unhappy in it when
decorating a platform or standing at a lectern. The first
stance served to emphasise social distance, the second
made plain the didactic intentions of rational recreation
- a further obstacle to its success.

Whatever its accessories, rational recreation was
basically and relentlessly didactic. As Heywood had
revealed, the entertainments at the Lyceums were devised
to sugar the pill of instruction. Once the revellers were
pinned to their seats by a great weight of tea and buns,
they became a captive audience for lectures on political
economy, or homilies on the virtues of a Christian home
life. Yet it is important to realise that Heywood was a
venturesome man in his day, for he was willing to allow
that popular recreation could legitimately embrace
pleasure, the pursuit of which was vilified in his own
culture as the road to vicious sensual gratification -
the mark of an unregenerate aristocracy and a recalcitrant
working class. He was also (against the wishes of his
fellow directors) prepared to serve beer ('the merry brown
bowl') at the mechanics' parties. He was, in fact, prepared to meet working-class culture half-way. That this

was exceptional may be judged by comparing Heywood's
tolerance with the forbidding severity of correspondents
to the 'Bolton Chronicle' on this question. 'Pro Bono
Publico', for example, advocated no amusements but such as
would impart a high-toned morality and pure devotional
principles. A letter from a tradesman on the Peel Park
proposal went thus: (47)

> The proper park for a Sunday afternoon is a tastefully
> laid out modern cemetery, where a conspicuous tablet,
> to the memory of Sir Robert Peel, or any other great
> and good man would preach a sermon upon the reward of
> virtue in the future.

It may be objected that letters to the editor notoriously
represent a sour sample of humanity but there is other
confirmation of the discouraging burden that improving
recreation was expected to carry. Henry Mayhew recommended 'wholesome amusements' to rescue the costermongers
from 'the moral mire in which they are wallowing' but
added: (48)

> The misfortune, however, is that, when we seek to
> elevate the character of the people, we give them such
> mere dry abstract truths and dogmas to digest, that the
> uneducated mind turns away with abhorrence.... we
> strive to make true knowledge and true beauty as for-
> bidding as possible to the uneducated and the unrefined
> that they fly to their penny gaffs, their two-penny
> hops, their beer shops and their gambling grounds for
> pleasures which we deny them, and which we, in our
> arrogance, believe it is possible for them to do
> without.

By the early 1850s, when Mayhew was writing, there
could be no doubt that big changes had taken place in
popular recreation. The study of a society at play was
held to be an especially revealing test of its moral
character, and several commentators were comforted by
England's record of improvement. But improvement was
essentially a middle-class concept and applauding its
progress was primarily an exercise in bourgeois self-
congratulation. Rational recreation could claim its
successes, but it had encountered a number of difficulties
which would not admit of easy solution in a class society.
Men in the field close to working-class life realised how
formidable was the task of remaking a whole culture. As
Tremenheere pointed out: 'To train a rising society in
the right way, is a process of comparatively little difficulty, but to change a great uneducated mass requires the
well directed effort of many years.' (49)

The New Leisure World of the Mid-Victorians: the Expansion of Middle-class Recreation, its Practice and Problems

In the years around the mid-century the Victorians entered a new leisure world. The Ten Hours Act of 1847 and the Great Exhibition at the Crystal Palace in 1851 were both in their various ways the concrete and symbolic pivots of this change whereby leisure in its modern form became progressively more plentiful, more visible, more sought after and more controversial. Something of the impact of this phenomenon (and the tensions it generated) is well caught in a leading article in 'The Times', 20 June 1876, which remarked tetchily on the importunate demands of 'Modern Amusements':

> The space we ourselves are from time to time compelled to surrender to this class of subject is in itself not the least proof of the importance they have attained ... a mingled mass of perfectly legitimate pleasures ever thrusting themselves forward in a variety of shapes, some known, some unknown, to our more easily contented ancestors, and all together making continually increasing demands upon our time, upon our money, and not least, upon our strength and powers of endurance.

As we shall see, the untutored workers whom Tremenheere had contemplated with such unease on the eve of this new era, were to participate in this 'mingled mass of pleasures', but it is a point of considerable importance that it was the middle classes who were the most substantial beneficiaries of the new bounty. Like their inferiors they were entering into the process of developing a new culture within the unique matrix of a maturing urban industrial society, and from the mid-century on leisure and its activities became a significant area of social innovation and fulfilment for the Victorian bourgeoisie. The increasingly prominent role of recreation in middle-class life, its effects upon the bourgeois

identity, the debate which such changes generated - all
these features of the new leisure world held important
implications for campaigns to improve the recreations of
the working classes. (1)

I

Leisure and its enjoyments were hardly a mid-Victorian
invention, but contemporaries were frequently moved to
draw a contrast between the more abundant leisure of their
own day and the meagre commons of previous decades. The
middle classes of the older provincial centres of England
had enjoyed a cultural life of considerable vigour and
sociability in the late eighteenth century, and many of
its institutions, if not perhaps its original élan, had
survived into the early Victorian period. In the new
towns too, middle-class life had not been all jejeune:
Bamford was as impressed by the literary and musical
interests of the Lancashire middle classes in the 1840s as
he was by those of the workers; a Bolton lawyer who took
articles in the 1830s recalled that hard work had taken
its reward in leisure hours enlivened by a constant round
of amateur dramatics, discussion clubs, much dancing,
singing and athletic exercise, together with the relax-
ations of fireside and garden. Such a life-style could
not have been unique to Bolton's John Taylor, but the more
general recollection of middle and late Victorians was of
an immediate past which was grey and joyless. 'We must
remember', wrote the novelist Walter Besant, 'how very
little play went on even among the comfortable and opulent
classes in those days.... dullness and a serious view of
life seemed inseparable.' It has been well said that the
Victorian bourgeoisie had had their own 'bleak age' to
endure. (2)
    Relief came with greater economic security and the
time, services and commodities that it could buy. Though
the business world was still visited by periodic crises
after 1850, fluctuations became less severe and the remarkable expansion of the economy in the third quarter of
the century did much to cushion middle-class incomes
against irreparable reverses; even when growth and prosperity seemed to suffer a more general contraction from
the mid-1870s on, the finances of a substantial element in
the Victorian bourgeoisie proved solid enough to resist
serious curtailment of expenditure and consumption. Such
good fortune was being actively enjoyed by the 1850s. Men
who had weathered the various exigencies of previous
decades could afford to rest awhile on a comfortable

plateau of prosperity, accompanied by wives whose domestic
duties were taken care of by a growing army of servants.
Constant attention to business was no longer necessary for
the successful, and a mellowing process suffused their
lives. We may take the Ashworth brothers of Bolton as an
example. In the 1840s they had struggled through a period
of uncertain profits; in the 1850s they felt secure
enough to delegate the running of their mill to subordi-
nates and allow themselves a series of travelling holidays. (3) Relaxation also became easier with the easing
of political pressures - the Ashworths had imperilled
their business by their preoccupation with the Anti-Corn
Law League and the 'Saturday Review' interpreted the new
taste for social pleasures as a reaction from the intellectual and political crises of the Great Reform Bill, the
Tractarian movement and the fight for free trade. (4)

The pursuit of leisure was more widely remarked because
it was becoming more widely spread; it was not only
master manufacturers who enjoyed the new bounty, but the
lesser lights in a middle class which was growing more
numerous as well as more prosperous. Henry Mayhew sought
to represent a new middle-class type in his account of
Cockayne, a very minor captain of industry, but one whose
thirty-five years in command of a soap factory in Clapham
had earned him a trip to Paris. This was in the 1860s, by
which time the process of bourgeois enleisurement was
plain to all. Its reach continued to widen throughout the
period and T.H.S.Escott gave this account of its operation
in the 1880s: (5)

A social movement quite as remarkable as that which has
been going forward among the better portion of the
English middle class, has been taking place, and is now
steadily progressing on a lower social stratum. This
class would once have been called the small shopkeeper
class, and its present condition is almost the growth
of yesterday.... Only the commercial prosperity of
England could have generated the new order from which
the chief patrons of theatres and outdoor amusements
are drawn.

There were always new recruits for the single-minded
pursuit of money, but the second or later generations of
successful business families were less disposed to answer
its imperatives. The younger Gurneys of Norwich were
'rather more inclined to stand before the fire with their
hands in the fronts of very good riding breeches' than to
attend daily at the bank. The 'Saturday Review' remarked
in the 1860s how rapidly the 'habit of enjoyment' had
spread among the young. 'It is', the journal maintained,
'an axiom with many young people that they have a right to

be always amused, or to be always going to be amused.'
Certainly the middle-class young (of whom more were surviving into early adulthood) enjoyed more free time than
their elders had done, for the increasing emphasis upon
public school and, to a lesser extent, university education as indispensable requirements for middle-class
gentility meant a prolonged freedom from the immediate
pressures of earning a living. Eventually put to work in
the family firm the son and heir often continued to exploit the generosity of the paterfamilias - 'stretching
his legs under the governor's mahogany' - and apply
himself more to play than business. This much is clear
from a lively debate on the 'young man of the day' in the
correspondence columns of the 'Daily Telegraph' in the
late 1860s. (6)

   The 'habit of enjoyment' was diffused and encouraged
through major improvements in communications. By the
early 1850s the major lines in the British rail system
were completed or under construction. Rail travel stimulated a general public curiosity and helped break down
regional insularities of mind and practice. 'The typical
John Bull', said the 'Cornhill Magazine', 'is fast becoming a legendary personage; his vegetative life and
stationary habits and local prejudices are all disappear-
ing beneath the stimulating influence of the railway, the
telegraph and the great cities.' Of parallel importance
was the growth of the cheap press and the increase in
newspaper advertising: the tax on advertising was
abolished in 1853, the newspaper duty of 4d a copy went
in 1855 and six years later the duty on paper was removed.
Escott recorded the effects: (7)

> The cheap press, with its ubiquitous correspondents and
> historians of all contemporary ranks and occurrences in
> the body politic, has transformed the severely domesti-
> cated Briton of both sexes, of all ages, who belonged
> to a bygone generation, into an eager, actively en-
> quiring, socially omniscient citizen of the world, ever
> on the outlook for new excitements, habitually demand-
> ing social pleasure in fresh forms.

II

What were the particular forms that social pleasure took?
Certainly a great deal of it took place within the ambit
of the home and family. The proliferation of newspapers
was part of a general flood of literature which kept the
middle-class public well supplied with its periodicals
and three-decker novels, either for solitary reading

(perhaps during the new 'enforced' leisure of the railway
journey) or to be read aloud to the family group. Cheap
sheet music was also published in increasing abundance
from the 1840s; mechanical refinement and improved production methods provided suburban villas with moderately
priced pianos upon which the ladies of the house could
display their talents - music was a fashionable, indeed
necessary, accomplishment for girls. There were many
other new diversions for the drawing room besides reading
and music. The 'Saturday Review' found 'the cleverness
and the laziness of the age aptly typified ... by its
ingenious contrivances for getting rid of an evening'.
Within the home these contrivances might consist of
private theatricals, quizzes and games newly devised for
the middle-class family market, or older pastimes such as
draughts and billiards - the latter now restored to respectability within the new canon of 'domestic athletics'.
(8) Cheap service and gains in space and comfort in the
middle-class home allowed of the increasing vogue for
entertaining guests, particularly at the dinner party,
whose growing extravagance was a prime indicator of rising
consumption levels among a class increasingly divorcing
itself from its heredity of thrift and frugality. Gardens
were also part of the improved amenities of domestic life;
here the family and its guests could play a set of lawn
tennis (an invention of the 1870s) or take a game of
croquet - as E.L.Woodward pointed out, 'Alice in Wonder-
land' affords a convincing demonstration that every
middle-class child could be expected to know the rules.
(9)

     The mid-Victorian middle classes were not, however,
permanently home-bound in their recreations, though they
did in general take their public pleasures en famille.
The railway gave them in particular a new mobility in
leisure, and the regular spate of advice and reports in
the press in the summer months testified to the growing
habit and ritual of the annual holiday. Old-fashioned
watering places were neglected for the attractions of new
seaside holiday resorts. Travel horizons broadened, and
by the 1860s Thomas Cook was running excursions, not only
to the Continent but to the USA and the Holy Land. 'The
quietest sort of people', so the 'Saturday Review' observed, 'are uncomfortable unless they, at least once a
year, tie themselves together in batches and go prowling
over the tops of unexplored Alps.' (10) Recreation out of
doors was generally brisker than the gentilities of domestic leisure, as a London lawyer and socialite recorded
in his diary in 1861: (11)

Muscular Christianity, the Volunteer movement, and
alpine climbing are in the ascendant. The affected
Dandy of past years is unknown. If he exists, he is
despised. The standard or average English gentleman
of the present day must at least show vigour of body,
if he cannot display vigour of mind.

Sport or, more specifically, organised games gave expression to this predilection for the physical. The newly
codified games spread from the reformed public schools to
the universities, and thence into adult life; national
bodies for the supervision and co-ordination of the major
new sports were formed in the 1860s and 1870s under
middle-class auspices. The Volunteer force, established
in 1859 in the face of threatening noises from the French,
also contributed to this particular impetus and direction
in middle-class recreation; the local corps promoted the
cause of physical fitness and the sports meetings which
enlivened the drills often became the basis for the formation of permanent athletics clubs. In addition the
fund-raising activities of bazaars and fêtes gave an
outlet for the leisure energies and talents of the womenfolk. Though middle-class involvement declined considerably after only a few years, the movement was an important
leisure stimulus - one contemporary credited the Volunteers with 'fostering a love of outdoor life that has been
utterly wanting among the great middle-classes for a
century'. Certainly the strainings of amateur athletes
and part-time soldiers provided occasions for new leisure
festivals for middle-class families: the Oxford and
Cambridge athletics meet, the Eton and Harrow cricket
match, the Volunteers' annual reviews, rifle meets and
sports tournaments at Brighton, Wimbledon and in the
counties - all were significant additions to the social
calendar. (12)

Public amusements of a less strenuous kind were also
plentiful; so much so that Stephen Fiske, an American who
worked in London in the 1860s, found the English at play
anything but the traditional dullards that other visitors
had judged them (Froissart's tag 'they take their
pleasures sadly after their fashion' was another cliché
of commentaries on national manners). Wrote Fiske:

Taking the average Englishman and the average
Frenchman, the former goes oftener to the theatres,
has more holidays, laughs more, and spends more
evenings where something besides a drink and smoke are
to be had for his money, than the latter; and yet the
average Frenchman is mistakenly held up to us as a
devotee of amusement.

These conclusions were based upon Fiske's experience as a

theatre manager in a capital city which was sucking up the
theatrical talent of the provinces and thriving on a
tourist traffic built upon the excursion boom of 1851.
Providing one was not in search of diversion on a Sunday -
Taine found himself ready for suicide after his first
sabbath in London - there was no gainsaying the long-
standing vitality of the metropolis as an entertainment
centre. (13)   But what of the provinces?

There are some forbidding memorials to the bleak tedium
of provincial towns, most notably in Dickens's descriptions of Coketown and Dullborough.   In his archetype
industrial town, 'You saw nothing ... but what was severely workful';   in his archetype small town, 'the preva-
lence ... of putting the natural demand for amusement out
of sight' strikes a sour but resonant note.   An Australian
visiting England in the mid-1860s offered further confirmation of the discrepancy between the capital and the
country at large.   Only in London, he concluded, could one
find company in 'idleness and pleasure seeking';   he found
life in all the great manufacturing towns 'as busy and
rather more anxious than it is in Australia or the United
States';   in the small provincial towns he found 'too much
exclusiveness for an Australian to penetrate into society
when on a short visit'. (14)   It is obvious that there had
long been a gap between the compendious attractions of the
capital and, say, the thinner pickings available to the
Mancunian;   but none the less, with all deference to
Dickens (who was often concerned over this question), the
natural demand for amusement was being met in the
provinces, if only yet in modest proportions.   The sophisticated Londoner on his reluctant prowl out of town
could overlook much that served the function of entertainment or recreation, hidden as it might be, for example, behind the deterring items on a lecture list. (15)
Besides, provincials might save their time and money for
pleasures elsewhere: in its growth from a small country
town to a London suburb, Croydon lost its taste for its
local celebrations as its inhabitants sought their diversions in the West End by cheap rail excursions. (16)
Thus the Londoner travelling out to the provinces might
miss his country cousins travelling in.

Mid-Victorian Bolton certainly provides clear evidence
that the middle classes in one large manufacturing town
knew a real expansion of leisure and recreation.   Bolton's
growing population enjoyed general prosperity in these
years - the relative diversification of her industries and
her specialisation in better quality textiles enabled her
to survive the cotton famine of the early 1860s better
than most Lancashire towns - and the middle classes showed

a substantial increase in numbers and wealth. The
'Chronicle' in the late 1850s considered the local
bourgeoisie 'scanty' compared with other large towns,
but correspondents pointed to the recent wave of professional and commercial men now assuming middle-class
status in Bolton, plus a disturbing new breed of 'fast'
young men. The 'Chronicle' was pleased to see the leisure
energies of these novitiates absorbed by the new passion
for outdoor sports and the pull of the Volunteer movement,
thus dispelling its fears that increasing affectation of
manners must lead to effeminacy. But refinement was as
fashionable as athleticism and found its expression in
exclusive subscription concerts at the Baths Assembly
Rooms and 'select and gorgeous' dinner parties in private
houses. Pub society had ceased to be respectable. John
Taylor took the teetotal pledge and pursued his love of
debate in a private club which met at members' houses -
the pledge was hardly fashionable but the retreat to the
drawing room was. Middle-class homes grew more palatial
and one local builder at least made his fortune providing
new residences for wealthy Boltonians at Southport on the
Lancashire coast. Southport was the fashionable resort
town for the north-west, but the biographies of Bolton
worthies show how much further their excursions ranged,
from Scotland to the Continent. (17)

III

Yet amid this vitality one soon detects a persistent sense
of dissatisfaction and unease on the part of both observers and participants in this new leisure world. Ana-
lysing the palsied progress of a middle-class dinner
party, Trollope concluded that the pursuit of leisure in
England was as laborious, affected and dull as foreign observers persistently made it out to be, and it was the
spectacle of bourgeois 'enjoyments' that moved Matthew
Arnold to ask: 'Can any life be imagined more hideous,
more dismal, more unenviable?' (18) By taking account of
the problems of leisure as well as its gratifications we
can more readily understand the fundamental novelty of its
presence in Victorian life.
     The problem of leisure for the Victorian middle-classes
was a many-sided one. In the first place they were dis-
covering that recreation in the railway age meant planning
and preparation; time-tables meant an increasing preoccupation with time-budgeting and the co-ordination of people
and services. In a moment of disenchantment with modern
'holydays' 'The Times' complained that the search for

enjoyment was often fatuous: 'It is work, and it is
tiring work.... it involves a perpetual attention to
time, and all the anxieties and irritations of that responsibility.' Even when the respite of true leisure was
reached, its satisfactions were impaired by that com-
pulsive regard for the precise and purposive ordering of
time that nagged the creatures of an industrial society.
'There is', remarked the 'Saturday Review', 'a sort of
mechanical style in our joys.' (19)

A further cluster of difficulties lay in the very
nature of bourgeois culture itself. As a class whose
immediate history celebrated the virtues of unremitting
industry, the Victorian middle class had only an attenuated leisure tradition to draw upon, so that the new life-
space they had won for themselves was something of an
embarrassment - 'We really do not know how to amuse ourselves', was the 'Saturday Review's' admission in an
article on 'Pleasure Taking', 4 June 1870. The leisure
of the aristocracy and the gentry - the aboriginal leisure
class of history - was rooted in the husbandry of their
landed estates and nourished by a high amateur tradition
in the civilised arts; the leisure of the common people
still echoed with the collective rituals of the folk community and the craft workshop, and evinced a ready taste
for pleasure. Yet it was these associations which had
made leisure such a suspect quantity in bourgeois ideology; in a work-oriented value system leisure represented
the irresponsible preoccupations of a parasitic ruling
class or the reckless carousing of an irrational working
class. Though the bourgeoisie had none the less at times
been enamoured of the aristocratic style, the clash of
political and economic interests and the strictures of
the evangelical revival had severely reduced its attractions during the early Victorian period. By the same
process certain once universally honoured convivialities
were also now disallowed, but the question of their replacement could no longer be ignored, as the 'Saturday
Review' explained in a piece on evening amusements, 4
January 1862:

> It is a very fine thing to have cured ourselves of the
> boosing [sic] habits of our ancestors; but there is no
> doubt that the moral conquest has left a formidable
> void in our social existence.... the gentlemen used to
> be drunk, and are now sober; and the mistress of the
> house, who got rid of them in the drinking days, has to
> bear the burden of their reformation, and find
> amusements to beguile the weary hours of sobriety.

A wide range of modified or newly contrived recreations
were pressed into service to fill the void, but it was

difficult to infuse such ad hoc devices with much sponta-
neity, particularly since the exercise of choice was
heavily constrained by that need for moral legitimation
which characterised bourgeois leisure in these early years
of new growth. As another commentator noted:

> A lingering asceticism of sentiment, a relic of the
> superstition which looked upon the body as the source
> of sin, still affects our modes of thought.... We do
> not proscribe amusement as previous generations have
> done, nor do we go heartily into them, as Paganism did
> and the Latin races do; but we indulge in them and
> apologise for them. We take some of our more pleasant
> and more needful recreations with a half suspicion that
> they are only half right.

A further discomfiture came from the apprehension that the
freedoms of modern leisure might prove too great a test of
the individual's capacity for responsible self-direction,
in the absence of that mutual public vigilance that
policed the life of the small community. The temptation
to delinquency was thought to be most acute for the young,
particularly among the army of rootless young office
workers in the great urban centres. 'The immense size and
total unlocalisation of life', wrote a correspondent to
the 'Daily Telegraph', 'tends to make the career of a
young man excessively individual.... he loses the fear of
censure that is the guiding idea of much life in smaller
places.' Compared to the disciplined structure of the
workplace and the home, leisure appeared to some a normative as well as a cultural void. (20)

As we shall see in the next chapter, there were other
tensions which attended the middle-class pursuit of
leisure, but enough has been said already to demonstrate
its ambivalence in bourgeois life. Moral integrity and
the code of respectability which defined its public face
were essential constituents of middle-class identity and
class consciousness. Resting on basically religious
sanctions reinforced by the teachings of political economy, bourgeois morality had, in the first half of the
century, provided its class with an effective platform
from which to challenge the aristocracy and subordinate
the lower orders. From the turn of the mid-century the
new and extensive bonus of leisure time threatened to
subvert the internal disciplines of the middle-class world
by its invitation to indolence and prodigality. Unwilling
or unable to deny the claims and attractions of leisure,
yet anxious to maintain a sturdy and coherent code of
values amid rapid innovation and social change, the Victorian middle classes sought a rationale which would
relieve them of the need to apologise for their pleasures,

yet still keep them within the bounds of moral fitness.
'Many people', observed the 'Saturday Review', 7 April
1877, 'are manifestly incapable of enjoying repose and
light diversion except on the understanding that they have
a right to do so.'

The question received considerable attention in the
periodical press, particularly during the summer holiday
season, when the correct disposal of such a conspicuous
slab of free time called special attention to the ethics
of leisure. A representative piece appeared in the
'Cornhill Magazine' for September 1867, written by Peter
W.Clayden. Entitled Off for the holidays: the rationale
of recreation, it moved on from the usual breezy bon
voyage to the summer holidaymaker, to a consideration of
the nature, method and purpose of recreation, 'a subject
only now beginning to be understood'. The author emphasised how modes of life had been transformed by Britain's
industrial progress. In response to the demands of modern
civilisation, Englishmen had developed 'magnificent
nervous organisations' which gave them an expanded capacity for work. This enabled them to continue to exploit the
opportunities of the nineteenth-century world, but the
cost of the new regimen was high:

> Our great-grandfathers ambled along with an almost
> restful movement; we rush along at high pressure, with
> fearful wear and noise. Their work was almost play
> compared with ours.... A kind of necessity is upon us,
> even at home, much more in our spheres of duty or ac-
> tivity, and all continuous necessity is a strain.

Readers could therefore rest assured that holidays and
recreation were necessary, as relief from this strain;
they allowed 'the rebound of an elastic nature from the
repression and constraint of civilised life'. The rebound
was best absorbed in recreation which afforded a total
change of pace, direction and environment, for 'work and
play, like day and night, are opposites, and the widest
unlikeness between them is the truest completeness of
each.' According to this principle therefore, men were
encouraged to seek recreations which provided the greatest
contrast to their normal occupations, and the article
sought to free holidaymakers of the oppressive fears of
ridicule which too often confounded this stratagem:

> We are dreadfully afraid of making ourselves ridiculous
> before one another. Public opinion ... persistently
> merges the man in his profession, keeps him perpetually
> on the pedestal of his status, and will on no account
> allow him to descend from it.

Such strictures could be safely ignored, according to
Clayden's dispensations.

Thus did one writer try to relieve some of the misgivings which attended the modern pursuit of leisure;
there were, however, some important qualifications to be
made. Mere rest was not true recreation, neither was
amusement: 'amusement merely occupies or diverts, while
recreation, as the word itself indicates, renews and re-
creates.' Work and play were best dissociated in time,
locus and content - 'renewal and recreation proceed on
the principle of antithesis' - but their functions were
complementary. In this way recreation was validated
primarily as an adjunct to work and its ideal represented
in terms of the vigour and purposiveness appropriate to
work. Play, explained Clayden, was change of work as much
as change from work. The sentiment became a commonplace
under the imprimatur of Gladstone, who maintained that
recreation was nought but change of employment, exemplifying the ideal in his retreat from the toils of office
to the arduous pleasures of tree-felling on his estate at
Hawarden.

For all his purposeful tone Clayden was alive to the
potential of leisure for the intellectual and cultural
enrichment of the individual, but many writers were only
prepared to justify leisure in its utilitarian role.
Writing in the 'Nineteenth Century', G.J.Romanes put the
matter succinctly:

Recreation is, or ought to be, not a pastime entered
upon for the sake of pleasure which it affords, but an
act of duty undertaken for the sake of the subsequent
power which it generates, and the subsequent profit
which it ensures.

There were other tests of acceptability, as W.H.Miller
outlined in his 'Culture of Pleasure'. The proper recreation should, he advised, 'bring back body and mind fitted
again for the business of life ... and it should ac-
complish its objects with the least expense possible of
time, strength and money.' Writing in the late 1860s,
John Morley thought that considerations of time and cost
operated as a more forceful limitation than religion:

Just as we have ceased to believe that pleasure is
fatal to salvation people start up to persuade us that
it is fatal to getting on in the world. The active
worldling is as ready to call every kind of amusement
by the evil names of frivolity and stupid self-in-
dulgence as the converted saint used to be.

There was still a general suspicion of pleasure. 'As a
legitimate object of deliberate pursuit', complained
Morley, 'it is invariably disparaged.' Education, he
maintained, taught that anything pleasant was wrong. Yet,
significantly, Morley felt able to record that 'Even

within the most contracted limits, the range of allowable
recreations is being extended.' (21)

The churches were particularly sensitive to the expansion of leisure. An early note of concern was sounded
at the Wesleyan Conference in 1855, which recorded 'with
sincere regret, the existence in some quarters of a disposition to indulge in and encourage amusements which it
cannot regard as harmless or allowable'. (22) By 1872,
when the prominent Broad Churchman, Henry Haweis, gave his
attention to the problem, it had become more alarming:
'Our streets are reeking with the abuse of pleasure; our
society is rotten with it; our social fabric is crumbling
beneath it; our best institutions are being shaken and
paralysed by it.' (23) It must be noted that despite the
apocalyptic tone Haweis was not condemning pleasure, but
its abuse. 'Pleasure', he allowed, 'is a legitimate
incident of life, but not a legitimate end', and he sought
some middle ground between 'the lean ascetic and the
bloated voluptuary'. While conceding the case for leisure
in modern life, Haweis was above all concerned to impress
upon his readers the need to subject its pleasures to the
strictest tests of conscience. It was a weighty matter,
of a piece with the great questions of biblical warranty
and evolution. Here is Haweis writing on Music and morals
in a two-part article in the 'Contemporary Review', December 1870-January 1871:

> The enormous importance of the distinction between
> right and wrong has been so branded by fire and stained
> in blood upon the page of history, that everything in
> modern life sinks into comparative insignificance by
> the side of morality and religion. No art or science
> is allowed to pass the solemn sentinels of the
> nineteenth century without getting some answer to the
> momentous question - What in its own deportment is
> really right or really wrong?

Men looked to the churches for guidance. A Nonconformist
minister noted how the young in particular sought answers
to the moral problem of leisure: 'Where is the rule which
settles where to conform and where to protest.... this
difficulty of adjustment meets us everywhere.' (24)

The question was a prickly one to judge from the trepi-
dation with which clergymen embarked upon its public
debate. In a sermon at Sheffield in 1860 the Reverend
G.J.Chester maintained that 'The subject of amusement is
of such importance and involves such tremendous interests
that I might well shrink from bringing it before you.'
This was obviously no imaginary fear, for another
Sheffield Anglican minister, Samuel Earnshaw, came close
to losing his living after delivering a sermon on the

subject in the same year. Chester had moved gingerly, but
Earnshaw had pressed a bold attack against the old evangelical proscriptions on games and sports, for which he
could find no scriptural warrant. It was, he argued, in
any case 'unnatural to resist the call of nature for exercise in honouring what were simply the commandments of
mere men'. Earnshaw appealed for a more charitable attitude towards the theatre and other public amusements,
endorsing the example of the Royal Family who, he said,
'openly do the very things which the arbiters of religious
opinions and models of Christian practice have pronounced
irreconcilable with a religious state of mind'. In all,
Earnshaw was trying to reconcile the Church with what he
obviously considered to be the tolerable peccadilloes of
a modern society. 'Is anything', he asked, 'permanently
gained by increasing the burdens and restraints of a
religious life?' (25)

Earnshaw was a minor, though significant, figure but
the importance of this matter can be better appreciated
when we consider the concern of the Birmingham minister,
R.W.Dale, chairman of the Congregational Union, and one
of the century's leading churchmen. Dale tackled the
problem before a wide audience in an article on Amusements
in 'Good Words', a middle-class family magazine, in 1867.
'What amusements are lawful to persons who wish to live a
religious life' was, he claimed, 'the question by which
many good people are sorely perplexed'. Dale was anxious
to redeem the old evangelical strictures from charges of
casuistry, and to explain them in terms of common sense
rather than scriptural sanction. He maintained that the
proscribed amusements had been condemned because of 'the
accessories with which they have been associated'. Thus,
he explained, racing had been excoriated because of the
gambling which was so much a part of it. At a less
obvious level, bagatelle had been acceptable because the
game demanded no expensive and therefore wasteful
equipment, and was usually played within the family home.
Billiards was condemned because the expensive equipment it
required would usually only have been provided in a public
house (Herbert Spencer, revealing his affection for
billiards in his autobiography, remarked 'those who
confess to playing billiards commonly make some kind of
excuse'). Fishing was permissible because it was solitary
and encouraged meditation and communion with nature.
Shooting, interestingly enough, was suspect not because of
any cruelty involved, but because it took place among
groups, which usually led to the unseemly conviviality of
the dinner party and heavy drinking. Dale was attempting
to argue out a revised catalogue of permissible

amusements, but in the last analysis he was not prepared
to make many specific rehabilitations;   he acknowledged
that there were some honourable exceptions in a sea of
otherwise perverse popular fiction, and condoned dancing
provided it was not excessive or tainted by 'unsavoury
social intercourse'. He remained opposed to the theatre.
But he did emphasise that 'each generation must examine
recreation anew', and urged a more charitable attitude
towards the recreations of one's neighbours - 'That may
be safe to them which is perilous to us.' Dale's church
took some of his teaching to heart, for the problem of
amusements was subjected to several re-examinations, the
most notable being a Congregational symposium called in
1879. Here again there was evidence of an advance in
tolerance, for none of the contributors favoured re-
enacting the old discipline against amusements, though
much of the hostility to dancing and the theatre remained.
There was, too, a general feeling that amusements were
best kept within the home. (26)

Thus the churches came to allow the legitimacy of
leisure, but there were still many conditions they attached to its pursuit. 'Recreation', warned the Catholic
'Dublin Review', 'should be more than even negatively
harmless, it should be positively healthy.' The Reverend
Chester urged that, 'As when men work, they should work,
according to Apostolic rule, with all their might, so when
they play, they should play with all their might.'
Pleasure-seekers were reminded that Christianity had a
high sense of the value of time, and that duty to others
should find a place in recreation:

> Thus the enchanting country walk may be rendered more
> enchanting still by the visit of mercy paid on the way
> to the cottage of the poor or sick; the trip to the
> seaside may be rendered doubly enjoyable by giving some
> invalid an excursion; and the ramble ... can delight

the memory by the useful book given away on its banks.
That the churches themselves should make direct provision
for recreation was a point frequently raised in the 1870s
and 1880s. A layman attending the Congregational symposium had urged that, 'it would be better to reclaim certain
amusements than to abandon them to those who abuse them',
and such remarks prompted the churches' considerable participation in recreation in the last quarter of the
century. But it was not easy for churchmen to unbend on
this matter and, as a Scottish minister observed in the
early 1880s, 'The Church has still to set herself right
with what is called "the world" in reference to her
oversight of amusements and recreations, and her providing
of such.' (27)

Entering into direct competition with the world of
amusements marked a climax in the churches' mounting
anxiety at the general erosion of their pastoral presence.
Halting dispensations on the range of permissible
amusements probably just added to this wastage for unless
they controlled them the churches were thereby simply
endorsing the counter-attractions to the religious life.
William Thomson, Archbishop of York, in a sermon on Sports
and pastimes in 1874, spoke of his fear that the church
was losing contact with culture at every level, and admitted that many Christians were failing to find relevant
scriptural guidance on the proper conduct of their recreations. Perhaps many no longer felt obliged to look in
the first place - it was in a sermon on Leisure time that
the Dean of Durham, while arguing that good works and
self-improvement were the proper constituents of leisure,
wryly noted 'the more common feeling that leisure is out
of the pale of religion altogether, a sort of neutral
ground which we may fairly call our own'. (28) Yet,
though the churches were to lose their struggle for do-
minion over leisure, their caveats against unproductive
or purposeless amusements reinforced a mid-Victorian
rationale of recreation which bristled with the highest
intentions.

Accordingly, the recreations which recommended themselves to respectable tastes were those with some manifest
moral or improving content. Much that took place in the
home was naturally so blessed, but the new family games on
the market took care to combine 'innocent amusement with
instruction' - a formula met with in Greenwood's Round
Games (Questions For Our Sunday Tea Table, Bible Quartets,
Scientific Quartets) which earned the endorsement of the
'Bolton Chronicle'. The fusing of recreation with instruction had been exemplified in the Great Exhibition
and the improving mixture was dispensed in penny packets
in public lectures and readings across the country.
Albert Smith drew huge crowds in the 1850s with his
lectures on the ascent of Mont Blanc, illustrated with
lantern slides and the equipment used on the expedition.
The retelling of an heroic exploit, the information on a
foreign country which was now within reach of the excursionist and the excitement of a night out proved an
irresistible combination. Travel was generally regarded
as wholesome: 'To have seen a mountain', averred the
'Chronicle', 'is a great step in a man's education.'
There was thus a great deal of recreation that came within
the pale by virtue of educational rather than spiritual
content, though there was a felicitous combination of both
in oratorios, whose considerable popularity in these years

was attributed to 'the prevalent religious sentiment of
the English middle classes'. Because of its non-represen-
tational character, music was generally thought to be the
least corruptible of the arts; even so, we may recall
that Haweis had warned of the need to refer it to moral
touchstones. (29)

The concern for moral legitimation remained a powerful
determinant of middle-class choice in leisure, but it was
not the only or necessarily the prime motivation, for
recreations answered a variety of needs, and though the
Victorian bourgeoisie plainly suffered under some vexing
inhibitions in their pursuit of leisure they none the less
proved capable of exploiting its dynamic properties. This
is evident, for example, in their new enthusiasm for
organised games, a set of recreations which met the tests
of moral propriety while serving as an important medium
for advancing middle-class social aspirations.
    Charles Kingsley's exaltation of muscular Christianity
provided the necessary moral gloss for organised games.
As a country vicar in the 1840s Kingsley had championed
physical health:
    The body, the temple of the living God.... There has
    always seemed to me something impious in the neglect
    of personal health, strength and beauty, which the re-
    ligious and sometimes clergymen of these days affect.
    I could not do half the little good I do do here if it
    were not for that strength and activity which some
    consider coarse and degrading.
Thus he had done much to dispel the suspicions of the body
as a source of sin, a staple of evangelical teaching which
Clayden and others had identified as an impediment to
physical enjoyment. Kingsley urged his young audiences
'to carry into them [games] the principles of honour and
religion', declaring bodily health a matter of personal
responsibility to God and duty to one's country. Neglect
of what he came to call 'the science of health' would, he
maintained, render Englishmen 'incapable, unhappy, like a
Byzantine Greek, filled up with some sort of pap'.
Herbert Spencer acknowledged Kingsley's leading role in
registering the importance of bodily exercise, and himself
used the language and imperatives of religion in empha-
sising that 'the preservation of health is a duty.... all
breaches of the laws of health are physical sins.' (30)
Kingsley's novels gave currency to such ideals, and inspired a whole school of imitators who were, in the words

of the 'Saturday Review', 'continually ready to build a
model hero, very good and very strong ... and free from
faults and fat'. As 'The Times' remarked drily of the
spread of athleticism: 'When you can at the same time
enjoy yourself and feel the consciousness that you are
doing a moral action, it is difficult to refrain.' (31)
   In games, the rhetoric of recreation and religion
tended to become one. Charles Box, an historian of
cricket, wrote 'sportsmen's homilies' to console athletes
obliged to interrupt their games in observation of the
sabbath. His 'Musings for Athletes' consisted of biblical
tales rendered in the language of the sports field, thus
'Jacob's Eleven versus The Stings of Defeat'. But in such
stilted compounds it was the religious content which
suffered, and the vocabulary of exhortations which emerged
from the new athleticism furnished the sentiments of an
increasingly secular morality. The ideal of muscular
Christianity yielded to that of manliness. Manliness as
a Victorian ideal derived in part from Coleridge, who conceived of it as that state of intellectual maturity which
marked the passing of childhood. It also carried strong
associations of physical courage and endurance in the
sense of the old eighteenth-century virtue of 'bottom'.
Kingsley in effect had combined the two usages and added
a dressing of aggressive religiosity. (32) But it was
Thomas Hughes rather than Kingsley who provided the most
popular model of the manly hero in Tom Brown, the archetype public schoolboy.
   In creating Tom, Hughes drew heavily on his own rural
upbringing in Berkshire, and the boy represented qualities
that the author much admired in the old squirearchy - accordingly Tom was jovial, gregarious and combative - but
in his later writings Hughes was anxious to commend a
manliness shorn of any suggestion of boorishness or ani-
malism. Though the Rugby boys in the novel 'mixed it'
with drovers at the fair and navvies from the LNWR (just
as the Rector's son in 'Vanity Fair' had slugged it out
with the bargees at Oxford) Hughes remarked of such
brawling that he had not himself shared 'this indiscriminate enthusiasm'. Thus he deplored the notion of manliness as mere brute force, and was much concerned to represent its essence as a moral action which could be found in
the physically weakest of men. Hughes's own personal
model in this regard was Christ, but he recognised the
declining enthusiasm for this feature of his philosophy.
(33)
   Historically the aristocracy had a long claim to manliness, but in several instances their conduct was found
wanting by the standards of the revised ideal. In 1854 a

court-martial at Windsor broadcast an example of dangerous
horseplay in the Guards officers' mess. Among the many
censures on such behaviour, the 'Era' for 10 September
declared:

> In that great middle class who form the most important
> element of English society the feeling is one of un-
> mitigated and contemptuous abhorrence of the coarse
> habits and disgusting language which prevail where we
> looked for elevated and chivalric notions of honour and
> the refined manners of a gentleman.... We shall
> nowhere in manufactories or workshops find such
> unmanly brutality.

In 1871 there was an outcry against the pigeon-shooting at
the fashionable Hurlingham Club. It was, said 'The
Times', 'practiced by aristocratic amateurs out of mere
wantonness and love of killing.... It betokens and en-
courages the restless levity and insatiable pleasure-
seeking of our younger nobility.' Haweis offered this
comment: 'With some illustrious exceptions there is not
enough real education among our upper classes, or we
should not find them gawping over sports that the middle
class have long abandoned as brutal and undignified.'
Vicious antics in the mess and the slaughter of captive
birds were unmanly offences against the spirit of the new
laws of organised games, and all the more offensive when
practised by the aristocracy. (34)

The hostility is, however, misleading. There was a
continuing radical animus against the aristocracy, exemplified in the campaign against the mismanagement of the
Crimean War but, in general, hostility towards the old
class enemy was diminishing. The guardians of the new
morality of recreation had no wish to ostracise their
betters, but sought rather to use the new code as a discreet vehicle for advancing their own class by redefining
the qualifications of a gentleman more in terms of conduct
than heredity. 'Manliness without coarseness, polish
without complacency, nobility without caste' - under
Hughes's definition, any public schoolboy might make
himself a gentleman, though he owed his education to his
father's trade in 'unmentionables'. And it was in the
public schools, not in the officers' mess, Tattersall's or
the Hurlingham that the new model gentlemen were being
made, for the schools were at once dynamos of the new
athleticism and hothouses for the precocious seedlings of
a newly aspirant gentility. Contemplating the games cult,
the 'Saturday Review' contended:

> Very many parents consider that the first requisite to
> success in life is the habit of associating freely with
> millionaires and their sons. They would, if possible,

get teaching too; but the first demand is that their
boys should go to the same schools with the sons of men
of wealth and rank.... a boy is sent to keep company
with lords.

At the local grammar school in Derby in the 1870s, so
J.A.Hobson recalled, 'Sport was encouraged as a means of
bringing us into the company of more reputable public
schools on the basis of equality.' (35)

The attractions of status were an obvious element in
the appeal of lawn tennis, an innovation of the mid-1870s.
The game was promoted without any moral apologia, and its
principal recommendation seems to have lain in the fact
that it could equip the suburban villa with some of the
resources of the country house, thus reconciling flights
of social fancy with the measurements of the back garden.
Major Wingfield, the game's inventor, advertised a list of
noble clients who had bought the necessary kit, together
with a letter of endorsement from a baronet; the
'Sporting Gazette' predicted with confidence that 'having
won its entrée into good society ... it [lawn tennis] will
be a popular pastime in every English home which can boast
a level piece of ground twenty yards by ten.' (36)

Looking back on the 1870s, Escott had this to say:

In all things the accredited exemplars of the latest
and most cosmopolitan mode were followed by the younger
generation of the classes that conveniently were still
regarded as strongholds of the ethical severity which
Puritan ancestors handed down.

To the 'Saturday Review', commenting on The pathos of
pleasure seeking, 29 August 1874, the 'eager attempts of
persons to wedge themselves into a slightly higher stratum
of the social formation by seizing on the favourite
amusements of that higher level' constituted one of the
more prominent features of contemporary leisure. In these
circumstances, reprimanding the aristocracy was something
of an anachronistic exercise, a ritual denunciation which
hurt no one and cost little by fixing on antique stereotypes rather than personalities. It was mostly the reflex
response of an older generation; in a new and ad hoc
leisure culture, fashion rather than custom conferred its
own legitimacy, and fashion was dictated by the rich and
aristocratic - the magical 'upper 10,000' - whose appeal
remained undiminished by the scandals for which a few of
their number were still notorious.

But middle-class leisure time was far from being
totally given over to the emulative strivings of so many
'bourgeois gentilhommes', however much the latter crowded
the pages of 'Punch' during this period. There was in
English society a process of long standing whereby promi-

nent bourgeoisie could be assimilated by their social
superiors, but in the middle years of the nineteenth
century there was a flood tide of middle-class men and
their families who could not be similarly accommodated
and, in many cases, were not sure that they wished to be.
For this large group leisure provided an opportunity to
confirm and consolidate their social standing rather than
redefine it upwards.

Building a community was a task which went hand in hand
with the confirmation of class identity, and helped determine the shape and nature of middle-class leisure in a
changing environment. Urbanisation had herded the working
classes into a gross proximity in the centre of the
cities; the same process relocated the middle classes on
the suburban peripheries. The once tight middle-class
world comprising a handful of families with more or less
permanent entrées into each other's company was multiplied, fragmented and flung outwards to crystallise into
large numbers of discrete and insular households (lacking
as yet the telephone, that great and in England almost
exclusively middle-class instrument of social communication). The dislocation of old patterns of neighbourhood
intimacy was compounded by the growing practice of board-
ing out children at school age; young adults returned
home to find themselves bereft of local acquaintances.
The solitary family was inadequate for social fulfilment
and the middle class, no less than the working class, had
to build its secondary associations to combat the strains
of the new environment. For recreation these might take
the form of private house or garden parties among business
associates or the extended family, but a major agent of
regeneration was certainly the formally constituted club
or society. These voluntary associations embraced a wide
range of activities: sports, amateur soldiering, literary
and scientific education and debate, the definition and
promotion of professional interests, and the pursuit of
reform - all, in varying degrees, performed an important
social function. 'In the Volunteer corps', observed Hugh
Shimmin, the Liverpool journalist, 'patriotism is a mask
for social relaxation; not only is each company or regiment as distinct a section of English society as a club,
but its most prominent features are those of club life.'
(37) Contemplating the annual meeting of the Church
Congress, 12 October 1863, 'The Times' was moved to
comment on congresses in general:

They are great social meetings to which people go to
see one another and become better friends, or to learn,
in a genial, offhand manner, the general course their
thoughts are taking.... this is the meaning of the

Social Science Congress. It is not scientific, and it
is not a congress, but it is social.
By such means did the mid-Victorian middle classes sustain
communities of interest which overcame the barriers of a
cellular suburban society.

Recreation through association appealed on many counts.
It appealed on practical grounds, since for every middle-
class arrivist bent on raising his status with the cheque
book, there were plenty with a nose for a bargain, in
leisure as in business. 'Most roturiers [self-made men]',
observed Escott, 'carry into private life the sound
business capacity that has made them so successful in
commerce.' Plainly, clubbing together spread the cost of
facilities and equipment - the exclusive gentlemen's clubs
of St James's were copied by rising professional bodies
for their economy and convenience as well as their associations of gentility. A club atmosphere also afforded
new opportunities for informal dealings in business and
politics. All this suggests heavy male dominance, but the
broadening choice of sports and outdoor activities provided increased recreational opportunities for the ladies
as well. Games parties and sports clubs provided cover
for courtship and flirtation, and the constant surplus of
women over men during this period accounts for female
enthusiasm for the mixed sports of lawn tennis and croquet
- the latter, we are told, offered 'fresh air and flirtation in agreeable combination'. The ice-skating boom or
'rinkomania' of the 1870s was clearly attractive to young
people anxious to escape the chaperone, as Escott also
noted:

> Not without a shock to her sense of maternal propriety
> did the English Matron of old fashioned ideas see, or
> hear of, her daughter being twirled in the arms of some
> youth just introduced, or perhaps without even the
> preliminary of that easy form.

Even matrons bold enough to take to the ice themselves
were no doubt easily out-skated, just as they were soon
to be out-bicycled. (38) Yet there were also ways in
which associations reinforced rather than slackened the
bonds of orthodox morality. For good or bad, they reproduced the kind of mutual vigilance which acted as a social
discipline in the small town milieu, but which tended to
break down in the anonymity and discontinuities of a big
city. One imagines that correctly ordered social clubs
would have recommended themselves to such moral watchdogs
as the journalist Ewing Ritchie, who was scandalised by
businessmen who drank heavily in town but passed as models
of respectability at home - the Jekylls and Hydes of
suburbia. (39)

Voluntary associations in general, and those for recreation in particular, met a variety of important needs in
middle-class life. A perceptive French observer offered
these remarks on this notable phenomenon: (40)

> This tendency of the English to form groups through the
> attractions of certain pleasures, deserves our at-
> tention.... In France men like to meet for the sake of
> meeting; the Englishman is perhaps less sociable: he
> requires an object, a community of tastes, a peculiar
> tie, which draws him nearer his fellowmen. Does not
> this explain how a nation founded in great measure on
> the principle of self, maintains itself so firm,
> compact, and united, without calling on the individual
> to sacrifice any of his liberties? The voluntary as-
> sociation in groups and series, is the great counter-
> poise of British personality.

There is a further point: in a literal-minded society
with a taste for the formulas of constitutionalism, few
associations were without their rules and regulations -
by such proper devices the Englishman could choose who to
join with or exclude from such associations.

The example of Bolton provides illustrations of several
of these themes. (41) Here there was no resident aristocracy to turn the heads of the town's burgeoning middle
class; but the new men abroad in business and the pro-
fessions, many of whose grandfathers according to a disgruntled local informant 'had sold sand, boiled tripe,
cobbled shoes, sold clogs, worked the traddles, or spun
cotton', needed to find some corporate identity, some
social expression for their new status. A correspondent
to the 'Chronicle' in 1865 declared the great need for a
club for gentlemen (the term itself was almost a new
designation in Bolton, for men like the Ashworths had
been proud to style themselves 'manufacturer' or 'cotton
spinner'). The town's gentlemen were soon accommodated in
the succession of associations formed in Bolton from the
mid-1860s: a rowing club was in existence in 1865, the
year of the foundation of Bolton's cricket club (whose
membership grew from 30 to 220 in six years); an amateur
athletic club formed in 1870, followed by an amateur
swimming club in 1871. A public school man, trying to
locate his kind in a town to which he was a stranger,
wrote to the 'Chronicle' in 1872 suggesting the formation
of an association football club, and Bolton FC was born
the following year. Subscriptions were beyond the range
of any but a middle-class pocket, and there were several
complaints about the exclusivity of the clubs, so much so
that a Liberal parliamentary candidate in 1868 tried to
make political capital out of the élitist pretensions of

the cricket club and the Volunteer corps which, he
claimed, were 'confined to a certain class' (mostly of a
disappointingly Tory persuasion). We have seen how John
Taylor, the Bolton lawyer (and sometime town coroner) no
longer took his recreation in the pubs by the 1850s but
entertained at home, and mention has been made of the
town's 'select and gorgeous' dinner parties, but a good
deal of socialising, for some perhaps even the greater
part, took place in groups outside the drawing room.
'Home sweet home', lamented one Boltonian in the mid-
1870s,

> does not form the centre of attraction it once did....
> We do almost everything in public ... every idea nowa-
> days assuming the form of a society - and these of
> course must all be supplemented by their music, their
> eating and drinking, and the inevitable speechifying.

The process of adjustment to the greater incidence and
opportunity of modern leisure was certainly more complex
than we have been able to explore here, for the Victorian
middle class was a social composite embracing men and
women of widely differing conditions and experience. In
general, however, the evidence does show the increasing
facility with which the bourgeoisie learned to incorporate
leisure into the normal pattern of their lives. Despite
the admonitions of a rationale which subordinated recreation to the priorities of work and Christian duty, the
old constraints were dissolving, and the public face of
leisure grew increasingly unabashed, particularly among
the young. Yet tensions between work and play, between
moral glosses and social reality still remained, and were
reflected in the dispensations of rational recreation to
the masses, themselves enjoying something of a modest
leisure boom in the less straitened circumstances of the
third quarter of the nineteenth century.

4

<hr>

Dispensing Recreation to the Masses
in the New Leisure World

<hr>

From the mid-century, many among the English working
classes found themselves sharing in the new bonus of
leisure and the expansion and diversification of popular
recreations. The middle classes had therefore not only
to decide upon their own response to the invitations to
worldly pleasure, but what to do and say about the multi-
plying pleasures of the masses. Social reformers gave
more attention to monitoring popular amusements during
this period than before, but though they increased the
facilities for rational recreation they fell far short of
the complete realisation of their schemes for improvement;
among the various difficulties they had to contend with
was that of a more competitive leisure market, and the
refusal of the middle classes to play the regenerative
role the reformers assigned to them.

I

The growth of working-class leisure in this period was
facilitated by a complex of changing circumstances, the
most dramatically felicitous of which were concentrated in
the decade of the 1870s. First, the workingman (and his
family auxiliaries) enjoyed more free time, as supple-
mentary industrial legislation in the mid-1860s and trade
union activism in the early 1870s brought a further reduction in working hours and the provision of a Saturday
half-holiday in an increasing number of trades. In turn,
the success of the Short Time agitation encouraged further
campaigns to cut working hours, including that of the
Early Closing movement for shop and office workers which
continued to register minor local victories. Measured
overall the gains were no doubt marginal; many occupational groups remained unprotected at law, and to one

informed workingman the half-holiday meant a rearrangement
rather than a diminution of hours. But the Saturday break
seems generally to have been savoured as a real bonus.
Certainly its increasingly common observance imprinted the
pattern of 'la semaine anglaise' with its fixed proportions of work and leisure more firmly in public habit,
and though St Monday was not yet extinguished, it was
Saturday night that was now installed as the ritual climax
to the average workingman's week. (1) The working year
also began to assume the familiar profile of the modern
industrial society. The Bank Holidays Act of 1871 guaranteed modest annual holidays for bank workers and the
dispensation spread to other groups. Commenting on the
institution two years later, 'The Times' noted: 'The
result seems to have been not merely to increase the
number of holydays, but to stimulate the observance of
them.' If the paper correctly discerned a new trend, by
the same token it was anachronistic in persisting with the
old spelling, for the Bank Holiday was significant as a
purely secular device with no counterpart in the liturgi-
cal (or agricultural) calendar. Company holidays also
became more common: in the late 1860s bank clerks in the
City could expect up to three weeks off after a certain
period of established service, and railwaymen with the
Great Northern in 1872 seem to have been the first
workingmen to receive regular holidays with pay. Employers in the north increasingly conceded 'Wakes Weeks'
as legitimate annual holidays which reinvigorated rather
than debilitated their workforce. (2)
   Improved communications broadened the horizons of
working-class life. The cheap press expanded social
consciousness here as it had done in higher levels of
society; similarly, the working classes shared in the
benefits of increased mobility conferred by the growth of
cheap rail travel and the excursion business. Provincial
workingmen and their families poured into London by train
for the Great Exhibition in 1851. Sometime in the 1860s
working-class families began to take breaks of several
days at the seaside, where distinctively proletarian
resorts were developing. A party of Bolton artisans went
to the Paris Exhibition in 1867 and a London journeyman
published advice on cheap continental holidays for
workingmen in 1878 - vacations, that is, as distinct from
the traditional working tours of the tramping artisan.
Savings clubs assisted in financing the more ambitious
trips, and the development of third-class rail travel in
the 1870s increased popular traffic. (3) Robert Baker,
factory inspector, noted approvingly: (4)

The working class are moving about on the surface of
their own country, visiting in turn exhibition after
exhibition, spending the wealth they have acquired
'in seeing the world' as the upper classes did in 1800,
as the middle class did in 1850, and as they themselves
are doing in 1875.

There were other gains in space and facilities inside
the towns and cities. As one observer recorded in the
late 1860s:

The lavish provision of public parks, pleasure grounds,
baths and free libraries in all the larger Lancashire
towns, testifies that the corporate authorities are not
unmindful of their obligations to promote the health,
happiness and culture of the industrial orders.

In Bolton and district, municipal and private initiative
increased the number of parks and indoor places of assembly. A vast new town hall, opened in 1873, looked down
upon the Free Library, the Chadwick Museum, a new Co-
operative Hall, a second Temperance Hall and a rash of
different clubrooms, institutes and coffee taverns. Of
course, what might appear lavish to a visitor may well
have been so only in comparison with his preconceptions of
 the industrial town as a Dickensian wasteland; in comparison to local needs, proper amenities were still in
short supply. In proportion to the number and density of
population in many big cities the provision of open space,
for example, was grossly inadequate, and modern research
suggests that the 'civic gospel' of municipal improvement
brought only modest recreational gains for the working
classes before the 1880s. Yet it remains plain enough
that the workingman had a wider choice of leisure resort
than simply that between church or pub which had previously obtained. (5)

Though constraints on time and space were considerably
eased, popular recreation could still not escape the
rebukes of its old opponents. The sabbatarian lobby
delayed the Sunday opening of art galleries until 1896, a
stand which exasperated many working-class leaders though
galleries may have been caviar to the general; more offensive in popular eyes, as we have seen, was the victory
of sabbatarians in closing down Sunday band concerts in
London parks and their threat to pub opening hours in the
1850s. There were several clashes in Bolton between a
sabbatarian rearguard and a popular party led by the local
secularists, who interpreted the issue of Sunday opening
in terms of class discrimination. 'The question of the
Sabbath', declared Simon Hilton, veteran Bolton radical,
'is never mooted but when the privileges of the humbler
classes are concerned.' Hilton's party secured the Sunday

opening of Peel Park in 1867; two years later Hilton led
the fight to allow the sale of refreshments in the Park on
Sundays - quoting John Stuart Mill to the hisses of the
Sunday school claque - and there were other contests in
later years. The Temperance movement developed a formidable national organisation in this period which secured
various curtailments of pub opening hours, thus cutting
back on recreational drinking. In Bolton, regular memorials from influential Temperance supporters to the annual
licensing sessions cut off the grant of new pub licences;
the same group, in alliance with the Sunday school lobby,
also took advantage of new requirements in Bolton's Corporation Improvement Act of 1872 to pressure the magistrates
into withholding a singing and dancing licence for the
Museum Music Hall, the descendant of the Star. In the
same decade, the increasing reach of licensing legislation
also made fairs and race meetings more vulnerable to official closure, though it was the music halls where the
clash of opposing interests was loudest. (6)

'The Battle of the Music Halls' made headlines in the
1880s, but there was another battle over popular recreation - the battle of the streets - which went on intermi-
nably, but whose communiqués were lost in the small print
of provincial newspapers. From one of many similar
reports from this forgotten front here is the case of a
certain George Healey of Bolton, charged with indecent
conduct on Chorley New Road in the spring of 1866. The
principal witness before the court was a Mr W.H.Wright,
a respectable tea dealer of the town: (7)

> on Saturday afternoon, about half past two, he was in
> his garden at Heaton, when he heard a noise in the
> road, and on turning round, he saw a man pass by
> wearing nothing except a pair of drawers; while di-
> rectly afterwards he saw the defendant running along
> the road in a completely nude state, with the exception
> of a handkerchief which was wrapped around his
> loins.... Witness ordered the defendant to dress
> himself, and then brought him to the police office in
> a cab. There were about fifty men and boys on the
> road. Witness added that he had been very much annoyed
> by this sort of conduct lately. Defendant said he was
> only running for exercise. Mr Wright: He told me he
> was racing for 5s.

The police superintendent commended Mr Wright on his zeal
and remarked on the frequency of such happenings: it was,
he said, 'the same all round the town'. This, then, was
an example of the 'Race Running Nuisance', as it was regularly characterised by the authorities; there were
several other nuisances, some of which have been noted

previously, which also gave rise to frequent arrests. The nuisances were often the desultory recreations of the loafers in the street, by many accounts a common, numerous and obtrusive constituent of the town's poor. On Sundays their presence was even more disturbing, and their contumely more offensive - 'crowds of men and boys', reported one observer, 'for the most part all in their deshabillé ... applying the expression "bloody" to almost every person and thing that came in their way'. Such congregations must often have unnerved the middle-class passer-by and they most certainly outraged city shopkeepers anxious for respectable custom, but in the case quoted above there was no threat to life, limb or property - a large and interested crowd (some no doubt with money riding on Healey's performance) gathered together on a Saturday afternoon (a legitimate time-off work for most) and watched without protest (there was apparently no bad language) while Mr Wright made his citizen's arrest. Healey's specific offence was that of indecency, a condition easily achieved within prevailing definitions of nudity - police witnesses thought it worth while to inform the courts whether or not defendants in such cases were apprehended with or without a jacket on - but his general offence was against bourgeois respectability, and he was only one of the countless many so indicted in this period. The police had not by any means abandoned their attacks on the more publicised and sensational unruliness of certain surviving traditional festivals, but it was in their more intensive surveillance of everyday life that their discipline of popular culture was most felt. Police harassment of popular recreations was compounded by the hostilities of petty officials: park keepers broke up games in the parks, and library attendants became minor ogres in working-class folklore. (8)

Active hostility to popular recreation was therefore still very much a reality in the mid-Victorian period, but on balance the working classes enjoyed a greater freedom and opportunity in their leisure than previously, not only in terms of time and space, but in terms of spending power, the greatest of emancipators. Average real wages rose gradually from the mid-century, and there was a pronounced upward swing in the 1870s; since there was as yet only a restricted choice of cheap consumer goods available to the working classes and few social incentives to save for some progressive betterment of living standards, much of the extra pocket money went on leisure. Though not all workers shared equally or simultaneously in the advance, in general popular demand became not only more numerous but more effective. (9)

Popular recreations in this period of growth often
evidenced considerable improvement in terms of regularity,
moderation and edification, particularly in the north,
where working-class life conformed more tidily than
elsewhere to the parameters of an urban industrial society. Such trends were exemplified in the careful year-
round saving which made the seaside holiday a regular
annual occasion for many Lancashire cotton workers. A
survey of Lancashire at play in the 'Pall Mall Gazette'
for 11 September 1884 reported that £60,000 had been paid
out by Oldham's works' savings committees on the eve of
Wakes Week, adding that holiday drunkenness had much
abated. Choral and brass band music flourished in the
north and midlands, and armies of choristers descended
regularly on London's Crystal Palace for the great choir
festivals. The more popular and commercialised music hall
that took root throughout the country never approached the
respectability of these offshoots of orthodox culture, but
its devotees were seldom profligates and several observers
discerned a decent, humanising influence in this burgeoning institution. The Volunteer force was a patently respectable movement that was soon drawing a surprisingly
large number of its recruits from the working class - by
the 1870s young workingmen comprised the majority of
members in a scheme originally conceived by and for the
middle class - and the modern historian of the force makes
it plain that it was the opportunities for recreation and
camaraderie, rather than the appeal to patriotism, that
pulled in these part-time soldiers. (10)
Thomas Wright, the 'Journeyman Engineer', also notes
the popularity of Saturday afternoon volunteering in his
1867 description of a typical working-class weekend -
typical, that is, 'among the general run of the real
working classes, the steady-going, regularly-employed
artisans and labourers, and their wives and families'.
Other young men, observes Wright, who draws his illustrations primarily from London working-class life, spend
their Saturday afternoon as members of workshop bands or
rowing clubs, while their elders attend to a little domestic handiwork, peruse the newspaper or address
themselves to some more solidly educational reading. For
the womenfolk, routine shopping is enlivened by the
purchase of some new finery or a piece of furniture for
the parlour. After a substantial tea comes the Saturday
'night-out', spent most commonly in the theatre gallery,
the music hall, the dancing saloon or the pub free and
easy. On Sunday morning the men luxuriate in bed while
the women dispatch the children to Sunday school. Then
follows a large and savoury breakfast, after which the men

climb into their Sunday suits and repair to the barber's
shop, obviously a social institution of some importance in
working-class neighbourhoods: here they gossip with their
mates, discuss the previous night's doings, take a
leisurely toilet and, if they are regulars, treat
themselves to one of the barber's famous 'revivers' - a
sustaining confection of spirits and other healing
cordials.   The day proceeds with the midday dinner, the
most imposing of the weekend meals both in size and cere-
mony.   This is a select family occasion, whereas Sunday
tea (taken after an interim walk or nap) is a time for
guests and hospitality, and significant in the furtherance
of budding courtships among the young.   For some, Sunday
is given over to a special excursion or outing;   for few
is it the automatic occasion for churchgoing.   The piece
is not without a certain disingenuous cosiness, but in sum
it carries conviction.   There is incidental gambling on a
fist fight, some clandestine tippling out of licensing
hours, and Wright introduces us to the phenomenon of the
proletarian dandy or 'working-class swell', but the general impression that he leaves is of the comparative seemli-
ness and decorum of so much of this family-based weekend
recreation. (11)

From elsewhere comes evidence of how workingmen with a
literary or intellectual appetite made good use of the
wider range of public resources.   Tom Barclay, semi-
skilled hosiery worker and self-styled 'bottlewasher',
enjoyed a fair choice of recreations in late-century
Leicester: dancing classes at the Spiritualist Hall,
lectures at the Secular Club, Gilbert and Sullivan at the
Opera House.   From London in the 1880s we learn of a
certain Edward Baker, 'who had a faculty for making the
best of the various organisations created for the elevation of the working classes ... a perfect directory of
free and cheap concerts and lectures all over London'.
From Leeds in 1870 a workingmen's institute reported the
proliferation of cheap concerts, penny readings, church
entertainments and public libraries in the town.   Old
showmen attributed the decline of their profession to,
among other things, the modern appetite for reading;   it
was, they claimed, destroying the public credulousness
upon which much of their business had been traditionally
based. (12)

It was, of course, far from true that popular recreations had succumbed en bloc to a new sophistication, for
many traditional styles and occasions retained their
appeal.   'In most of our provincial cities and boroughs',
so the 'Saturday Review' maintained in 1869, 'the fair and
the race-meeting are the two great festivals of the local

calendar, the two seasons from which the mass of people
date forwards or backwards.' Though fairs declined in
number, recent research demonstrates how one at least -
St Giles' Fair in Oxford - proved capable of enhancing
its attractions, by utilising the modern technology that
one may too readily assume to have spelt its doom.   In
Lancashire the term 'Wakes Week' was borrowed to describe
the seaside holiday the workers increasingly preferred to
the local summer fairs, but the spring fairs remained
great occasions for neighbourhood visiting (though May Day
celebrations seem to have been appropriated for displays
of municipal pride - parades of corporation dust-carts and
the like). Bolton's New Year's Fair was still a two- or
three-day holiday, celebrated in more extensive fashion
than Christmas. (13) The number of race meetings in the
country actually increased, particularly in the vicinity
of the larger towns;   their provenance is clear from the
disparaging label of 'publicans' races' awarded them by
the racing establishment. The Turf was becoming more
commercialised: admission charges were introduced as a
growing number of courses were enclosed;   more exciting
programmes were devised to tempt spectators to pay for
their pleasure;   the bookmaker appeared in force, and
gambling on and off the course was further serviced and
encouraged by the cheap racing sheet and newspaper supplement.   The sport at the minor tracks was still rough and
ready and in general much working-class sport of the 1860s
and early 1870s remained unreconstructed.   Contemplating
the sporting press of the 1860s, one journalist remarked:
(14)

'Bell's Life' tells us, not what ought to be done by
Englishmen, but what, as a matter of fact, is done.
It shows what a large balance there still is versus
that crushing respectability which threatens to overwhelm us - it tells us how much of the animal pleasures
of savage life survives in the heart of civilised life.
Animality, excess, certainly boisterousness - these
were still notable features of popular recreation. Some
of their typical manifestations had been driven underground, as in the cock and dog fighting which survived
only in clandestine encounters, but a good deal of popular
amusement in the old style could not be kept from the
public eye.   The Sayers-Heenan fight in 1860 offers a
notorious case in point, and most historians of mid-
Victorian England have their favourite horror stories
of brutal or violent episodes which passed for recreation;
public executions continued into the 1860s, and elections,
despite reforms, were celebrated as popular holidays cum
licensed brawls throughout the period. A Lancashire

speciality was 'purring', a form of single combat by
kicking, which still produced occasional fatalities. (15)
The violent delights of Derby Day continued to jolt the
confidence of the most generous anglophiles, and from the
mid-century Boat Race Day occasioned similar popular
bacchanalia. August Bank Holiday seemed to encourage more
of the same - 'For days the streets are full of
stragglers,' recorded a Frenchman living in England, 'it
is a whole week lost, drowned in beer.' As suggested
earlier, there was a certain rawness and urgency in popular recreation which marked the reflex action to the
rigours and privations of much working-class life. Thomas
Wright thought there were times when the London workman in
particular was driven to a craving for excitement in his
amusements by squalid and over-crowded housing, and Taine
considered the licence of Derby Day 'an outlet for a year
of repression'. (16)

     But it was not all quite so manic: violence bespeaks
frustration but prodigality answers to other less desper-
ate explanations. From 'Gammer Gurton's Needle' to Harry
Champion's 'Boiled Beef and Carrots', the message of folk
wisdom to those who lived near the poverty line was to put
any extra money in the belly and not on the back. There
were in any case still relatively few competing alternatives to food and more especially drink for the spare cash
in the workman's pocket. The consumption of alcohol
reached its highest level in Britain in the mid-1870s and
it seems reasonable to assume that in working-class life
this represented a considerable increase in social
drinking in the pub rather than that done for physiologi-
cal or dietetic reasons in the workplace or at home.
Heavier drinking in these years may have been due to the
shortage of other leisure-time commodities or things to
do, but it must also surely have been an activity often
relished in itself, and much of the drinking behaviour
among workingmen that middle-class consciousness registered as excessive would have been well within their physical
tolerance. Drinking was also part of the unique and
continuing attraction of pub life; the licensed trade was
still under attack and the number of drink outlets began
to level off during the 1870s, but publicans and archi-
tects devised ways of making existing premises more com-
modious and their style and ambience yet more seductive.
(17) Though certain ritual obligations to drink were
declining, particularly in the workplace, the sentimental
drinker might still be propelled by some powerful traditions, for great things were still claimed for beer, as
this snatch of popular oratory from the 1860s reveals:

Beer and wine met at Waterloo: wine red with fury,
boiling over with enthusiasm, mad with audacity, rose
thrice against that hill on which stood a wall of
immovable men, the sons of beer. You have read
history: beer gained the day.

Strong ale and its legendary compeer roast beef were not
merely the stage properties of an erstwhile Merrie
England, but sacraments in a continuing mythology of
national superiority and class identity. The English
workman was the great ale-swiller and meat-eater whose
industry and stamina put the puny continentals to shame
or flight, in work or war - thus was the lesson of
Waterloo repeated in the prodigious exploits of Peto's
navvies on railway construction in the Crimea and France
in the 1860s and 1870s. (18)

Though not every day was Derby Day, there were a good
many occasions for celebrating its minor relative the
'beano', the 'spree', the 'blow-out' - all terms of popular currency in mid-Victorian England. The national
meeting of the Friendly Society of Ironfounders held in
Bolton in 1866 provides an example. The society enjoyed
a strong local following for iron workers constituted the
town's second largest occupational group next to textile
workers, and though it was in the process of transformation from a trade friendly society to one of the new
model unions, it obviously retained a strong emphasis on
good fellowship. The chairman opened proceedings by declaring they were met for two principal objects - 'enjoyment and pleasure, and to show the country that the
ironfounders were not behind other bodies of workpeople
in this age of improvement'. Improvement here was
measured on a different scale from that used by poli-
ticians and reformers - it came by the bellyful. In a
pavilion in Peel Park a local publican provided the
following spread:

1000 lbs. of beef, 400 lbs. of mutton, 500 lbs. of
lamb, 300 lbs. of salmon, 100 rice puddings, 150 plum
puddings, 200 cheese cakes, 200 small and 100 large
blackcurrant, damson, strawberry and gooseberry tarts;
6 loads of potatoes, 12 doz. of cauliflowers, 36 doz.
of cabbage, 24 bags of peas, 150 4 lb. loaves, and 1200
cobs of bread, in addition to cheese.

To cater to the thirst of the 1,500 delegates 'the whole
length of the west side of the pavilion had been appropriated to a refreshment department, in which were to be seen
a multitudinous array of glasses, jugs and beer barrels.'
Afterwards the ironfounders and members of local allied
trades disported themselves with 'singing, dancing and
reciting, and other amusements which continued until the

dawn of day'. The friendly societies in general provide
an interesting example of the continuing strength of
traditional recreational priorities in institutions which
mostly commended themselves to middle-class observers as
improving agencies in working-class life. 'After all
their drawbacks', concluded the 'Bolton Chronicle' in a
review of the Lancashire societies in the late 1870s,
'they ... provide an education in the duties of citizenship through the practice of self-government.' (19)

Thus rationality and old-style conviviality were not
necessarily irreconcilable qualities in popular recreation, a point given further exemplification in a suggestive piece by Thomas Wright called Bill Banks's day
out, published in 1868. (20) Bill is a railwayman who
goes 'St Mondaying' with his wife and friends to Hampton
Court. They meet outside a local pub, admire each other
in their best dress, and start the excursion with a
morning pint. They travel out to Hampton Court by hired
van, complete with cornet player to enliven the journey.
On arrival they tuck into a dinner provided by the van-
owner at 2s 6d a head - 'a first-rater; beef and mutton
and ham, and any quantity of rolls, and lots of fruit-
tarts, in the way of eating, and bottled ale and a small
cask of porter to wash 'em down'. The harmony of the
occasion is disturbed when Bill, somewhat flushed with
drink, takes exception to the superior airs of a young
shopman in the company (Wright himself detested 'counter-
jumpers'); after a scuffle, peace is restored and the
party continues, finishing up in late evening back in
town, at the Alhambra, the famous Leicester Square music
hall. Bill and his wife together with two friends share
the cost of a cab home, enjoying the prospect of scandal-
ising the neighbours by returning in such style.

Retailed in the first person, the piece has an internal
consistency which suggests how a workingman at play could
move through several different roles, all reconcilable,
but each in turn likely to be interpreted by an outsider
as the behaviour peculiar to a distinct, separate and
exclusive type within the working classes. On the evidence of his home life Banks would pass as the self-
improving artisan: he is a considerable and intelligent
reader who borrows books from the local institute to
supplement his own small library. Thus he belongs to the
tradition recorded by Bamford and lauded by the students
of working-class progress. In taking an excursion (albeit
on St Monday) Bill appears at first to be a further credit
to his class. His expenditure can be reckoned at between
10s and 15s for him and his wife, yet the day out is not
the reflex action of a poor family gobbling up a sudden

windfall, but the happy product of careful budgeting
which, so we gather, owes something to Mrs Banks's good
management (Wright, in company with other commentators,
attributed many of the miseries of working-class life to
inefficient housekeeping). Hampton Court, an historic
house on which Bill is well read, represents a 'rational'
choice for a visit, and in their concern with their appearance the party display that 'pardonable vanity' which
Slaney had once recommended as a tonic both for trade and
self-respect. Thereafter, however, Bill Banks's respectable image disintegrates, as he regresses into the time-
honoured role of the English workman on a spree. To a
middle-class observer he would then appear drunk, glutton-
ous and unruly. Detected among the music hall crowd he
would serve as an example of the feckless new breed of
workingman who surrendered himself to the temptations of
the 'fast' life. If Bill Banks is at all representative,
the pattern of his day out can, at a later point in this
chapter, help us understand the gap between ideals and
achievements in the work of those who worked to reform
popular recreation. It is to their continuing endeavours
that we now turn.

II

The concern to encourage rational recreation for the
working classes which had awakened public attention with
the passing of the Factory Acts in the late 1840s continued to grow in the following period, finding a firm
place in the general vocabulary of most social reformers.
'There is', wrote Professor Stanley Jevons in a much-
quoted article in the 'Contemporary Review' for 1878,
'hardly any other method [of social reform] taken sepa-
rately, to which greater importance should be attributed
than to the providing of good moral public amusements.'
This greater sensitivity to popular leisure clearly came
from the growing realisation of its significance as the
workingman's major area of free choice. As the Christian
Socialists pointed out in the house journal of the London
Working Men's College: 'Our work, whatever it might be,
was for the most part assigned to us by circumstances over
which we had very little control; but with respect to our
amusements much more was left to our freedom of choice.'
This fact gave leisure hours 'a value for the formation
and development of character which cannot be estimated too
highly'. (21) Since leisure was now assumed to be a
common possession, the manner of its proper disposal was
a frequent topic for debate at all levels of the press,

from the detached commentaries of the critical reviews to
the crusading journalism of men like Mayhew and George
Godwin (editor of the 'Builder') in London, and Hugh
Shimmin in Liverpool.

Working-class reformers and writers were generally more
concerned with the achievement of the essential prerequisites for leisure - time and money - than with its proper
content. They were, however, worried that immoderate indulgence in amusements and holidaymaking would reduce the
political consciousness of the workingman. In a well-
known commentary upon Lancashire in 1870, Thomas Cooper
discovered that affluence had reduced many of the heirs
of his unkempt Chartist heroes of the 1840s to political
indifference, and he stood aghast at the spectacle of
Lincoln workmen pawning their beds to take a railway excursion. Wright, too, had some misgivings about the
Londoners' insatiable taste for amusements. The recommended corrective was that of rational recreation, both
to continue the political and educational improvement of
the class and, through public good manners, to oblige the
other classes to respect the workingman. (22)

Faced with declining congregations the churches interested themselves more actively in the question of popular
recreations. This was particularly noticeable in the
Church of England which was shrugging off its discomfiture
in the presence of the urban masses and moving in to
tackle a wide range of social problems. The activists in
recreational improvement were only a minority, but a very
vocal one which pushed its case hard at the annual Church
Congresses that met regularly from 1862. The Established
Church also reassumed a prominent role in the Temperance
movement, which expanded its work of providing counter-
attractions to pub-based recreations. (23)

The commonest platform for reformers of all stripes was
that of the National Association for the Promotion of
Social Science which met in annual conference from 1857.
Meetings of its department of social economy received
regular reports on recreational reform projects. The
reformers in the field were mainly churchmen, local nota-
bles, occasional municipal officials, and a number of
middle-class women. The audience included most of the
leading contemporary 'friends of the working classes':
new model employers such as Mundella and Morley, Christian
Socialists such as Kingsley and Maurice, civil servants
such as Chadwick and Tremenheere, reconstructed aristo-
crats such as Lords Shaftesbury and Lyttelton, reform MPs
such as Slaney and Ewart. The tone of proceedings was
earnest but non-sectarian, the rationale that of gradual-
ist social engineering serviced by philanthropy. The as-

sociation was a good deal less rigorous and hard-headed in
its promotion of social science than its propaganda proclaimed, but it provided the most important single forum
for middle-class recreational reformers. (24)

Rational recreation widened its brief in one important
respect as reformers addressed themselves to the problem-
atical social life of the young clerks and shopmen whose
number increased dramatically in this period. Although
concern for their welfare echoed something of the traditional concern for the town apprentice, this group
constituted a new phenomenon, an overnight creation of
modern urban society; the clerk, maintained Charles
Kingsley, 'is distinctly a creature of the city; as all
city influences bear at once on him more than in any
class, we see in him at once the best and the worst effects of modern city life.' Clerkdom occupied a decidedly
marginal and ambivalent position in society; from within
its ranks one Liverpudlian wrote that it 'presents di-
vergencies as wide, and peculiarities as interesting as
does any other class of a great labouring community'. In
Edward Hodder's cautionary tale, 'The Junior Clerk: A
Tale of City Life' (published in 1862 and recommended to
employers for distribution among their young men), the
hero is well educated and confident of an eventual
partnership, but below the articled youngster with good
connexions stretched an army of young men with careers
ranging from middling to destitute - Shimmin, another
practised observer from Merseyside, included clerks and
shopkeepers' assistants in the working classes. (25)
Generally, however, reformers defined the social problems
of this group in terms of its urban environment rather
than its class identity. Young and impressionable, often
living in lodgings away from the restraints and affection
of home, 'their hours of business constantly shortened and
relaxed to suit faint inclinations for work', according to
one sardonic but not untypical estimate of the achievements of the Early Closing Movement, clerks were considered exceptionally vulnerable to the temptations of fast
company - juvenile 'swells' and 'cads' who had yielded
to such corruptions figure in most contemporary descriptions of music hall clientèle and the loungers in
city cigar-divans. (26) Organised rescue work had begun
with the founding of the Young Men's Christian Association
in 1844 in London and YMCAs multiplied throughout the
country in the next decade. Although at first these
institutions were narrowly evangelistic - 'Amusements are
not necessary to your happiness, religion is' - they began
to broaden their activities in the 1860s with cautious
doses of recreation. (27)

As debate increased, the lineaments of rational recreation for the masses became clearer. In the calmer
climate of the mid-Victorian era there was less preoccupation with recreation as a distraction from mob politics.
In any case, as we have seen, the idea of recreation as a
safety valve whose cathartic effect justified the sus-
pension of normal social disciplines was unacceptable to
men primarily concerned to maintain control and conformity. Play was not to be allowed any form of special
licence; rather it had to be firmly and unequivocally
integrated with the rest of life and securely anchored in
orthodox morality. Ideally - rationally - recreation was
an adjunct and complement to work. The literal implications of the word itself were repeated: 'Recreation is
the RE-creation, the creation anew of fresh strength for
tomorrow's work'; and again, 'Amusement, to be legitimate, wholesome, innocent, must be useful, in refitting
the body or mind for its duty.' Accordingly it was 'of
WORKERS only that there can be RECREATION'. (28) In this
prescription work and play were antithetical in form only;
in purpose they were part of a single natural process at
the service of God and society. It was however made clear
that of the two constituents work was sovereign: work
disciplines had to be projected into play, not vice versa.
As the house journal of the Christian Socialists' London
Working Men's College put it: 'The question is not, are
we to have all work and no play, but what sort of work can
we find pleasant enough to be made play of?' (29) To
invert the relationship would be destructive, as the
Bishop of Winchester warned a workingmen's meeting at a
Church Congress in the 1870s: (30)

> We have been considering how best to get the workingmen
> leisure hours and I myself am bent upon it. But why?
> That they may in their leisure hours raise their own
> physical force - I don't forget that we have a body as
> well as a soul - then their family, then their intel-
> lectual, and above all their spiritual being. That is
> the use of having these leisure hours, and if the ad-
> ditional hours should be spent by the workingmen of
> England in dissipation, riot and drunkenness - if they
> should be spent in learning himself and teaching others
> not to be satisfied, not to understand that work is
> glory, and that doing the work he is set to do is the
> glory of man here, and will be the elevation of his
> faculties - then better by far that they should not
> have hours of leisure.

The address reveals the tension which attended most
debates on the place of leisure in working-class life.
Leisure was a necessary condition for physical refreshment

and progress towards the good life, but without moral vigilance its practice would threaten the priorities of work and social discipline. The discussion of leisure was still characterised by the weight of cautionary advice it was made to carry. Leisure was time - ideally a third of men's lives, according to reformers in the Early Closing movement who resurrected King Alfred's formula of eight hours' work, eight hours' play, and eight hours' sleep - and time was valuable. Members of the YMCA (which was started by employers) were reminded that 'their masters would naturally be chary of curtailing the hours of labour unless they could see the leisure of their young men PROFITABLY employed.' Profit was tangible in work, but how was it to be made a recognisable quantity in play? Young men at the YMCA were advised to apply a simple cate-chism to their recreations: 'Are they likely to make us better sons, brothers, husbands and fathers, better servants or masters, better citizens, and better Christians?' (31)

At this point it might well be asked how the precepts outlined above differed from those urged upon middle-class audiences. The answer must be that there was little difference in basic teachings - the Victorian rationale of recreation was not in itself specifically discriminatory - but that the stronger tone employed in addressing the working classes betrays fundamentally different as-sumptions regarding the capacity of the particular classes for recognising and acting upon moral imperatives in recreation. A society based upon a paramount belief in the benevolent operation of free will had to concede the right and capability of the individual to practise and police his own leisure activities for, according to the commonest of contemporary analogies, 'Free trade, free religion, free art and free self-culture are all bound up in the same bundle, and stand or fall together.' Never-theless, it was as yet only the middle classes who in the nature of things could be expected to apply the appropri-ate moral calculus to their pleasures. Reformers were generally agreed that most workingmen still lacked the education and elementary accomplishments of 'social econo-my' - the proper management of time and money - which would qualify them to assume the responsible status of free agent in the dangerously open-ended world of leisure time. (32) Fears for the working classes' ability to apply the necessary controls in leisure grew sharper in the 1870s, when observers noted that gains in free time and spending power seemed generally to promote increased drunkenness rather than self-improvement. 'The period of transition from low to high wages, and from incessant toil

to comparative leisure', warned Goldwin Smith, 'must be
one of peril to the masses.' (33)   Faith in the powers of
formal education gave hope that the recent educational
reforms would produce a better disciplined younger generation, but there were still wide areas of working-class
life untouched by any effective control mechanisms.   Education in the necessary leisure disciplines had to be
taken to the masses.   It was, declared Jevons, 'a positive duty on the part of the middle and upper classes to
frequent the well-conducted places of popular recreation'.

The question of precisely who was to set the correct
example was no longer contentious.   Neither the aristocracy nor the bourgeoisie now contested for social or
political leadership in the terms of a class dialectic;
philanthropy in particular afforded opportunity for the
middle classes both to savour the snobbish frisson of
rubbing shoulders with nobility, and to advance their
claims to share in the common gentility which identified
a new composite ruling class.   The agreed denomination for
exemplar of rational recreation was that of gentleman.
Example-setting by superiors and the common association of
ranks in recreation was a formula well rehearsed during
the previous period, but it was now being urged more
forcefully.   In the first place observers argued that the
superior classes had need to be put on their best behaviour as a corrective to their own infatuation with the
lure of worldly amusement and the seductions of materialism.   Obliging them to fulfil their reform role would be
mutually beneficial and arrest the degeneration which
faced society as a whole in its transition to a leisure
culture.   'Raise the workers', wrote one reforming
journalist, 'and the masters will be shamed into morality.' (34)   A further and more prevalent argument for
securing an upper-class presence in popular recreation was
that it would achieve a return to what many believed to
have been a pristine state of fraternity among all the
classes.   The bitter alienations of the previous period
seemed to have subsided but industrial strife still advertised the hostility between capital and labour, and urban
dispersal and the physical segregation of the classes
threatened general social disintegration.   Rational recreation could help rebuild a community of common sentiment
and interest.   This was the formula of the Christian
Socialists, as explained by the secretary of their London
Working Men's College to the Social Science Association.
The promoters sought to overcome diversities of birth and
education by appealing to

the weight of common interests which bind together
fellow strugglers in the race of human progress....

they work on the principle of a direct personal relationship ... on the principle, in short, that in
order to do any good to or for a man you must first
make a friend of him.

The Christian Socialist cultivated only a select corner of
working-class company, but there was general agreement
among reformers that some such exercise on a broad scale
was necessary to integrate and humanise mass society. (35)
As the 'Bolton Chronicle' put it in more down-to-earth
manner: 'If the working classes cannot have equality,
they can at least have fraternity.' (36)

   What was the best setting for this fraternal exercise,
this restoration of a community of feeling? The semi-
rural industrial colonies which had furnished the milieu
for reform experiments in the previous era were mostly
defunct; there were continuing experiments in building
model industrial settlements - Titus Salt built Saltaire
near Bradford in the 1850s under the spell of Disraeli's
picture of Trafford of Wodgate as the ideal employer - but
this form of patently proprietorial philanthropy carried
less weight than previously in reform thinking, which
looked now for something less isolated and more accessible
to general membership. (37) The search passed by some
seemingly obvious alternatives, for the middle classes
were unwilling to throw open their homes or relax the
exclusive regulations of their clubs and societies. There
was a long-standing concern with the alleged breakdown of
the working-class family in industrial towns and reformers
urged the prior claims of home life as a salutary and
necessary recreation for the workingman, but his home was
too small and ill-equipped to afford a common meeting
ground and homes in general were in any case becoming
increasingly respected as desirable sanctums of privacy.
(38) In this regard the home also lacked what reformers
came to hold as a vital property of rational recreation -
visibility or, in its contemporary usage, publicity, the
condition or fact of being open to public observation or
knowledge. Teaching by example was done most effectively
and economically in open congregation. Public assembly
under proper restraints and of the right social mix
exerted a collective moral vigilance - 'the coercion of
public opinion', 'a police of good understanding', as it
was variously called by reformers. (39) It was therefore
of little use to clear the streets of its various
nuisances if the workingman retreated to the impenetrable
bolt-hole of the home or, much worse, the pub.

   There were suggestions for taming the pub (and other
places of entertainment) by constructing the front entirely of plate glass so that its denizens would be visi-

ble to those outside and thus shamed into moderation and respectability, but reformers generally preferred that the milieu of improvement be of their own making. (40) In an age which remained awestruck by the scale, logic and success of the Great Exhibition's Crystal Palace, schemes for some kind of grand mechanical solution were regularly offered: People's Palaces - built at Muswell Hill in the 1860s and the Mile End Road in the 1880s - were attempts to provide a Great Eastern, as it were, of rational recreation. (41) There was support, too, for public gardens on the model of the German Volksgarten or Copenhagen's Tivoli. Foreign travel introduced an increasing number of middle-class reformers to the continental Sunday; its moderation and easy mingling of the classes in public promenade won many new converts and encouraged the growing opposition to sabbatarianism. A People's Garden Company issued a prospectus in London in 1870, and there were regular appeals in the press for the opening of the many private city squares to the public. (42) But the most favoured device for improvement was not the people's palace or the people's garden but the smaller association of the club or institute. Although the pub was still anathema to most reformers, its ubiquity and popularity in working-class life made it an inescapable model, and rational recreation tried in many guises to reproduce its human scale and convivial intimacy of spirit away from the contagion of strong drink and the corrupting benevolences of the publican. Accordingly it was the smaller institutions of rational recreation which grew considerably in number from the mid-century.

There was considerable debate among reformers as to precisely what fare these institutions should offer in the name of rational recreation. Given the moral purpose it was meant to serve it was, as one interested party neatly observed, a very difficult task to provide recreation that was 'pure, yet not dull; relaxing, yet not enervating; invigorating, yet not too exciting; popular, yet not vulgarising, and much more besides'. Since the early Victorian period improving institutions for workingmen had concentrated on solidly instructional fare. Where the pill of 'useful knowledge' had been sugared with entertainment, the more serious purposes had often been thwarted; this had been so with the Lyceums in Manchester, as we have seen, and it held true for the London Mechanics' Institute in the 1850s. (43) But as popular demand for amusement rose steeply in the 1850s and 1860s reformers were forced to acknowledge it. In 1861 the London Working Men's College felt it necessary to hold a conference on the 'Amusement Question', although

in this particular confrontation between the claims of
seriousness and frivolity, as J.M.Ludlow chose to charac-
terise it, seriousness prevailed.   Three years later, at
the YMCA's annual conference, workers in the field
impressed upon senior officials how important it was that
they offer amusement as well as instruction in order to
boost the association's appeal.   Temperance audiences
demanded and got comic relief as well as exhortation. (44)
British Workman pubs (dry facsimiles of the real thing,
started in Leeds in 1867 and copied in many northern
towns) and coffee taverns and palaces (offshoots of a
movement established in 1874 with the formation of a
London Coffee Tavern Company) from the outset placed a
major emphasis on amusement and relaxation as well as the
provision of cheap refreshments.   By 1879 a People's
Entertainment Society was in operation in London and
within a year its example had been followed in three major
provincial cities. (45)   Such ventures were expected to
pay their own way and met with mixed financial fortune.
Their premises and fare varied considerably in attractive-
ness, but some of them clearly strove to give their
message of rational hospitality a certain gusto, to judge
from these lines written to celebrate the opening of a
Birmingham coffee house of the period: (46)

> Throw open your doors with a flourish of trumpets,
> Let the generous tea urn run frothing and free.
> Oh! toast the rich muffins, and butter the crumpets,
> We pledge the promoters in mocha and tea.

Dating from the 1860s there was in fact a significant
retreat from unrelieved didacticism in most schemes for
recreational improvement.   Reformers were learning that
successful competition with the growing range of leisure
attractions meant making some attempt to approach popular
culture on its own terms, taking the workingman for what
he was, rather than for what he ought to be.   James Hole
in Leeds had indeed arrived at this realisation some years
previously: (47)

> It is no longer a question of social morals, but of
> supply and demand; not of the elevation of popular
> taste, but of gratification.... It is not drink, much
> as our people are given to drinking, which attracts the
> majority. The singing saloon supplies what neither the
> gin-palace, nor the beer-house supplies - amusement....
> Exclude the workingman from the opportunity of spending
> a leisure hour unprofitably if you like, and you shut
> the door of your institute on half of those who now
> enjoy its advantages. To raise the workman, we must
> take hold of him where he is, not where he is not.

As Shimmin remarked from Liverpool in the same period, 'An

improvement of manners has been attempted without duly
considering the man to be improved.' (48) Hole and
Shimmin were men who knew working-class life at close
hand, but the good sense of their message impressed itself
on others further removed from its actualities. Explaining the Working Men's Club movement to the Social Science
Association in 1865 Lord Brougham emphasised, 'Nothing can
be more erroneous than the notion prevailing in some
quarters that the object of these clubs is for education
.... the primary objects are relaxation and amusement.'
Methods had changed, as another speaker impressed on a
later conference of the Association; 'Their object', reported James Airlie, 'was to instruct through amusement
instead of amusing through instruction.' (49) It is
likely that this tactical volte-face was due to something
more than a changing appreciation of the realities of
working-class culture - due in good measure to the more
relaxed mores of middle-class life. As Walter Besant
remarked of this latter transformation, the days had gone
when employers of leisure disallowed merriment among the
poor because they themselves were content to be dull. (50)
    It is obvious, however, that whatever the changes in
style and method, rational recreation remained a very
serious business for its proponents, who still spoke in a
strongly missionary tone. The dilemma they now faced was
that the admission of lighter and more entertaining fare
would dilute or obscure the moral message which lay at the
heart of the reform design. Churchmen were particularly
sensitive to this problem. The churches' concern for
recreation was partly a defensive operation against what
the Dean of Manchester identified as a 'non-Christian
humanitarianism', and partly a determination to rid the
clergy of the kill-joy image which hampered the fight to
hold and expand congregations. It was attended by a real
effort to understand popular needs - to recognise, as
Bishop Fraser of Manchester put it, 'the actual instincts
and appetites of the human beings with whom we have to
deal' - and Anglican reformers in particular (with the new
wave of Christian Socialists in the van) moved forward in
the 1870s and 1880s to endorse the claims of dancing, the
theatre and even the pub as humanising institutions which
might yet serve as proper vehicles for social and moral
improvement. In such a spirit did a certain Canon
Woodhouse propose to update John Wesley: 'If the devil
ought not to have all the good tunes, why should he have
all the popular amusements?' (51) But many clergy and lay
workers were disturbed by the consequences of entering
into competition with the outside world on its own terms.
The Sunday schools enlivened their meetings with songs and

sketches, but according to one Bolton minister, who
claimed to detect the same syndrome in all the local
churches and chapels, the additional recreation failed to
hold young people for the senior church:

> Where are all the scholars that pass through our Sunday
> schools? How is it that they do not find their way
> into the church? My answer is, you have created in
> them an appetite for something else, and if you want to
> find them, visit our theatres and singing saloons, and
> you will find them there in thousands.

A lay worker noted that occasional booms in Sunday school
attendance were directly attributable to the announcement
of some treat or excursion and were never sustained beyond
that date; 'Pleasure seeking', he concluded, 'is so
rampant on every hand that it crushes out all desire for
mental progress and produces indifference to religious
matters.' (52)

Disillusionment and disappointment provided a persistent counterpoint to the reformers' faith in the ultimate efficacy of rational recreation. After the conclusion of a debate on recreational improvements in the
Social Science Association in 1866, Lord Shaftesbury
remarked wearily: 'It has exhausted the subject but it
has devised no cures.' (53) A dozen years later Jevons
was no more impressed with the progress of reform. Undoubtedly much of the reformers' disappointment can be
attributed to the difficulty of realising expectations
that were markedly at odds with the cultural process at
work in urban popular society. Rational recreation was
meant to supplant all 'irrational' recreation and thus
establish a moral monopoly in working-class leisure. But
in the absence of coercion the workingman still retained
the right to choose his recreations, and on the evidence
of Bill Banks his choice was indiscriminately rational and
irrational. We are not told how Bill Banks spent his
Sundays, but even though he may well have been no
churchgoer he passed as a man of rational taste in respect
of his intelligent literacy and the good management of his
home - in several other respects he could be seen as a
pleasure-seeking yahoo. Bill Banks reflects the nature of
his culture, which was predominantly additive rather than
substitutive, and exclusively responsible neither to
fashion nor ideology. In an expanding working-class
leisure world recreations were not all equally attractive,
but they were all equally legitimate. In such circumstances it was most unlikely that rational recreation
could effect total victory.

III

Other problems which the reformers faced in reaching and
holding working-class attentions are considered more fully
in subsequent chapters; this chapter concludes with a
consideration of the middle-class response to rational
recreation, bearing in mind the important role assigned to
them in the reform design.

It seems clear that the reformers' propaganda did much
to convert the middle-class public to recreational improvement in the 1850s and 1860s; recreation grew to be
accepted as a necessary amenity, a basic overhead in the
maintenance of an industrial society. The opening of new
facilities were occasions for much official self-congratulation on the theme of progress. The inauguration of Peel
Park in 1866 moved the 'Bolton Chronicle' to recall how
leaders of the people had once made the poor find
amusements for themselves, whereas now the poor were
increasingly well provided for in any number of schemes
across the country 'which may fairly be qualified by the
adjective disinterested'. Editorialising on the Working
Men's Club movement of the same period 'The Times'
commented that 'such institutions stand upon the modest
and unassailable ground of simple convenience', opining
that, aside from a little neighbourly assistance, 'we see
no necessity for a gentleman going much out of his way or
putting his hand very deep into his pocket.' (54)

If this was the language of encouragement it was also
the language of disengagement, marking a general middle-
class reluctance to favour popular recreation with
anything other than an occasional subscription or platform
speech. Letters to the 'Chronicle' in the 1870s pointed
out the still inadequate facilities for rational recreation in Bolton. There was, remarked one correspondent,
no shortage of moralising on the workingman's condition,
but a real shortage of practical assistance: 'moralisers
in general never "knuckle down", that is, propose much
more worthy substitutes for recreating the plebeian order,
seldom go beyond a sort of Infirmary-recommend' (the
latter was a sour local joke referring to the long delay
in building a much-needed hospital in the town). Bishop
Fraser assailed the Bolton middle classes for their
neglect of what he called 'the great question of the day',
chiding them for their self-righteousness as they sat over
nuts and claret deploring the crudity of working-class
behaviour. They had, he said, no sympathy or interest in
the unfortunate yet remediable environment in which
workingmen lived. (55) Certain employers provided their
workpeople with reading rooms and sports facilities, but

as the big masters withdrew to Southport or farther afield class contact had diminished; the day-to-day running of the mills passed to a new class of managers with little interest in the lighter side of industrial welfare, and the heads of firms only met their hands for celebration of the major dynastic events of marriage and majority, and occasional beanos in the run-up to elections. On the evidence of the factory inspectors' reports (which, with the increase in legislation, covered a greater number of establishments) the country's employers generally paid less attention to their workers' social welfare than in the 1840s. (56) Thus, with the exception of some sporadic largesse and the endeavours of a handful of local philanthropists and churchmen, the behaviour of Bolton's bourgeoisie conformed to what the reformer Ellice Hopkins identified as 'the selfish indifference of the higher and educated classes to the people's amusements'. (57)

Indifference might be better rendered as distaste, for the period witnessed a growing middle-class impatience with the workers. There had been something of a honeymoon period in class relations following recovery from the alarms of the 1840s: the working classes had distinguished themselves by their good behaviour on the 'shilling days' at the Great Exhibition, the workingman in arms had won admiration for his courage and steadiness in the Crimea and the Lancashire millhands had earned great praise for their stoic bearing during the cotton famine in the early 1860s. No doubt, too, others besides Mr Gladstone were heartened by the accumulating deposits of small investors in the Post Office Savings Bank. With the revival of reform agitation and the passage of the 1867 Reform Bill the working classes came under more critical scrutiny as 'Our New Masters' (a somewhat apprehensive designation), and it was discovered that the workingman was being paid too much, scamping his work, striking indiscriminately and spending his 'overplus' in reckless style. In 1873 'The Times' remarked tetchily that 'More wages and more idle time furnish this abundant leisure which is indeed the luxury of the so-called working classes.' 'Workingman worship', so the 'Saturday Review' reported in the same year, 'has abated'; the workingman had become 'rather tiresome and exasperating'. (58)

The conspicuous pleasure of the masses gave particular offence where it was maintained in the face of financial exigencies in the business and professional world. The author of a theatre article in the 'Daily News' in 1868, writing for an audience still presumably shaken by the collapse of the financial house of Overend and Gurney two years previously, confessed himself irritated by in-

creasing working-class patronage of the theatre and music
hall, at a time when 'the critical nature of commercial
affairs demands that the middle-class man must ration the
visits of his family in the interests of economy.' Such
comparisons became more frequent and invidious as the
economy met with later difficulties which threatened to
halt the rising standard of middle-class living by the
relative stagnation of their incomes. Reviewing the expenditure in an East End music hall in 1880, the
journalist Ewing Ritchie was indignant that 'In these bad
times, when people in the middle ranks of life are in
despair at the hard prospect before them, here were these
workingmen spending their two hundred pounds a night at
least.' (59)

The offence was compounded when the workingman made his
mass breakout from the urban ghetto and thrust himself in
upon the privacy of his betters. After four weeks in
Southend, reported Ritchie, 'I began to tremble at the
very sight of an excursionist.' In the following
childhood recollection of the descent of the 'townie' upon
rural Derbyshire, the novelist Ouida expressed her re-
pugnance more fully:

> The excursion trains used to vomit forth, at Easter and
> in Whitsun week, throngs of the millhands of the
> period, cads and their flames, tawdry, blowzy, noisy,
> drunken; the women with dress that aped 'the fashion',
> and pyramids of artificial flowers on their heads;
> the men as grotesque and hideous in their own way;
> tearing through woods and fields like swarms of devas-
> tating locusts, and dragging the fern and hawthorn
> boughs they had torn down in the dust, ending the
> lovely spring day in pot-houses, drinking gin and
> bitters, or heavy ales by the quart, and tumbling pell-
> mell into the night train, roaring music-hall choruses;
> sodden, tipsy, yelling, loathsome creatures, such as
> make a monkey look a king, and the newt seem an angel
> beside humanity - exact semblance and emblem of the
> vulgarity of the age ... vulgarity likely to live and
> multiply, and increase in power and in extent.

The magazine 'Fun' provided regular graphic illustration
of the boorishness of the workingman's leisure seen
through middle-class eyes. In a representative cartoon on
The rough's holiday, a suitably wart-encrusted blackguard
confers with his mate: (60)

> Well, we ain't done a bad 'oliday 'ave we? We've broke
> lots of trees an' 'edges, an' spiled a luvley garding,
> an' trampled down some roses an' things, an' ruined all
> the lanes about here. Now let's set fire to a Common
> an' go 'ome to supper.

Yet, in one sense, reducing the workingman to this loutish stereotype may well have been comforting; a little gratuitous hooliganism was better than the fury of a Communard, and was small price to pay for its implicit confirmation of bourgeois superiority of manners and morals. The reality, however, was more insidious, for the broad advances in working-class leisure (in company with marked economic and political gains) threatened to obliterate the social differential between the classes. Contemplating the prospective 'plebification of art' in 1866, the journalist Matthew Browne remarked that 'social boundary lines are not so sharply drawn as they used to be.... In other words the old "cordon sanitaires" have snapped under the pressure of the multitudes, and we have not yet succeeded in twisting new ones.' This advance of the multitudes was more clearly defined by another writer, Keningale Cook, in a consideration of 'The Labourer's Leisure' in 1871:

> From being machines, fit only for machine work or inert quiescence, the masses are given the liberty of being men - gentlemen indeed, if in that term be applied the possession of leisure, the power of being 'at large' - a coveted attribute of gentility.

By the 1880s the implications of this development had made themselves very clear to the middle classes, for as Walter Besant noted, (61)

> they have perceived that their amusements - also, which seems the last straw, their vices - can be enjoyed by the base mechanical sort, insomuch that, if this kind of thing goes on, there must in the end follow an effacement of all classes.

In such circumstances the middle classes stood ready to defend the line of their own gentility with a judicious mixture of discrimination and neglect, and the reformers found themselves pulling against the stream. The latter were proposing to alleviate the tensions and degeneration in society through the fraternal association of all classes in leisure, at a time when the middle classes were acutely concerned to reinforce, not reduce, social distance.

5

◇◇

Rational Recreation in Operation:
the Working Men's Club Movement

◇◇

The Working Men's Club movement provides the most prominent example of rational recreation formally organised on
a national scale. Fostered by the Working Men's Club and
Institute Union, founded in 1862, the movement derived its
momentum from middle-class initiative and support, yet by
the 1880s the clubs had become exclusive working-class
preserves, and the original designs of its mentors had
been all but frustrated. The history of the movement
provides further illustration of the social philosophy of
rational recreation, while demonstrating the problems of
putting it into practice. (1)

I

The idea of providing workingmen with social clubs which
emphasised good fellowship rather than adult education
clearly finds its antecedents in Heywood's Manchester
Lyceums of the 1840s. Charles Knight, the publisher, also
recalled a club in Birmingham in 1848 which was run by a
hosiery manufacturer called Brookes, who advertised it as
his own Ministry to the Poor, providing cheap food and
reading rooms 'in an attempt to penetrate down to those
classes which Mechanics' Institutes and Benefit Societies
have never yet reached'. This sounds more like an
exercise in relief than recreation, but the attempt to
reach beyond the established working-class public for
improvement and mutual assistance was one of the principal
objectives of the Club movement as it developed. In
Brighton in the same year, the Reverend Frederick
Robertson founded a Working Men's Institute which, though
short-lived, provided some early inspiration for Henry
Solly, the subsequent founder of the CIU; its primary
emphasis was on formal education, but Robertson's Insti-

tute has been awarded the title of the 'first recognisable
workingmen's club'. (2)

Of the twenty or so clubs which emerged in the 1850s
and satisfied the CIU's later search for a pedigree, the
majority were rural. They were the creations of paternalist landlords and clergymen anxious to counter the beershops, whose spread had excited much more opposition from
local authorities in the country districts than in the
towns. The Reverend Sidney Godolphin Osborne, a shrewd
observer of rural society (and, as S.G.O., an indefatigable correspondent to 'The Times') wrote in 1852 of the
need for 'moral beer-houses', painting a picture of 'a
simple retreat, furnishing warmth and light, bread and
cheese, baccy and beer under the superintendence of a
steward with no interest in beer sales'. Osborne's description soon came to life in the establishment of
Bastard's Club in Blandford, Dorset (named after its
founder and not its members, as Cole and Postgate enjoy
telling us) and several other clubs were in existence in
the southern counties by the middle of the decade. At
Littlemore, near Oxford, the local vicar formed a club
for farm labourers which progressive churchmen hailed as
a timely experiment. At Rothamsted in Hertfordshire, Sir
John Lawes, the pioneer agricultural chemist, established
a club for the workers on his estate. The success of his
experiment attracted a visit from Dickens, who recorded
his approval, noting that the sale of beer in the new
club - in limited amounts - had put the local village pub
out of business. Such a victory was the battle honour
reformers were proudest to display, but the mortality rate
among these early village clubs was high, and the few
details of their careers which survive show clearly where
they were most vulnerable to working-class disaffection.
The prohibition of beer which prevailed in most of these
pioneer establishments was much disliked, but the greater
offence of the first club promoters in the eyes of members
was that of their intrusive supervision of club affairs, a
particular failing of the clergy. (3) These problems
bulked large in the history of the developing Club
movement.

A handful of town clubs were also started in the 1850s.
Temperance was a common guiding light - literally so in
the case of the Notting Hill Workman's Hall where a
working model of the Eddystone lighthouse guided the converted to its doors - and clergymen were the commonest
promoters. (4) Among them was Henry Solly, who founded
a Working Men's Mutual Improvement and Recreation Society
in Lancaster in 1860. The organised games at least
pleased the local police sergeant - 'If this thing goes

on, sir, there'll soon be nothing for us to do' - but the
experiment was short-lived, and provided Solly with hard
evidence of the difficulties of establishing a constructive rapport between middle-class patron and working-
class members. He found the latter's behaviour alternate-
ly encouraging and exasperating, as he reported to Lord
Brougham on the progress of his scheme; one week he was
warmed by their 'earnest, brotherly zeal', the next week
he was depressed by their 'miserable apathy'. Such
vagaries no doubt bedevilled other town clubs, for they
were not noticeably hardier than their country cousins.
(5)

     But Solly held faith with the club ideal, and it was
largely through his energies that the CIU was founded in
1862, to encourage, supervise and co-ordinate the establishment of Working Men's Clubs across the country.
Solly had found the ideal platform for propaganda in the
Social Science Association, and it was in the course of
its annual congress in London that year that his lobbying
produced a meeting with other interested parties which
established the Union. (6) The other founder members
included philanthropic businessmen such as Edward Rathbone
of Liverpool, the MP James Heywood, Edward Clarke, a young
London lawyer interested in social reform, and the
Reverend David Thomas who had pioneered clubs in the
capital. Two workingmen were present among this predominantly middle-class assembly, one of whom, John Bainbridge, had been Solly's friend since the 1840s. Solly
prevailed upon Lord Brougham to be the first president of
the CIU, an early example of his success in attracting
aristocratic patronage. But the real work of the Union
was done by a small secretariat, and its early history is
dominated by successive secretaries. Of these, Solly
himself, who held the post intermittently from 1862 to
1872 and remained an influential figure for several years
thereafter, is most important. He embodied the CIU, and
his credo exemplifies much that was common thinking behind
rational recreation.

II

Solly's interest in working-class improvement was con-
ditioned by his first-hand experience of class conflict
in the 1840s. Born in 1814 into one of the well-educated
and commercially prosperous London dissenting communities,
Solly had been educated at London University and was
destined initially for the family business; he chose
instead to enter the Unitarian ministry, which took him

to the West Country, where he became involved in the
Chartist agitation. This was his first contact with
working-class life and politics. He discovered a sympathy
with the local Chartists who, as moral force men, impressed him by their intelligence and restraint as well as
the basic justice of their case. It was in this company
that he met Bainbridge, who later moved to London and
served as something of a mascot for Solly in the early
years of the CIU. Bainbridge clearly represented all that
was best in working-class life for Solly, and was most
likely the model for the eponymous hero of Solly's novel
'James Sandford, Carpenter and Chartist', a workingman who
takes William Lovett for his hero and admits the good
sense of working with rather than against middle-class
reformism. After the excitements of the Chartist years,
strenuous self-help brings Sandford the proprietorship of
a small business, the happy-ever-after dénouement of the
bourgeois prescription for working-class contentment.
During the course of his progress, Sandford meets with
and resists the appeals of the dark forces within the
working-class community, represented by the physical force
Chartists with their credulous infatuation with Feargus
O'Connor. Thus for Solly the confrontations of the 1840s
revealed two distinct and contrary faces to the working
class. (7)

During these years Solly also learnt at first hand of
the gulf between the classes; The elders of his church
in Yeovil had been so affrighted by Chartism that they had
threatened to withhold Solly's stipend when they learnt of
his implication in the movement. Solly was a natural
convert to Joseph Sturge's Complete Suffrage Union of
1842, which was formed expressly to effect a reconciliation between middle and working classes behind a reform
programme free of all associations with O'Connorite militancy, and he enlisted as one of the movement's mission-
aries. His appetite for political reform subsided after
the 1840s, and under the influence of Christian Socialism
he turned to social questions. His continuing concern
here was that the classes should work for improvement in
concert, and thus preclude a return to the dangerous
divisions of the Chartist years.

Solly's ambivalent attitude to the working classes
persisted into the 1860s. At his most optimistic, Solly
cast them as 'the new Greeks', whose genius for association would, when effectively released, renovate national
life, which he considered dangerously decayed owing to the
reckless competition and materialism of both the aristocracy and the middle class. But this same canker which
was demoralising the upper levels of society was liable

to disrupt those of the working classes necessarily cast
as helots or worse:

> Every advance in material prosperity presents increased
> temptations and facilities to the destitute and crimi-
> nal classes for more DIRECT violations of the eighth
> commandment. What would a force of eight or nine
> thousand police be against the 150,000 roughs and
> villains whom, on some sufficiently exciting occasion,
> the metropolis might see arrayed versus law and order
> .... we must not conceal from ourselves the possibili-
> ty of Londoners having to live from time to time under
> the protection and even rule of the military; that
> again might raise the labouring classes throughout the
> country, and give us a civil or servile war.

The garotting scare in West End streets and a recent bread
riot in the East End moved Solly to raise this spectre of
insurrection in an address in 1868 to the Royal Society of
Arts, and his warnings reflect the underlying nervousness
among his class at the continuing combustibility of the
masses, particularly in the capital. (8)

To Solly the achievement of a well-ordered and harmonious society depended upon educating the working classes to
recognise that the existing system offered the best, and
indeed the only guarantee that the interests of both
capital and labour would be well and equitably served.
The better elements among the workingmen would come to
this realisation voluntarily if they could find sanctuary
from the ignorant clamour of the pub and the baseness that
lurked among their fellows; 'the more prudent, worthier
members of the working class', noted Solly, 'are too often
dragged down by their reckless, drinking, cowardly or
dishonest neighbours.' The club was the right milieu
within which the necessary education of the workingman
could proceed; it provided firstly for recreation, which
Solly recognised as a basic need of social welfare, but it
also constituted an informal teaching situation into which
more serious matters could gradually be introduced. The
principle was explained in Solly's theory of the inclined
plane:

> Begin by meeting the workingmen's humblest social wants
> for relaxation and amusement, and you may lift our
> hardworked brethren by degrees up to very respectable
> heights of knowledge and education.... You fail if you
> present the thick end of the plane first.

Accordingly, he explained, some incidental discussion on
news of the day could lead to regular classes which, had
they constituted the only item on the club programme,
would have been impalatable to the average workingman.
Head of the list of suggested topics was political econo-

my. 'If they [workingmen] were asked at the outset to
join such a class', Solly maintained, 'they would never
consent; but if they once attended such classes, they
would discover that political economists were not striving
to enforce laws of their own or anybody's making, but
simply seeking to interpret the laws of God.' Solly chose
the word club for its associations of sociability and
relaxation but the inclusion of institute in the Union's
title was meant to indicate its serious educational intentions, and there was never any dissembling as to its
ultimate purpose of social indoctrination. (9)

    The success of the scheme was, in Solly's mind, very
much dependent upon the participation of the middle and
upper classes. They were to provide the initiative, the
'stimulus ab extra', as he called it. Working at the
local level they would establish clubs according to the
guidelines recommended by the CIU. The workers themselves
were expected eventually to take over the complete management of the clubs, but the practice of social contact
between the classes would by then be firmly implanted.
It was an express purpose of the clubs: 'to form a centre
of communication between men of all classes interested in
the welfare of the people; to bring about a better understanding between men of different occupations and
standings'. Communication would be facilitated by in-
structing workingmen in the proper forms of address and
conversation - 'getting rid of that which makes men re-
pellent in ordinary intercourse', as the wealthy Christian
Socialist E.V.Neale explained in his club lectures on True
Refinement. Cordiality and good manners would then allow
such practical returns as the arbitration and conciliation
of industrial disputes and 'the interchange of kind
services'. (10)

    Solly was indefatigable in pursuing his dream ('This is
Mr Solly,' Henry Fawcett remarked drily to his wife, 'who
thinks Heaven is made of working men's clubs') but his
single-mindedness was a mixed blessing to the movement.
Benjamin Hall, the CIU's first official historian, wrote
that Solly had two jobs to do in his capacity as Union
secretary: he had to obtain support, financial and moral,
from non-workmen; and he had to interest the workmen
themselves. He was more successful in the first task.
Hall, who was not wholly uncritical of his predecessor,
was none the less dazzled by Solly's skill in raising
subscriptions, declaring that 'so comprehensive a list
of distinguished men and women of the Victorian era, led
by Lord Chancellors and Archbishops, was never before or
since attracted to any scheme.' The tenacity with which
Solly pursued aristocratic patronage bemused and ultimate-

ly exasperated Lord Lyttelton, who succeeded Brougham as
president. Lyttelton confessed to the latter that he had
allowed himself to succumb to 'our persevering friend',
and be used 'as a jackal to get letters and opinions from
the nobility'; he finally rebelled after 'ten years of
ridiculous gyrations'. (11) There was something of the
social climber in Solly which may have been anxious to
compensate for the occasional ostracism he had suffered
as a Unitarian, or may more simply have reflected the
characteristic desire of his class for lordly contact and
recognition; in any case, it is clear that he was more
solicitous of noble than working-class company. Within
the council of the CIU he rode roughshod over Thomas
Paterson, the most prominent working-class member, and
in 1870, when Solly was at issue with the council as a
whole and attempted briefly to form a rival organisation,
it is noticeable that though he contrived to redirect the
subscriptions of most of the dukes and earls to his new
scheme he was unable to command the allegiance of the
rank-and-file club members. Paterson is an obscure figure
and it would be too facile to interpret his clash with
Solly in exclusively class terms, especially since the
latter was told by James Hole that he was 'without exception the most deficient in tact of any man in a public
capacity', a deficiency which, as we have seen, could
exasperate an aristocrat as easily as an artisan. (12)
But the court revolt against Solly was against his
authoritarianism, and it is plain that this characteristic
alienated workingmen with whom he worked in other improvement schemes. As one of them wrote: (13)

> Mr Solly's different attempts at similar movements have
> not recommended him to the working men. He has never
> worked unless allowed the entire lead as well as good
> pay. And has never been over-scrupulous in obtaining
> his ends.

It is doubtful if the lordly guineas that Solly attracted
were always sufficient compensation for the ill-feeling
generated by his often irascible missionary zeal.

III

The CIU grew but slowly during its early years and Hall
identified various general difficulties that impeded its
progress. Of these, 'The Great Beer Question' and the
complications of patronage weighed heaviest. Beer was
central to working-class culture but mostly abhorrent to
middle-class reformers. Solly himself was an active
teetotaller, and though the original prospectus for the

CIU disclaimed any connexion with the Total Abstinence movement it recommended prohibition of the sale of liquor, and Solly mailed a copy of the prospectus to every Temperance society in the country. (14) Many of the clubs of the 1850s had been strictly teetotal and Hodgson Pratt, Solly's successor to the secretaryship, recollected that local cadres of Temperance workingmen, backed by discreet subsidies from wealthy sympathisers, had founded a substantial number of the new clubs following the inception of the Union in 1862. Pratt also recalled how unpopular these 'temperance shops' had been with other workingmen. (15) Brougham and Lyttelton of the Union council had from the outset advised Solly against enforcing prohibition. Lyttelton, who was an enthusiastic supporter of the CIU, took his model for the workingmen's clubs from the gentlemen's clubs of Pall Mall and St James's, and argued that drink in moderate amounts had a natural place in social life. (16) As a peer, he was more likely to prevail with Solly than other council members, but what seemed finally to effect the latter's conversion to tolerance on the beer question was the respectable character of those clubs which had ignored the CIU ruling and sold beer to their members from the beginning.

At several conferences in the mid- and late 1860s Solly heard the workingmen's case: that they drank beer for the company rather than from an unmanageable lust for beer; that tea and coffee were inadequate refreshment after a shift down the mines or in the steel mills; and that the clubs would foster moderation by moving men out of range of the publican with his encouragement of traditional customs of 'treating and tossing'. (17) These arguments were not new - they were mostly common enough counters to the Temperance case - but now they were proven in practice, and were supported by club patrons who had been won over from an initial hostility to strong drink. Union officials tried to promote coffee as an alternative beverage and took club secretaries on tours of the coffee taverns, but the clubmen were unimpressed by the 'black dose of chicory soup' as a source of refreshment or good cheer, and by 1871 Henry Solly was to be found urging the Social Science Association to recognise the fact that the great majority of British workmen were 'moderate drinkers' who would never join a club without beer. Thus the CIU came to accept the sale of beer on club premises and, indeed, yielded to another experiment in homeopathic therapy in these years by allowing card games for moderate stakes. (18) The young Lord Rosebery endeared himself to clubmen by delivering the final blow for tolerance at the thirteenth annual meeting of the Union four years later.

As guest speaker he declared that each club 'should be
free from all vexations and childish restrictions on the
supply of intoxicating drinks and all similar matters.'
(19)

The patronage issue constituted a more obstinate
problem than the Great Beer Question, though the two were
closely connected, for the prohibition of beer exemplified
the tight control which most early patrons considered appropriate for club members. Drawing on their experience
of other promotions, several speakers to the Social
Science Association had warned of workingmen's resentment
of manipulation and autocracy, but club patrons were
confident that they knew best. As Ben Hall remarked:
'It may be taken for granted that what took place in the
majority of clubs in the first year of our Union was not
what the members wished, but what was ALLOWED.' After
ten years' acquaintance with the CIU an artisan reported
to 'The Times' that little had changed; the clubs, he
maintained, offered only a secular version of 'the cup of
tea and tract formula'. Solly was aware of the members'
criticisms and in one of the Union pamphlets explaining
club philosophy to prospective patrons he reproduced one
of the workingmen's complaints: 'We have masters all day
long, and we don't want them at night.' The motto of the
movement, emphasised Solly, must be 'Supplement, not
supersede'. The middle classes must prime the pump, but
the workers were to be given every encouragement to work
towards independent management, and Union policy recommended that at least half the members of any club's
governing committee should be bona fide workingmen.
Patrons, advised Solly, must conduct themselves as
friends, not masters. (20)

Solly's own overbearing manner reveals how difficult it
was to reconcile this prescription with existing class
roles; moreover, however much confidence Union propaganda
expressed in the workingman, Solly and other middle-class
supporters of the movement had considerable misgivings
about his ability to initiate or maintain an orderly and
efficient organisation. As one otherwise encouraging
article on the clubs pointed out when the CIU was formed:
'if such institutions are left entirely to the working
classes they will be deficient in power, method and stability, and for want of the conservative element will be
ever in danger of falling to pieces.' (21) At the inaugural tea party of the Bolton WMC Edmund Ashworth warned:
(22)

We shall always find a number of men, perhaps, whose
education has been acquired in the pub, and the impro-
prieties of such characters will be difficult to

control, except you have a vigorous committee and an
absolute authority to enforce good order. You may
find sometimes a little difficulty but I suggest that
absolute authority be placed in the hands of one individual and that the committee be always at hand to
support his authority.

In recounting the history of the early years Hall confessed: 'As we know now, failure lay principally in the
fact that the clubs were not spontaneously originated and
democratically controlled.' In explanation he offered the
standard apologia that workingmen then 'were little capable of the thought of, or the power to originate and
manage clubs until taught and inspired by others.' (23)

Certainly, outside support was often invaluable in
establishing clubs; granting premises, guaranteeing rents
and mortgages, advancing loans, providing a legal umbrella
- these were services the working classes could not easily
provide for themselves. But members objected to the
further tutelage they were obliged to accept, 'the cup of
tea and tract formula' that included censorship of entertainments and a ban on all political discussion. (24)

The CIU oligarchy was particularly anxious to keep
politics out of the clubs. Solly had promoted the club
ideal as non-sectarian in matters of religion and politics
- 'a green spot', as one of his supporters once put it,
'where all shades of opinion, creed, or calling can meet
in harmony with one another'. Though he was sympathetic
to the London junta of trade union leaders he shut George
Howell out of the CIU council in 1866 as an undesirable
agitator, and in 1870, when he was joint editor of the
'Beehive' for a few months, he tried hard to counter-
balance the radical views of George Potter, the founder
of the famous working-class paper. 'Politics', Solly once
declared, in a desperately ingenuous remark, 'should be
studied without reference to politics.' He feared that
the working classes would return to the political ad-
venturism of thirty years before and destroy the likeli-
hood of achieving the fraternal class consensus he yearned
for. (25) W.T.Marriott, QC, a long-standing supporter and
council member of the CIU, told a union soirée in the
early 1880s that he would say nothing against political
clubs, 'but he much preferred social clubs, because in the
latter there would be more fair play (loud cries of 'No'
and 'Yes')'. Fair play in the early years of the CIU had
meant no play; in the 1870s, as middle-class control of
individual clubs was supplanted, many of them provided
strong political content, and by 1881 Solly estimated
their number at between 500 and 600. (26)

Friction between patrons and members appeared least in

small towns, and it was this type of club which fared best
in the first years of the CIU's history. In a list of 103
clubs known to the Union in 1869 only nine were in the big
towns or manufacturing districts; two years later,
despite an overall increase in number, the proportions had
scarcely changed. It was a small town which provided the
Union executive with its model club - Wisbech WMC in
Cambridgeshire. Hodgson Pratt awarded Wisbech first prize
after a tour of clubland in 1870, and it represented the
ideal to him and Solly for more than a decade. Its
patrons were drawn from the prominent local Quaker family,
the Peckovers, and in a town of 9,000 it enjoyed a membership of over 800 workingmen. It incorporated its own co-
operative society, savings bank, library and allotment
scheme; it stayed teetotal and, in Solly's words, 'es-
chewed polemics'. Strong traditions of deference and a
marked community identity gave the club its stability.
The other successful clubs which impressed Pratt during
his tour were in Bridlington and North Ormesby, and one
of the few enthusiastic reports from workingmen in these
years came from Scarborough, another small urban centre.
(27)

The halting progress of the movement in the large towns
and cities reflected the tensions of a more divisive class
society. CIU reports attributed slow growth in the
capital to the fragmented nature of its working-class
community and the abundant rival attractions of a great
city. Solly felt that the root of the problem lay with
the trade societies. The Union encouraged workmen to use
club premises for their trades' and friendly societies
meetings rather than the pub, but London trade societies'
leaders feared the employer's hand in this, for during the
1859 builders' strike the masters had attempted to set up
workingmen's institutes to supplant the existing houses of
call and shelter and indoctrinate non-unionised labour.
Solly met with the trades' leaders and went some way to
appeasing their fears, but there were still considerable
working-class misgivings about the motives of the Union
patrons, and the annual meeting of 1866 remarked on 'the
suspicion with which the great mass of workmen view the
Union'. (28)

Just as the workingmen held back, so too did those 'men
of higher social position' whose assistance the CIU considered so necessary to success. Few of the vice-presidents whose names adorned the Union's prospectus sponsored
their own clubs. The treasurer of the Wellclose Square
WMC in the East End of London reported on 'the utter indifference of most of the wealthy employers of labour who
amass their money here, but spend it elsewhere'. The in-

difference was not confined to London, and appears as much
a measure of studied retaliation as of insensibility, for
the annual report of 1873 acknowledged that 'In several
localities we have found a determination on the part of
employers to refuse any aid towards the establishment of
these clubs - the result of the unfortunate disputes which
have arisen between them and those they employ.' When the
first Working Men's Club in Bolton was in a state of immi-
nent collapse in 1869, the 'Chronicle' warned that its
members could expect no subvention from employers while
industrial relations were strained. Thus were the new
clubs afflicted by the very problems they were supposed
to remedy. (29)

But the club idea met real working-class needs and
workingmen gradually overcame the problems of absent or
overbearing patronage by founding their own clubs or dis-
charging the original middle-class promoters as redundant.
Some workingmen had formed their own clubs in the first
decade of the CIU's history, but the practice became
noticeably widespread in the mid-1870s; the annual report
for 1873 which remarked on the hostility of employers also
noted the increasing number of applications for CIU advice
from workingmen - 'The idea of no patronage', it noted,
'grows fast.' As examples the report referred to the establishment of an independent WMC in St Austell in
Cornwall, and the emancipation of the Wednesbury WMC in
Staffordshire, where members had succeeded to self-
government by kicking out their 'sluggish' gentleman
patrons. Established clubs assisted their new neighbours,
and members pooled their trade skills to convert and
furnish premises whose amenities were often thus superior
to those provided by patrons - as one observer remarked,
'Many friends of the working classes think that they have
done all that is necessary when they have provided a
building like a cab stable or a wash-house.' (30)

The sale of beer was of great assistance in the development towards worker control of the movement, for it
provided valuable revenue. From Maidstone, the local
Working Men's Clubs made the following report to the
Union's house journal in 1873: 'The members have made
the discovery that the profit on beer is about 30%, and
brings them double what they have to pay for rent, though
the quantity sold does not average two pints per person
per week.' Once a club was self-supporting it could
become self-governing. So went Maidstone WMC, and so went
many others. (31) It should be noted here too that the
sale of beer indirectly encouraged a greater responsibility among club members, for it obliged the clubs to fight
a long defensive action against the publicans' trade pro-

tection societies which contested the legality of club
liquor sales. Good order and scrupulous attention to the
conditions of membership were thus necessary to assure the
clubs of their continued status as private institutions
exempt from official licensing requirements. (32)

By 1878 an outside observer estimated that 52 per cent
of the clubs were wholly self-supporting, and five years
later Pratt put the figure at 75 per cent. Membership
figures indicate the overall growth in the same period:
in 1874 membership was put at 90,000, in 1878 at 150,000,
in 1880 at 320,000 and by 1883 was estimated to have
passed the half-million mark. The expansion was particularly marked in the London area where the number of clubs
rose from 82 to 120 between 1876 and 1882. (33)

It was the London clubs which took the lead in attacking the last stronghold of patronage. For though the
clubs increasingly controlled their own affairs, they were
almost completely unrepresented on the CIU council. A
handful of the more politically minded London clubs began
to protest the middle-class monopoly of council offices by
refusing to contribute to CIU funds and forming a virtually independent London branch of the Union in 1881 (the
forerunner of the Metropolitan Federation of Radical Clubs
of 1886). The withholding of subscriptions hurt the
Union. Solly complained to the Social Science Association
that it was being 'mischievously crippled', and by 1883
the council realised that it could no longer survive on
the hand-outs of honorary vice-presidents and agreed to a
conference on the question of finances and club representation. Here the longstanding complaints of club members
found full and forcible expression. One working-class
delegate put it thus:

> The Union has reached a crisis in its history. It must
> either be patronising or self-supporting. It cannot be
> the former and must either become the latter or cease
> to exist.... A great deal has been said about abolish-
> ing class distinctions but under the present system
> these existed in the constitution of the Union itself.

Another workingman registered 'a strong protest versus
patronage', before meeting criticisms which must have been
used to block working-class representation before:

> The working men have a right to work out their own
> aims. It is absurd to say they cannot maintain and
> work the Union - they must take it in hand at once,
> for at present there was no faith in it.

Council members repeated the Union's aims of eradicating
class feeling, talking bluntly of the need to deflate the
bigots in fustian as well as in broadcloth. Solly was
afraid that a sudden working-class takeover would alienate

subscribers to Union funds. But the working-class delegation claimed that such dependence was not only demeaning
but unnecessary if the CIU could command the complete
allegiance of its members, and, following a series of
meetings in committee, the delegation carried the day with
the passage of New Model Rules, which secured direct club
representation on the CIU council. J.J.Dent became the
Union's first working-class secretary on the resignation
of Hodgson Pratt. (34) In Manchester there was to be a
similar victory over the class exclusiveness of the
district headquarters, and at the annual general meeting
in 1884 Thomas Brassey pronounced the Union justly de-
mocratised. (35)

IV

Who were these first generations of clubmen and what was
club life like? Hard evidence is difficult to come by,
but it seems that the movement attracted members from
across a wide range of working-class society. The CIU had
never recommended imposing any test of membership (or conditions of dress) and advised only a lower age limit of
eighteen years. Henry Mayhew, whose categories are generally reliable, visited London clubs where membership
comprised 'lower middle class, well-to-do artisans and
petty tradesmen', others where membership was 'confined to
the labouring rather than the artisan class'. Some club
secretaries agreed in recognising a caste distinction
between mechanics and labourers which determined local
membership, but the majority of references suggest a broad
mix of members within each club. The Scarborough club
reported that its members included 'the better class of
workmen, the indifferent, those who spend their spare time
in drinking and loose company, and some of the off-
scourings of society'. The Leeds club ran the gamut 'from
respectable artisans to the low fellows who may be seen
leaning against the walls of public houses'. On the evidence of the minutes of the Newcastle upon Tyne WMC it may
have been true that it was the skilled craftsman who
dominated the club committees, but it seems likely that
in general the clubs recruited by neighbourhood rather
than particular trades. (36)
    The self-evident fact of the clubs' exclusively male
membership should not go unremarked, for it seems to have
been a matter of popular preference within the movement
as much as it was part of the original design of the
middle-class founders. Union officials do appear to have
been somewhat embarrassed on this point; they justified

the exclusion of wives and families on simple logistical
grounds, claiming none the less that in insulating the
head of the family from bad company and raising the moral
tone of his recreations they were contributing indirectly
to the improvement of home life among the working class.
The membership in general does not seem to have been
anxious to reverse official policy, for though the
question of the admission of womenfolk was raised at two
successive annual conferences in the mid-1870s it provoked
little in the way of popular response. (37)

There was some adverse comment on the quality of club
membership. Hodgson Pratt complained in the 1880s of 'the
lack of some sort of intellectual or educational backbone'
to the movement, and was disturbed at what he felt was a
'complete separation' between the clubs and other working-
class organisations such as the co-operative societies (of
which he was himself an active supporter). Frederick
Rogers, in what seems to be the only contemporary working-
class autobiography to record club life in any detail,
maintained that 'the clubs did not attract the more intellectual of the working classes; these were in the trade
union movement or the co-operative world.' (38) Such
comment is not to be disregarded - particularly since this
kind of charge became more common by the 1890s - but
neither should it be left unchallenged. At Newcastle and
Wisbech, for example, local co-operative societies used
the Working Men's Clubs' premises, which argues some
mutual acquaintance, and during the campaign for the
Third Reform Bill in 1884 the 'Club and Institute Journal'
reported that 'the affiliated clubs formed no mean part of
the procession, although somewhat short of numbers through
the fact that many of their members fell in with the various trades unions.' James Beal, the middle-class chairman
of the Metropolitan Municipal Reform Association, found
that the clubs in Chelsea at which he lectured were com-
posed of 'the most intelligent workingmen of the district
in all cases', and Stan Shipley's researches into metropolitan club life reveal programmes of lectures and discussions which fulfil his claims that certain of the clubs
constituted an artisans' university. (39) The vigorously
intellectual club was no doubt an exception in the
movement as a whole, and would have been too iconoclastic
in the content of its debate to recommend itself to Pratt
and the Union council, but the weekly reports in the club
press record a regular diet of literary and scientific
talks, dramatic readings and discussions, which demonstrates that club life was far from mindless. Perhaps
it was the unabashed informality of the clubs - the
constant traffic, the cries of the pie-boy and the

pot-boy, the smoking and bantering - which produced a bad
press among middle-class visitors. For Rogers, fired with
the enthusiasm of the working-class auto-didact, disenchantment came in the middle of his Sunday morning lecture
on Shakespeare, when the club chairman called a break to
let the man come round with the beer. (40)

Certainly in these years the clubs were not passive
institutions, and as patronage receded they made themselves heard on an increasing range of public questions.
The Newcastle upon Tyne club petitioned Parliament on
several occasions in the 1860s: on the franchise
question, the Alabama Dispute and the Contagious Diseases
Act. Several clubs in London and the provinces applied
for membership of the republican-flavoured Land and Labour
League in 1870, and there was considerable protest from
metropolitan clubs at the grant of funds to the Prince of
Wales for his Indian trip in 1875. The London clubs also
spoke out against sabbatarianism and the anti-music hall
lobby, and took a considerable interest in local municipal
politics. There are echoes of this kind of activism in
Lancashire. (41)

But the main function of the clubs was to provide for
'the humbler wants' of its members, and this they did
admirably. They provided a set of permanent premises for
recreation to an extent which no other organisation or
movement could match. Illustrations of club interiors
seem cheerless to us, but the rooms were kept clean, well-
lit and warm, a far remove from the condition of much
working-class housing. They were genuine recuperative
refuges, free from commercial pressures, ritual drinking,
police harassment, district visitors and the wife and
family. (42) With their lectures, concerts, indoor and
outdoor games, excursions and picnics, Christmas clubs,
coal clubs and sick clubs, they provided, at modest cost,
the facilities of the public library, music hall, pub,
playing field and friendly society combined.

The spare and functional aspect of the clubrooms was
relieved by the feeling of community generated by the
members, a factor that impressed otherwise critical
visitors such as Rogers and Walter Besant. This had not
been an instant accomplishment. In the early years
members had missed the commanding central figure of the
landlord and the familiar atmosphere of the pub - one man
complained that he missed the pot-boy in particular, for
here at least had been someone he could order about after
a day of taking orders. When drink was introduced the
Union urged club stewards to play the part of the host,
but as simple dispensers of beer they lacked the traditional substance of the publican. (43) The style of

the Working Men's Club as it evolved was much less mono-
centric than that of the pub, and management by committee
made authority more self-effacing. Something of the
essence of club life and of the typical clubman is conveyed in this character sketch by Rogers of James Lowe,
the greatly respected president of the Hackney WMC: (44)

> He was a man with a good fund of general information
> but was not in any large sense an educated man. He
> was not a great orator; he was a moderately good
> speaker, and that was all.... He had the frank
> geniality which the workman loves, knew his own limi-
> tations and never presumed on his position, devoted
> himself absolutely to the well-being of the club and
> its ideals, and in his interpretation of them was only
> just a little ahead of his followers.

Club government was none the less forceful for being
by committee. Mayhew had remarked on the perfect decorum
in the clubs he visited on his London tour. He had, he
said 'witnessed NOT ONE single case of drunkenness, nor
riot, nor coarse language'. At the Newcastle upon Tyne
club, which was self-managed, the committee appointed a
superintendent who patrolled the clubrooms, alert for
drunkenness, 'ungentlemanly language' or petty corruption
on the part of the bagatelle marker. The club hired up
to a dozen policemen to keep order at the annual picnic.
Members who were expelled or suspended for some breach of
the regulations anxiously solicited for reinstatement,
for membership was obviously highly valued and the rules
generally respected. This concern for good order and good
manners fulfilled something at least of the original
intentions of Solly and his friends.

How close had the CIU come to realising its founder's
designs? The clubs' historian provided one answer: 'The
sphere of the workman's club', wrote B.T.Hall in 1912,
'is smaller in circumference than was at first projected
by the Pioneer, and immeasurably smaller in its results.'
(45) Measured against Solly's expectations, this would
also stand as a fair judgment of the reach and progress
of the organised Club movement in the first twenty years
or so of its life. The good order that obtained was
obscured by the fug of tobacco smoke and the clatter of
glasses, and if club members were not barbarians they
would hardly yet have passed as the new Greeks. The
workingmen who gradually assumed control of the clubs
were bent on improvement, but though they moved up Solly's
inclined plane they were bound for a different destination
and - most disappointing of all - they expressly rejected
the guiding hand of their social superiors. The reso-
lution of class differences through 'the friendly dis-

cussion of capital and labour' clearly begged too many
questions about the outside world of the 1870s and 1880s,
and in struggling to construct their own life within the
clubs the members revealed the instincts of an authentic
class consciousness and the continuing strengths of an
independent culture. Yet in their willingness to allow
beer in the clubs Solly and other bourgeois patrons had
come closer to an informed and committed tolerance of
that culture than the great majority of their fellows,
for they had after all been prepared to modify social
patterns to accommodate behaviour that others tried simply
to eradicate. It was ironic that it was this concession
which gave the working-class members the economic self-
sufficiency that enabled them to unship their mentors.

6

Rational Recreation and the New Athleticism

One of the more remarkable features of the expanding world
of mid-Victorian leisure was the innovation of organised
and codified athletic sports - a broad category of activities which comprised primarily the athletics of track and
field events, as the term is understood today, together
with a reconstructed version of football, and the
previously reformed game of cricket. In the 1860s public
school men began to carry their enthusiasm for the reformed canon of athletic sports through into adult life,
and by the Jubilee year of 1887 Gladstone was pointing to
the popularity of these sports as a measure of the
nation's improved taste in recreation. 'For the schoolboy
and the man alike', he observed, 'athletics are becoming
an ordinary incident of life.' (1) Thereafter the
practice spread still more widely and moved one reputable
historian of the period to contend that 'the suburban
middle class made organised games rank among England's
leading contributions to world culture.' (2) In today's
world sport is recognised as a powerful instrument for
commanding social conformity, with a unique role to play
in counteracting divisive forces such as class and race.
(3) How did it commend itself to the Victorians, and what
part did it play in the prescriptions of rational recreation?

I

There were those contemporaries who were persistently
hostile to the growing cult of organised games, but they
need not detain us long; the intellectual strengths of
their case could do little to check the tide of popular
enthusiasm. John Ruskin, Matthew Arnold and Wilkie
Collins were among those who attacked the worship of

athletics as boorish and dehumanising. In 1869 Collins
enjoyed considerable literary success with his novel 'Man
and Wife' in which the central figure, Geoffrey Delamayn,
is an athlete whose life is brutalised by his sport.   In
the preface Collins makes it quite clear that Delamayn
represents a new type, 'the rough in broadcloth', who
constitutes a serious menace to society. (4) Recalling
this indictment some twenty years later, Montague
Shearman, barrister, athlete and author of discerning
and respected handbooks on sport, commented that the
English public had admired the story but refused to
swallow its message; to Shearman it was by then self-
evident that 'the athletic movement has benefited the
people at large.' (5)

For the most part the new-style athleticism won a good
press and recommended itself as an eminently rational,
even spiritual, recreation. In mid-Victorian England, in
particular, the preoccupation with the maintenance of
national military preparedness led to a new respect for
physical education. In the 1830s and 1840s reformers had
talked of the Health of Towns; the capitalised imperative
in following decades became the Health of the Nation. The
shift is significant. The previous concern had been that
the disease and misery of the new manufacturing towns
would demoralise the working classes, make them easy prey
for the political agitator, and lead them to subversion
and revolt. After 1848 the fear of the governing classes
was of assault from without, more than from within. In
1850, contemplating the welter of self-congratulation at
England's escape from the fires of the continental revo-
lutions, John Stores Smith, a Manchester businessman, declared England 'the forlorn hope of European life'. Smith
was impressed less by the fact of her survival than by the
extent of her vulnerability which, in the light of his
study of other once-great nations, suggested the danger
of immediate decline. This theme gained currency. In
1852, in the course of reviewing the activities and publications of the growing number of vegetarian and homeopathic societies, the 'Westminster Review' - while enjoying itself a little at the expense of the 'potato gospel'
- pointed out 'how unfailing an accompaniment of the
decline of empires is the depreciation of the national
habit of body'. A proper concern for the nation's health,
continued the journal, came 'just in time for that great
contest with European tyranny during the remainder of the
century, which is apparently to be the part of England
and America'. (6) The Crimean War, the invasion scare of
1859 and the dramatic rise of Prussia increased alarm at
the imminence of such a contest, and gave new emphasis to

the traditional utility of sport in preserving the fitness
of the nation's physical stock. Thus the Volunteers
played their games in the service of England's security.
(7)

The call for effective exercise was addressed to town
dwellers of all classes, for the debilities of city life
seemed to threaten rich as well as poor. Of the former,
Leslie Stephen noted in 1870:

> The class which does not live by manual labour, and
> which at the same time has very little opportunity for
> hunting and fishing, has increased in an enormous
> ratio, and is still increasing. We are living more and
> more in towns and treading closer upon each other's
> heels.

Though he was apprehensive at the dangers that the popularity of athletic sports posed to intellectual life at
the universities, Stephen allowed that they met the need
for physical recreation ('some good stupid amusement') for
the urban middle classes. Some traditional prescriptions
were in any case now simply impractical - as John Morley
pointed out, 'the persistence of doctors in urging horse
exercise is, to the majority, absurd.' (8) Among this
majority were the clerks and shopmen, whose work, according to 'The Times', demanded only the slightest of
physiques: 'Civilisation wants light men - they don't
want six feet to vault over counters and run up steps at
a draper's shop.' At the time of the Crimean War the
paper warned that the nation could not rely upon such
insubstantial material to win future Inkermans, unless
nimbleness was reinforced with muscle and stamina. Thirty
years later, in a survey of modern English sport,
Frederick Gale concluded that only organised games had
saved the 'counter skippers' from effeminacy. (9) The
working classes were never in danger of effeminacy, but
city life blighted their health to an extent which alarmed
doctors and disappointed recruiting sergeants. William
Hardwicke, medical officer for health in Paddington in the
1860s, urged the case for state promotion of games and
gymnastic exercises to halt this degeneration, and Lord
Brabazon, chairman of the Gardens and Playgrounds Association, moved the same case twenty years later on the evidence that nearly half the recruits seeking enlistment in
the services were rejected for physical incapacity. (10)

Physical recreation received further endorsement from
major contemporary figures. We have seen in a previous
chapter how Charles Kingsley imparted a spiritual gloss
to sport and bodily exercise. His emphasis upon their
necessary practice as a duty to one's country became more
insistent after his conversion to Darwinism (an ideology

whose popularity increased the general concern over
national health). Another Darwinian, Herbert Spencer,
maintained that 'the contests of commerce are in part
determined by the bodily endurance of the producers.'
(11)

Under the influence of such teachings sport became a
medium for training the young to meet with the diverse
challenges of a naturally harsh and competitive world -
'Games', declared the physician to Rugby School, produce
a just ambition to excel in every phase of the battle of
life.' (12) The language of games became the language of
adventure and the highest endeavour, designed to sustain
the young under fire, whether from fast bowlers or in-
surgent tribesmen. A Scottish divine expressed his
delight at a youthful game of cricket in the following
terms: (13)

> How I love to mark the quick, watchful glance of the
> eye as the ball comes speeding on which will decide
> for 'our Club' the honour of the day, and to mark on
> the faces of those who go out, the look which was on
> that of François I as he wrote to his mother after the
> battle of Pavia, 'Tout est perdu hormis l'honneur.'

In Newbolt's popular poem 'Vitai Lampada', it is the voice
of a schoolboy that rallies the ranks during some desper-
ate desert action: 'Play up! Play up! and play the
game!'

The public school was the principal laboratory in which
the young were exposed to sport as a test for greater
things to come, and it was here that the games ethos was
refined. Men like Dr Arnold at Rugby had promoted organised games to instil discipline and self-government in
schoolboys who, in the unreformed public schools of the
early nineteenth century, had often sought their recreation in organised riot. (14) The full returns on this
practice stood out clearly by the 1880s when Edward
Lyttelton considered the merits of public school athletics: (15)

> Firstly by being forced to put the welfare of the
> common cause before selfish interests, to obey implic-
> itly the word of command, and act in concert with the
> heterogeneous elements of the company he belongs in;
> and secondly, should it so turn out, a boy is disci-
> plined by being raised to a post of command, where he
> feels the gravity of responsible office and the diffi-
> culty of making prompt decisions and securing a willing
> obedience.

Personal courage tempered by the team spirit, and a
respect for authority under the governance of fair play -
these were the key values in the new rationale of sport,

and also served as important social controls off the
field. Devotees of sport internalised its values:
N.L.Jackson, a prominent and influential athlete of the
1880s and 1890s, decorated his memoirs with an ample
definition of sportsmanship, to which he attributed
lessons in self-control, compassion and honesty, maintaining in conclusion that 'it unconsciously directs every
action of your life.' 'Athleticism', asserted Charles
Box, cricket writer and popular philosopher, 'is no unim-
portant bulwark of the constitution.... /it/ has no
sympathy with Nihilism, Communism, nor any other "ism"
that points to national disorder.' Contemporaries felt
too that the values of the games field could be fed back
into business life to correct the unrelieved materialism
and excessive appetite for speculation that seemed to have
superseded what were represented as the essentially moral
endeavours of the pioneer heroes of nineteenth-century
capitalism. (16)

    Sport could be effective in indoctrinating hoi polloi
as well as public schoolmen. A testimony on this count
comes from H.B.Philpott, an early historian of the London
School Board: (17)

    It is as true for the children of mechanics and
    labourers, as for the children of merchants and
    professional men, that manly sports, played as they
    should be played, tend to develop unselfish pluck,
    determination, self-control and public spirit. Observe
    a group of Board School cricketers after they have
    undergone a period of friendly supervision.... No one
    quarrels with the placing of the field.... the young
    captain does not bawl 'butter fingers' or 'silly
    fathead' whenever a catch is missed.... the batsman
    bowled for a duck neither shouts that 'it ain't fair'
    nor punches the umpire.... No, they have learned to
    'play the game'. And the change is not a matter of
    cricket only; in becoming better cricketers they have
    become better boys.

Philpott also remarked on the 'moral salvation' effect-
ed by football, but it is significant that he should pay
most attention to the social therapies of cricket, for it
was this game which was constantly made to serve as a
metaphor for the ideal society. Although there was a
thorough-going commercial sector in cricket, the general
banishment of gambling from the game recommended it as a
reformed sport. It carried with it long-standing associations of a bucolic, pre-industrial society; it was
in fact a perfect vehicle for the myths of Merrie England.
Cricket, wrote one representative commentator in the
course of a political reform tract of the late 1850s,

afforded 'a happy and compendious illustration of English
characteristics and English social institutions.... the
truly English republican element of a mixture of classes
with the right man in the right place, is nowhere better
exemplified than in the cricket field.' (18)   The game was
applauded as a civilising influence in the new towns, not
least because it was credited with disciplining the spectator as well as the participant. Recording progress in
Yorkshire, John Lawson observed that 'it is not uncommon
now [1887] for the people of Pudsey to be seen applauding
their opponents by clapping hands' (the reactions of sixty
years previous had been somewhat more curmudgeonly). (19)

Thus the new model athletic sports boasted some im-
peccable credentials: they provided a regimen which
brought physical fitness to the individual, toughening
him against the debilities of city life and maintaining
his readiness for armed service; they also provided an
education in self-discipline and team work which acted as
a moral police over the individual's life at large;
adapted to the new circumstances of modern society they
yet retained sentimental historical associations of social
harmony and the fraternity of all classes in sport. At
the very least they were recommended as an antidote for
what, by all accounts, seems to have been the common
complaint of Victorian town dwellers - indigestion.

II

Given then the patently 'rational' nature of athletic
sports or organised games we would expect them to have
been widely promoted among the working classes. Yet such
was not the case. As H.A.Butler-Johnstone, MP, pointed
out to the House of Commons in 1875, 'it is no answer to
the complaint that large classes are deprived of the
advantages of athletics and outdoor sports to say that
other classes are devoted to these exercises.' It was
only in the late 1880s, and then with doubtful enthusiasm,
that Shearman could record: 'The athletic movement which
commenced with the "classes", and first drew its strength
from the Universities and public schools, has finally,
like most other movements and fashions, good or bad,
spread downwards to the masses.' (20) The story of the
cultural spin-off during these years records the obstacles
in the way of achieving in sport the social liaison which
had long been preached by those interested in the reform
of recreation.

First, there was little provision or encouragement for
athletic games in the educational world outside the public

schools. Clearly one of the problems was lack of space.
An assistant commissioner enquiring into popular education
in the 1860s deplored the absence of playgrounds and
organised games in working-class schools, and Thomas Okey,
who was a boy in Spitalfields at this time, echoed the
complaint of many a working-class autobiography in recalling that the streets were the only playing fields of
his youth - as athletic practice he swam in the canal, for
there were no games at his National School. The Education
Act of 1870 did little to remedy such deficiencies.
Philpott, whom we have quoted on the beneficent effect of
properly supervised sport on board school boys in London,
nevertheless found physical education 'one of the least
satisfactory features of the Board's work' and described
some of the problems impeding its progress. The
children's interest in and capacity for playing sport was
restricted by deficiencies of diet and of pocket money,
and in the long absence of playing fields their cultural
traditions stopped short with the games of the street.
Some teachers had worked hard to promote sport, said
Philpott, but most of them were too intent on the struggle
of bringing each scholar up to the point of passing the
government inspector; under the system of payment by
results it was difficult for them to introduce anything
not encouraged by the official code. (21)
     The neglect of games in elementary schools was not,
however, due simply to the dearth of play space but also
to the specific social function assigned to these schools
in educational policy. The Clarendon report on public
schools in 1861 had recognised the value of sport in
character training, but in terms of the State's provision
it was training reserved for society's leaders, not the
led. Physical education for working-class children meant
not games, but drill. Edwin Chadwick was prominent among
those who made a strong argument for drill in the 1860s
and pressed their case upon Forster, the author of the
1870 Act. Drill would provide industrial training for
each new generation of the labour force and paramilitary
training for a potential citizens' army. The economics
of the scheme were spelled out in detail - with such
training, claimed Chadwick, three might eventually do the
work of five and, if a boy was taught to walk with a more
even step, he might make do with one less pair of boots
over the year. Drill found its way into the schools'
curriculum and, unlike sport, qualified for a grant. The
school boards welcomed drill: it helped control unruly
classes; it made efficient use of limited space (drill
could be practised in the classroom gangways if there was
no playground at all); the children often enough enjoyed

it, and it was not unpopular with parents (a man who was
in school in Swindon in the 1880s recalled forming squares
and doing elementary rifle drill with broomsticks - 'My
father, a John Bright liberal, didn't object'). Gymnastic
exercises provided an occasional supplement to drill but
there was no teaching of athletic skills which might later
enrich the adult life of board school children. Indeed,
one authority talked as though physical education during
schooldays was the only such training most working-class
children would receive, 'in as much as, after an early
age, they have little or no time for recreation like those
socially above them.' (22)

In the adult world, even where time was available,
working-class participation was limited by the restrictive
rulings of the new governing bodies of the various athletic sports. As an example we may take the policy of the
influential Amateur Athletic Club, formed in 1866 'to
afford as completely as possible to all classes of
Gentleman Amateurs the means of practising and competing
versus one another without being compelled to mix with
professional runners'. For the AAC an amateur was further
defined as (23)

> Any person who has never competed in an open compe-
> tition, or for public money, or for admission money,
> or with professionals for a prize, public money or
> admission money, and who has never, at any period of
> his life, taught or assisted in the pursuit of athletic
> exercises as a means of livelihood, or is a mechanic,
> artisan or labourer.

The barring of mechanics, artisans and labourers was also
standard policy for the Amateur Rowing Association and the
Bicycle Union. The justification for this common barring
clause was that those whose habitual mode of life involved
physical labour would enjoy a built-in advantage in athletic contests which would preclude genuine competition.
We may recall too the principle of antithesis in the
Victorian rationale of recreation which maintained that
the most appropriate recreations were those which provided
the greatest contrast with a man's work. By this test it
could be argued that the leisure needs of the muscular
workman were best served by mental rather than physical
exercise.

Some members of the new athletic clubs were anxious to
keep out the lower orders to spare themselves the embarrassment of an unwonted physical intimacy in the
dressing tent - 'a matter of some importance to a
sensitive person' (24) - but a more basic explanation
for the discrimination against the mechanic, artisan or
labourer lay in the fundamentally new attitude of the

middle class to the practice of sport. This gave a
further emphasis to the distance between bourgeois and
popular cultures, and is exemplified in the contrast
between the new model athletic sports of the AAC and the
popular athletics of 'pedestrianism' - the sub rosa world
of professional running and walking races.

Pedestrianism was eccentric and undisciplined. Its
contests were frequently bizarre - walking backwards,
racing in heavily weighted clogs, picking up stones (or
eggs) at regular intervals over a long distance, trundling
barrow loads of bricks - and often seemed little removed
from traditional rural feats of brute strength and endurance. (25) The sport had a long previous history of
gentlemanly patronage - masters had chosen footmen for
their running prowess, and backed them against those of
rival households in matches which they themselves had
often joined (26) - but upper-class interest and participation had waned considerably by the 1850s. In an article
on Gaming, betting, lotteries and insurance, 4 December
1852, 'Chambers's Edinburgh Journal' reported:

> In pedestrianism ... we occasionally hear of gentlemen
> whose emulation impels to a contest, which they may
> spice with a bet of 100 guineas or so; but the com-
> petitors, in most instances where money passes, are
> poor men, who literally walk or run for their bread;
> the match is generally concocted by a tavern-keeper,
> who plans it so as to make it a matter of business.
> The individuals who outrage nature by walking 1000
> miles in 1000 successive half-hours, and such like
> feats, are mostly publicans' protégés.

While shedding its old patrons, the sport had become
extremely popular. The élite among the professionals,
bearing heroic and flamboyant names - the Gateshead
Clipper, the Norwich Milk Boy, the Crow Catcher, and the
like - raced for championship cups and belts before crowds
of several thousands at major pedestrian enclosures in the
big cities. It was an unruly business, to judge from the
notices of pedestrian meetings appearing in the sporting
press of the period. From a match promoted by the
landlord of the Yorkshire Stingo at Mr Roberts's ground
in West London, the 'Era', 5 January 1862, reported: 'The
betting was heavy, the sport admirable, the management
insufferable.... not until half the proceedings were over
did the Proprietor send for the police to keep order, as
is usual on all running grounds.' As we have seen, pedestrianism was a sport of the streets as well as the
running grounds - an 'indecent nuisance', condemned by
respectable citizens, harassed by the police and punished
by the courts. The world of its champions was recorded in

the pages of 'Bell's Sporting Life', the principal organ
of a great underground of popular sport. A contemporary
acknowledgment of the paper's significance is worth
requoting: (27)

'Bell's Life' tells us not what ought to be done by
Englishmen but what, as a matter of fact, is done. It
shows what a large balance there still is versus that
crushing respectability which threatens to overwhelm
us - it tells us how much of the animal pleasures of
savage life survives in the heart of civilised life.

Supporters of the new athleticism would not have represented their games as celebrations of the savage life; in
many ways they were institutions abstracted from life,
whether savage or civilised. Despite the aggressive style
of language which coloured debates on health and athletics
in the context of social Darwinism and national survival,
there was a sense in which the games field served more as
a refuge from the competitive strains of real life than as
an extension of it. The doctrine of fair play provided
for competition, of course, but suspended the absolute
judgments of success or failure, affluence or bankruptcy,
which could befall commercial or professional life. The
vindictive laws of Nature which were judged to govern a
man's working life were to be barred from his play. Sport
was now a laboratory in which men could test themselves
under precise and uniform rules, not an arena where, to
recall the phrase in 'Chambers's Journal', men were
incited to 'outrage nature'. (28) The old sports had
about them the flavour of gladiatorial contests (in pedestrianism as much as the prize ring) and were reported
in an arcane vernacular of epic and arresting style; the
new sports had their heroes, and the heroic style of
reportage survived in modified form in the flourishing
world of boys' periodicals, but the typical sporting paper
which appeared in the 1860s and 1870s to service the new
athleticism was a journal of record, rarely an essay in
melodrama. Thus was sport represented as a neutral,
scientific exercise, an alternative world of physical
improvement and achievement which could be exactly
measured, safe from the harsh and often adventitious
sanctions of working life; the members of its fraternity
enjoyed a sense of competitive striving which stopped far
short of self-destruction. In team games in particular,
reckless individualism was restrained by the insistence
upon team spirit and co-operation. Sport was not,
however, to be allowed to engross life; a magazine
article in 1881 which criticised the proliferation of
prizes in amateur athletics did so because they tended
'to exalt recreation above its limits into a substitute

for work', leading to a situation where 'selfish competition prevails rather than the sense of wholesome membership in sports.' (29)   Thus pedestrianism was abhorrent to
amateurs because it was professionalised and therefore a
kind of work.   It was on such grounds that the governing
bodies of the reformed sports contested the participation
of professionals in their meetings, in a running controversy which dominated the athletic world from the 1860s
onwards.

Also central to the case against professionalism was
the contention that it encouraged gambling.   Gambling was
reviled by middle-class opinion on several grounds.   It
was a matter of perpetual scandal to the man of business
that the society gambler would honour his gaming debts
though scorning to the last the claims of the honest
tradesmen among his creditors, while betting among the
lower orders was regarded as a constant threat to property
and social order.   Young gentlemen were advised that 'The
moral healthiness or unhealthiness of any recreation may
generally be estimated by the extent to which it has
become the subject of bets.' (30)   The gentleman patron
of traditional sports had backed his protégés as a matter
of course, and 'The Times', 30 May 1868, could still
defend betting in the 1860s with the argument that, with
a few reckless exceptions, the nobility knew how to bet;
their vulgar imitators, said the paper, should be caution-
ed but not proscribed.   But the railways and telegraph had
produced a national sporting market in which the aristocratic backer had been superseded by the bookmaker;   the
presence of a gentleman had allegedly ensured fair play,
whereas the bookie provided no such guarantee. (31)   The
'roping' or rigging of contests by the gambling interests
was notorious at pedestrian meetings, and as far as the
amateurs were concerned such chicanery distorted the
neutral frame of reference within which sports should
ideally be conducted.   'The pedestrian circle', asserted
one of the new wave of athletic papers, 'is too much
surrounded by a halo of beer and skittles, and amenable
to the low art of the bookmakers to make it either a
healthy or an improving place of resort, or a reliable
gauge of man's physical powers.' (32)

Such associations were to be avoided at all costs if
the new sports were to be made socially respectable.   The
enthusiasts who founded the AAC and like bodies had some
initial difficulties in persuading their elders that the
practice of athletic sports outside the confines of public
school and university was not vulgar and morally ruinous -
Walter Rye's fiancée was forced to break off the en-
gagement when her mother discovered that he took part in

athletics, 'sharing with my own parents, as she did, the
then prevalent idea that athletics meant pot-housing'.
It was to avoid such opprobrium that early amateurs wore
masks and competed incognito. Even in 1868, Anthony
Trollope considered modern football and athletics too
parvenu to include in his survey of British sports and
games, explaining that 'we have felt that they have fallen
somewhat short of the necessary dignity.' (33) Once such
prejudice was dispelled, everything was done to maintain
a respectable tone by securing amateur athletics against
interlopers from lower stations in society.

The new world of amateur sport was therefore an exclusive one. Discrimination against the older sport and
its practitioners was based on rational and moral grounds
- what could be more irrational than walking backwards,
or more immoral than gambling? - but the concern for respectability emphasises the strong element of class discrimination. In a review of the amateur versus professional controversy on 26 April 1880, 'The Times' noted
that

artisans and mechanics have, by almost general consent,
been shut out from the privileged inner circle, and
have been counted as in every case, professionals....
Their muscular practice is held to give them unfair
advantage over more delicately nurtured competitors.

'The Times' thought such an argument had become rather
obsolete but spoke up for discrimination on other grounds:

The outsiders, artisans, mechanics, and such like
troublesome persons can have no place found for them.
To keep them out is a thing desirable on every account.
The 'status' of the rest seems better assured and more
clear from any doubt which might attach to it, and the
prizes are more certain to fall into the right hands.
Loud indeed would be the wail over a chased goblet or
a pair of silver sculls which a mechanic had been lucky
enough to carry off. The whole 'pot-hunting' world
would be simply so much the poorer, to say nothing of
the ridiculous nature of such a defeat, and of the
social degradation which the contest would have
implied, whatever its results had been.... No base
mechanic arms need be suffered to thrust themselves
in here.

The most difficult problem in maintaining exclusivity
lay along the margins of the class line; it was, presumably, fairly easy to distinguish and therefore exclude the
base mechanics or professionals - even though the latter
occasionally adopted false whiskers and false names to
plunder a few cups (34) - but in large metropolitan communities with a high rate of social mobility the screening

capacity of the ruling cliques was severely reduced, and
the ex-public school and varsity men faced a takeover by
the lower middle-class tradesman and clerk. This situation produced a further refinement of the definition of
amateur in an attempt to reserve the higher social reaches
of sport for the 'gentleman amateur', as a letter to the
'Sporting Gazette' in July 1872 serves to emphasize: (35)

> Sports nominally open to gentleman amateurs must be
> confined to those who have a real right to that title,
> and men of a class considerably lower must be given to
> understand that the facts of their being well conducted
> and civil and never having run for money are NOT suf-
> ficient to make a man a gentleman as well as an
> amateur. They have a hundred and one tradesmen's
> meetings to fall back upon, and what more can they
> want?

Nor was it to be expected that sporting skills would
secure an entrée where civility and good conduct on their
own were insufficient credentials; as an editorial in the
'Referee', 27 January 1878, laid down, 'The fact that a
man is exceptionally brilliant as a player is in no way an
excuse for the assumption of unwarranted social rank;
quite the reverse.' It appears that those most recently
qualified as gentlemen were the most assiduous in pulling
up the ladder behind them; as one observer remarked,
'From enquiries I have made I find that nearly all the
members of the athletic clubs calling themselves "Gentleman Amateurs", and who exclude tradesmen are, IN REALITY,
TRADESMEN'S SONS.' (36) If sport was indeed the great
leveller, its social utility to the established or aspiring bourgeoisie was that it might level up, not level
down.

III

Given then the limitations on working-class participation
in the new games in the schools and those associations
best equipped to provide for and encourage athleticism,
by what process did athletics 'spread downwards to the
masses'? In particular, what role did reformers allot
to sport in their promotion of rational recreation?
   Reformers certainly recommended physical exercise to
the working classes. Samuel Smiles advised 'abundant
physical exercise' in his programme of self-help. William
Lovett prescribed the same in proposing a physical regimen
which he believed would assist the improvement of his
class, and other working-class reformers contributed to
the delineation of a new model physique - trimmer and more

ascetic than that derived from the publican and the prize-
fighter. (37) The preservation of open spaces attracted
attention among reformers in the 1870s: trades union
leaders and middle-class friends of the working classes
formed the People's Garden Company in London in 1870, and
by the middle of the decade Octavia Hill and other philanthropists had established the Open Space movement,
whose manifestoes emphasised the common man's need for
healthy outdoor sports. As we have seen, Lord Brabazon
and others urged the same case in the interests of
national military preparedness. (38)

A growing number of athletic churchmen urged their
colleagues to develop games skills as a means of reaching
and extending their working-class congregations. As noted
previously, Kingsley's teachings had helped to make sport
more respectable (though Kingsley himself kept to fishing
and leap-frog rather than football and cricket) and the
new-style sporting parson was well enough known to suffer
Dickens's mocking attentions by the 1860s. (39) The
cricket field was the most frequently recommended setting
for the clergyman's exercise in fraternity - in Bolton by
1867 about a third of the cricket clubs were connected to
a religious body (40)) - but he was active in other sports
too. One knowledgeable modern historian of British
football finds that 'the curate, and often the vicar,
inspired by his own early education, frequently set out
to claim souls with a Bible in one hand and a football in
the other.' There are some well-known examples of this
provenance in the histories of today's major football
clubs, and the contention receives further support from
another detailed local study of the period - about a
quarter of the clubs in the Birmingham area in the 1880s
had some connexion with religious organisations. (41)

The Church was one of several institutions that provided physical facilities for sports (the most welcome
form of assistance) such as changing rooms and playing
fields. In the 1870s and 1880s young workingmen (and
such clerks and shop assistants who shared their enthusiasms) were able to meet together in YMCAs, friendly societies, Working Men's Clubs, public houses, schoolrooms and
the workplace to form their various sports clubs. In
Bolton in the 1860s a number of local employers provided
their workers with a cricket ground; many of the clubs
formed in this way followed the common national pattern
of fielding a football side in the winter to maintain
their association, thus further extending the practice
of organised sports among workingmen.

But Butler-Johnstone's statement to the Commons, quoted
above, should alert us to the extent to which active en-

couragement and provision by the wealthier classes was the
exception rather than the rule. The Open Space movement
provided a standing acknowledgment of the chronic shortage
of playing room in the towns. Where public parks existed
sport was often prohibited - Farnworth Park near Bolton
was not unexceptional in banning cricket and allowing
games 'of a quiet nature only'. (42) Church patronage in
sport was not yet convincing enough to dispel the image
of the clergyman as kill-joy, and the sporting churchman
was in a minority in a profession which remained generally
suspicious of popular sport as a corrupter of morals,
despite the new and respectable models. 'Despite all the
talk, fashionable as is the so-called muscular Christianity,' complained W.T.Marriott, 'still little is DONE for
their [the working classes'] improvement.' In any case,
according to some observers from within the Anglican
Church, athletic clergymen often used their games skills
to ingratiate themselves with the upper classes rather
than with workingmen. (43) Moreover, church-sponsored
sports clubs were subject to built-in limitations on
membership, for the latter was often made conditional upon
church attendance. Similarly, some business firms restricted passes to recreational functions to 'reputable'
employees. (44)

Yet the role of the upper classes must still be recognised as an important one. Despite the reservations which
some of their number continued to hold, the simple fact
that athleticism was practised by the respectables made it
legitimate practice for the lower orders. Certainly there
was a new tolerance for sport which had not existed in the
1830s and 1840s. The new codes of play and conduct were
the work of middle-class administrators who could secure
them almost immediate national recognition through that
intimate community of interest which the English know as
the old-boy network, an institution for which there was
no good working-class equivalent. There is some indication too that working-class boys absorbed the new
teachings of fair play and good sportsmanship from reading
schoolboy papers written for the middle-class market
(though the new code must often have sat uneasily beside
the laws of survival learned in a slum culture). (45)

What the substantial middle class did not provide in
any abundance was a direct presence. Even in the case of
the many football clubs associated with church or chapel,
it is clear that in several instances the initiative came
from within the church membership rather than from the
church officers. The latter were often of less assistance
than other members of the community, and once established
the teams seem to have quickly severed the religious con-

nexion. The original members of Aston Villa (a club
referred to as a church team in standard histories of the
game) were 'connected with' the Bible class of a Wesleyan
chapel. Their playing field was provided by a local
butcher and their dressing room by a local publican.
Members of a Church of England school team in Wolver-
hampton, later the Wolves, derived more support from the
publican father of one of the boys than from their clerical headmaster, and themselves took the initiative in approaching a local industrialist for his backing. Members
of the Christ Church Football Club in Bolton deserted
their mentor, the Reverend J.F.Wright, four years after
he had formed the club; they walked out of a meeting in
the church schoolrooms, crossed the road to the Gladstone
Hotel and reconstituted themselves as the Bolton Wanderers. Tottenham Hotspur was a team originally associated
with the YMCA, but it was formed by a small group of
enthusiasts who approached the Association for assistance,
rather than responded to any initial lead from that organisation. In the practical and eclectic fashion of their
culture, workingmen used such institutions as a socially
neutral locus for the formation of their clubs and teams;
the function of institutions was more one of convenience
than of direct encouragement. (46)

The popular expansion of the new sports in the 1870s
and 1880s derived a great deal of its impetus from below;
workingmen generated their own encouragement, and showed
also how little they were deterred by explicit discourage-
ment. There had always been a considerable popular appetite for sport in England, and it had been far from extinguished by the deficiencies of diet, income and space,
and the attenuation of cultural continuity that Philpott
later remarked. As Will Thorne recalled of Birmingham in
the early 1870s: 'One of the remarkable things about
those times was that, no matter how hard men and boys
worked, they were whenever possible always anxious to take
part in sports.' (47) Such was the pressure of popular
interest in athletics that it became difficult for governing bodies to enforce any distinction other than the basic
one between amateur and professional, where the former was
defined simply as a competitor who was not dependent on
the sport for his livelihood (the matter of legitimate
expenses for the amateur was an early problem which did,
however, continue to obscure the issue). Some officers
in the London hierarchy had begun canvassing for the
deletion of the clause excluding mechanics, artisans and
labourers in the 1870s, though the appeals were sometimes
less than gracious. Arguing that 'The common republic of
sport does not admit of such invidious comparisons',

H.F.Wilkinson of the London Athletic Club went on to
instance examples from other sports of the happy combination of 'the lord, the lout, and the merchant'. (48)
The lout was in fact turning out to be less of a threat
to the new sporting ethics than had at first been feared.
The Northern Counties Athletic Association, formed in
1879, dropped the mechanics clause and threatened to
boycott the AAC championships which were traditionally
held in the spring. The timing here was made to fit in
with the university calendar but caught the bulk of
working-class entrants unprepared; they could not train
during the day and needed the long summer evenings to
reach optimum fitness. Faced with this crisis the AAC
went into dissolution, to be replaced by the more democratic and less élitist Amateur Athletic Association in
1880 which followed the provincial associations in de-
leting the mechanics clause and recognising athletics as
primarily a summer sport. (49)

The popular participation which opened up the amateur
running tracks to all comers was not, however, of such a
volume to provide the regular market opportunities for
commercial speculation which might have led to eventual
professional domination of the sport. For some time the
pedestrian world contined to co-exist with amateur athletics, still attracting large attendances on occasions,
but otherwise alienating its supporters by the overt
corruption of the 'gaffers', the backers who put up the
stakes and manipulated the betting. (50) In any case the
big crowds were being lured away by football, the most
dramatic in growth of the new organised games, and a mass
spectacle by the mid-1880s.

The middle-class officials of the Football Association,
founded in 1863, had at first felt no need to stipulate
the status appropriate to those who wished to play. The
old game of football was an occasional and irregular
affair, and there was no flourishing professional sector
of the game to threaten the new code as had been the case
with athletics. Moreover, the nature of the game itself
allowed for a covert and largely inoffensive form of
discrimination. Athletic clubs received entries for
their meetings from individual competitors rather than
from clubs en bloc, and then more often by post than in
person, so that comprehensive screening was very difficult; football clubs could choose their opponents at
will. For almost the first twenty years of its life,
therefore, major wrangles within the FA centred on differences over the rules of play, as the administrators sought
to reconcile the several variations emanating from the key
public schools which had fostered a revised version of the

game - the issues were those of technical, rather than social, discrimination. (51)   But the early enthusiasts were mindful of the need to give football a respectable tone, for it was but a few years previously that the headmaster of Shrewsbury had dismissed the game as 'fit only for butcher boys', and we have noted above Trollope's misgivings about the lack of dignity in football.   In Sheffield, an early stronghold of the game, the managing committee of the first established football club in 1854 stated its intention to confine activities to gentlemen, an intention echoed in the following advertisement for the post of secretary to the local football association in the 1880s: 'Besides possessing great educational ability, the secretary should be a gentleman of good position, with whom distant officials would not deem it derogatory to correspond.'   Frederick Wall, secretary of the FA from 1895, recalled the game in its early years as 'a joyous revel for the middle classes', and so it remained with little need to police its boundaries until the mid-1870s. (52)

It was the inception of the FA Cup competition in 1871 which opened up the game, simultaneously disarming the freedom of preference the early clubs had been able to exercise in selecting opponents and inducing a cumulative excitement throughout the season which multiplied popular interest.   The Cup competition was conceived initially as an extension of the system of public school house matches, but its subsequent history rapidly dissolved this recherché image.   Northern clubs with a predominantly working-class membership and following entered for the Cup, and thus broke into London and the south where the idea of football as the gentleman's game was strongest. To travel to the south, the northern clubs were often obliged to raise a public subscription, and the problem of meeting their players' expenses grew as the range and frequency of matches increased.   Competition in the north, particularly in Lancashire, became so intense that the leading clubs began to import players from Scotland, already productive of notably gifted 'professors' of the game. (53)

The signs of incipient professionalism were soon noticed - the sovereign in the boot, the mysterious deliveries of free coal, the easy tenancy of a pub - and the FA moved to defend the amateur status of the game. The debate between supporters and critics of professionalism had grown heated by the early 1880s, and the football world was convulsed in the autumn of 1884 when the governing body introduced a ruling effectively banning professionals from playing in the Cup competition.

The Lancashire clubs saw themselves as the principal
target of such a move and expressed their resentment in
class terms. The football correspondent of the 'Bolton
Chronicle' put it thus: (54)

> In the South the players are mainly of the 'upper ten'.
> They can afford time and money for training, and
> travelling, and playing. In the North the devotees of
> the game are mainly working men. They cannot play the
> game on strictly amateur lines.... They cannot afford
> to train, or to 'get in form', or whatever other name
> you like to call it. Besides, they command big 'gates'
> and they naturally think they have a right to a trifle
> from it.

A Preston official writing to the 'Athletic News', 29
October 1884, voiced the popular opinion that the covert
professional was a workingman denied the full fruits of
his labour. Those who paid to see the game were willing
to pay its players and abhorred the system which sought
to preserve the fiction of amateurism; it was absurd and
unjust to reward the coal miner with a talent for football
with 'the occasional supply of a set of dessert cutlery'
when the man would be better served as an open professional in a new and superior employment. 'To the "upper
crust", no doubt', concluded the correspondent, 'it is
annoying to see "cads" attaining excellence and equal
powers to themselves.' Class resentment was compounded
by a provincial hostility to the metropolis, from where,
in northern eyes, the game was being manipulated by 'a
few mashers who wish to have the English cup back in
London'. (55)

The north formed its own British Association in November 1884, announcing it as a democratic alternative to
the peremptory oligarchy of the FA, and promising to regu-
larise professionalism within the game. (56) Faced with
the open secession of Lancashire and considerable disaffection in the midlands, the FA executed a remarkable
volte-face and gave official sanction to professionalism
in football in the summer of 1885. (57) Though the
northern clubs were thus prevailed upon to accept the
continued jurisdiction of the FA, the mood of grass-roots
assertiveness persisted in the local Lancashire Football
Association where there was an outspoken campaign to
remove Lord Hartingdon as president - 'the day of orna-
mental officers', said one critic, 'has passed.' (58)

Professionalism did not, however, mean the end of
patronage, but rather a change in its pattern and provenance. Professionalism, increasing gates and the inception of a national league in 1888 brought new problems
of management without necessarily guaranteeing financial

viability for the clubs. Men with longish pockets were
needed in these years when professionals were contracted
to individual members of club committees rather than to a
club itself. Such men could provide jobs and housing for
the pros, as well as stand as trustees for club grounds
with expanding amenities and services. (59) The early
enthusiasts who had encouraged workingmen to take up
football had been men of a solid middle-class background
or above. Probably fewer in number than has previously
been allowed, they were none the less moved by considerations of social and moral responsibility and, in many
cases, a player's love of the game. The new patrons who
fastened on the sport in the 1880s seem more likely to
have been marginal or self-made members of the middle
class: successful tradesmen, small businessmen, aspiring
publicans. William Sudell of Preston North End was a mill
manager. William MacGregor of Aston Villa, the instigator
of the new Football League, was a prosperous shopkeeper of
humble origins. John Davies, who at a later date rescued
Manchester United from bankruptcy, was a publican turned
brewer. (60) Few clubs could have been without one of
their kind. In one sense they represented a traditional
source of support, heirs to the countless publicans and
other middling men who had encouraged the new game of
football as they had previously encouraged all manner of
other working-class games and contests. The new patrons
revealed much the same motivation as their forerunners -
serving sport won prestige in the working-class community,
a prestige flattering for men who still regarded themselves as of the people, and useful too in local council
elections. But though often fanatical in their enthusiasm
for their teams and football itself, the institutional-
isation of financial control in the game made these men
more hard-nosed and proprietorial than their predecessors
from either their own class or the public school élite.

At the top, the FA continued to be officered by gentlemen, but in general the middle class withdrew from the
game which they had once proclaimed an instrument of moral
salvation and social order. The practice of professionalism, the related growth of mass spectatorship, and the
growing commercialisation of the game made association
football (soccer, as it became known) increasingly distasteful, and the middle class retreated to the more
select world of rugby football. By the 1890s, commentators were attacking soccer as 'a moral slough' and 'the
acme of athletic horrors'. The top players were, it was
claimed, the objects of extravagant popular adulation and
were better known than local MPs. The professional game
generated 'an epidemic excitement' among the crowds. 'As

a rule', remarked one observer, 'they do not go to see
football; they go to see their own side win, and that is
all they care about.' The referee was an immediate ritual
scapegoat in the working-class game, a symbolic proxy for
the rent collector or school board man who suffered
frequent abuse and assault. Reports of brawling in the
crowd and altercations on the field were common, and
seemed proof that ideals of fair play and gentlemanly
conduct had given way to 'a fashionable brutality'.
'Football', concluded another disillusioned witness, 'is
a passion, not a recreation.' (61)

Herbert Spencer crystallised much respectable contemporary opinion in representing football as a prime example
of what he termed the 're-barbarisation' of society. (62)
The modern game was in many ways far removed from the
hectic clashes of its folk predecessor, but those of its
features which excited the adverse comment of middle-class
witnesses were strongly reminiscent not only of the older
game but of much unreconstructed popular sport in general.
The occasion of modern football was now strictly limited
in duration, and regularly scheduled within the legitimate
free time of Saturday afternoon; players and spectators
were clearly segregated, and the activities of both contained within purpose-built stadia, admission to which was
governed by turnstiles and entrance charges; play was
limited to a small, fixed number of participants policed
by a referee in common acknowledgment of a standardised
code of rules. Yet the fierce expressions of group or
neighbourhood loyalties conveyed in the crowd's partisan
identification with team and players, and the general
function of spectatorship as an act of collective participation showed how, even within its new structure, the
sport retained much of the emotional temper and spirit of
an earlier society. (63) For such manifestations was association football generally disqualified from the canon
of rational recreation.

In contrast, cricket maintained its respectable image.
Professionals had been an accepted part of the game since
the early years of the century and, though cricket expanded greatly from the 1860s onward, they continued to
play alongside the amateurs without corrupting the equable
spirit of the game. (This held good despite occasional
strikes among the top professionals in the 1880s and 1890s
and the emergence of the more highly competitive and professionalised game of League cricket in the same decades.)
(64) Professionalism in county cricket, argued the
latter's many champions, did not produce the vicious
rivalry and bad sportsmanship which had marred pedestrianism and now corrupted football, because control rested

firmly with the gentleman amateurs; their presence
carried a traditional authority derived from that of the
landowner in the rural society whence the game had originally sprung. Furthermore, the good manners on the field
communicated themselves to the spectators, whose conduct
was irreproachable beside that of the football crowds.
There was something in this. The nature of the game was
less combustible than other sports, and the absence of
physical contact meant that to a large extent the normal
terms of social address could be maintained at play.
Patrons of the game no longer recruited professionals
exclusively from the workers on their estates, but they
clearly did regard the pros as servants who were assigned
functions within the game appropriate to their station.
Thus the pro would spend most of his time fielding - the
chore given to fags in public school cricket - and bowling
in the nets to give the gentlemen practice. The professional with Bolton Cricket Club in the 1860s bowled in
clogs as if to acknowledge his status, and the distinction
between amateur and professional or Gentlemen and Players
(after the famous annual match inaugurated in 1806 and
played until 1962) sat so easily on the game that it impressed itself upon the national vocabulary as a synonym
for mutual and amiable discrimination. A Tory politician
seeking to specify Disraeli's status within the Conservative party concluded thus: 'We know he does not belong to
our Eleven, but we have him down as a professional
bowler.' (65)

Much of the practice of sport in England remained
segregated along class lines. The new athleticism had
provided sport with credentials which gave unprecedented
emphasis to its capacity for imparting the highest moral
and social values. Despite these recommendations, there
had been no extensive move to propagate the new games
codes among the masses. The middle-class enthusiasts of
the new athleticism mostly discouraged working-class participation, in order to prevent contamination from the
corrupt practices attributed to popular sport, and to
reserve the new games as a medium for defining class
status. In the much vaunted 'republic of sport', only
cricket received special dispensation as the one game
whose mystique resisted popular corruption and kept the
base mechanicals in their place; otherwise, the working
classes were to be left the basic commons of military
drill and callisthenics. Despite the antipathies of its
self-appointed governors, the working classes took up the
new athleticism with avidity. The process of diffusion
needs further research and explanation, but it seems clear
that reformers played a more limited role than has previ-

ously been suggested. There was a strong appetite for sport among English workingmen and, while they took readily to the new models, they showed in the case of football a determination to adapt them to the circumstances and needs of their own culture.

7

Rational Recreation and the Entertainment Industry: the Case of the Victorian Music Halls

---

While organised sport increased its following among the
working classes, it was undoubtedly the music hall which
dominated popular recreations in the second half of the
nineteenth century. (1) Developed from the singing
saloons by a new breed of publican entrepreneurs, this
prototype modern entertainment industry provides a strong
example of the capacity of working-class culture to meet
the leisure needs of its constituency. Middle-class observers reacted to the demotic vigour of the halls with
mixed feelings: some derived a measure of encouragement
from the new phenomenon, but the bulk of reformers were
disturbed by the halls as a further manifestation of the
generally debased tastes of the masses. Next to the pub
the music halls became the most embattled institution in
working-class life, as reform groups strove variously to
close them, censor them or reproduce their essential
appeal in facsimile counter-attractions purged of vulgarity. Though the halls proved remarkably resilient, they
did yield some ground to the pressures of rational recreation; significantly, the more effective pressures came
from within the industry itself.

I

The take-off in growth for the music halls came in the
1850s. In recognition of a growing popular demand for
entertainment, some of the more enterprising publicans
expanded the operations of the singing saloon. They
abolished the refreshment check in favour of a straight
admission charge thus de-emphasising the trade in liquor,
and relying on the pulling power of the entertainment and
the superior appointments of the new establishments - the
music hall label was meant to indicate an advance in taste

and amenities upon the singing saloon. A certain Thomas
Harwood (member of a family later prominent in East End
music hall management) explained to a government licensing
committee in 1852 how realisation of the potential of this
new formula had prompted him to open a new concert room:
(2)

> I was about leaving business, and it always struck me
> that the working classes could have a better de-
> scription of recreation, supposing a person could
> speculate sufficiently largely, and give the recreation
> at a low price.

The smell of big money was in the air in the licensed
trade; increased business in the 1840s had accelerated
capital accumulation, and the publican was well placed to
subsidise his ventures into music hall proprietorship from
other enterprises such as sports promotion or outside
catering in food and drink. (3)

The best known of the new wave of publican entrepreneurs ('caterers' in contemporary jargon) was another
Londoner, Charles Morton, who opened his Canterbury Hall
in 1851 in Lambeth. Originally an annexe built on the
site of his pub's skittle alley, the hall proved such a
profitable success that Morton reconstructed the whole
premises in 1854 at a cost variously estimated at between
£25,000 and £40,000. The new hall had a capacity of over
1,500 and boasted its own library, reading room and
picture gallery; admission charges started at 6d. In
1861 Morton duplicated his success when he opened the
Oxford in Oxford Street, the first purpose-built music
hall, complete with a fully equipped stage and fixed stall
seating (the latter a significant change from the free-
standing tables and chairs of most halls). The lavish
appointments of the Oxford were the talk of the West End;
not the least attractive feature was its bevy of remarkably handsome barmaids. (4)

But the leading showpiece of the new era was the
Alhambra in Leicester Square (the choice of Bill Banks
and his party for their night out in the late 1860s).
Converted from the Panopticon of Science and Art into a
3,500-capacity music hall in 1860, the Alhambra eventually
outdid the Oxford in the scale and spectacle of its pro-
ductions and the range of its amenities, and claimed a
yearly attendance outstripping South Kensington Museum or
the Zoo. It retained the patronage of a solid core of
working-class Londoners, but also benefited from the
capital's increasing tourist traffic (there was a further
Exhibition in 1862). In 1864 it became the first music
hall operated by a limited liability company, and proceeded to pay handsome dividends. (5)

The introduction of limited liability in 1862 released
a flow of venture capital into music hall promotion, encouraged by the flourishing examples of the Oxford and
Alhambra. By 1866 when the boom seems to have levelled
out, the solicitor to the London Music Hall Proprietors'
Association could list thirty-three large halls in town
with an average capitalisation of £10,000 and an average
capacity of 1,500. (6) The existence of such an association is a further indication of the success of the halls,
for it was founded to protect proprietors from legal
actions brought by theatre interests in central London
who were suffering from the competition of the new entertainments (informers laid information that the halls were
offering episodes of straight drama which encroached upon
territory reserved for the legitimate stage under the
Theatre Act of 1843). At the hearings before the select
committee appointed to reconsider theatrical licensing in
1866, it became clear that the music halls were incompa-
rably better appointed and better run than the theatres.
From his experience of theatre management in London,
Stephen Fiske, the American, concluded that 'almost the
only managers who display extraordinary enterprise and
ability are those of the music halls and east end
theatres.' (7)
There was also considerable growth and enterprise in
music hall promotion outside London (though this has been
mostly ignored by historians of the halls, past and
present). There were, it seems, problems of under-
capitalisation, but the number of provincial halls more
than doubled during the 1860s, and the big establishments
in the midlands and the north rivalled those of the metropolis in size and popular success. Indeed it was the
provinces that produced entrepreneurs like Moss, Stoll and
Thornton who built up the big syndicates that began to
take over the London halls in the 1890s. (8)
Below the larger halls stretched a dense undergrowth of
smaller establishments, mostly pub music halls still
operating by refreshment check, many of them probably
without the necessary music and dancing license. The
Licensed Victuallers' trade paper, the 'Era', calculated
that there were between two and three hundred small halls
in London in 1856. Figures derived from a sample of
entries in Howard's inventory of London's halls indicate
that their mushroom growth ended in the early 1860s when
they went into a general decline; the great number of
entries of only two to three years' operation suggests
an extremely hazardous and competitive market. There was
a further abrupt fall-off in the late 1880s when the
London County Council began the rigorous enforcement of

safety requirements under a Board of Works act of 1878
and the concert areas in many pub music halls reverted
to billiard rooms. Municipal improvement also threatened
the small fry in the provinces. (9)

The big establishments consolidated their grip at the
expense of their smaller rivals, and the opening of the
rebuilt London Pavilion in 1885 signalled a new bout of
investment in music hall properties. The 'Financial News'
recommended the music hall for those investors recently
frightened off the foreign market and confided that:

wherever it has been decently and prudently managed,
it has yielded large fortunes. If it paid well ten
years ago it should pay much better today, for many
more people now frequent it and people of a better
kind than formerly - if it continues to refine itself
and to heap novelty on novelty as it does, it will go
on growing.

Given such encouragement the money poured in, and within
a decade or so the publican and his check-taker were
finally superseded by the theatrical capitalist and his
accountant. (10)

II

The Victorian music hall qualifies as a prototype modern
entertainment industry, not just because its capital investment allowed economies of scale which secured it a
mass paying audience, but because of the thorough-going
commercialisation which accompanied its growth and affected all facets of its operation. Commercialisation
had, for example, important consequences for the performers, who were reconstituted as a fully professional
labour force. At the top were the stars, already by the
1860s earning some extremely handsome salaries, and enjoying some useful perks - allowances from wine-shippers
for the champagne which was the indispensable fuel of the
'swell', free suits from tradesmen in return for a mention
in the act and royalties from publishers' agents anxious
to push a new song. (11) Among the lower ranks of performers, rewards were often niggardly and the competition
much more severe. The pub music halls provided a constant
flow of aspiring talent which kept the profession permanently overcrowded. Though the halls paid better than the
theatres, performers found themselves increasingly
squeezed by managements. One example of the monopoly
effect exerted by the big halls was the turns system,
introduced by Morton when he opened the Oxford. He filled
his bill with artists already employed at the Canterbury

who thus played in Lambeth and Oxford Street on the same
night, crossing the river by cab. It became customary for
an artist to do four or five turns a night, and the system
played into the hands of the big proprietors and agents
who could secure exclusive control of performers where
they enjoyed an interest in more than one hall. Artists
had to meet their own expenses for costume and transport
between turns, and the practice of matinées (legal after
1866) and twice-nightly performances (introduced in the
1870s, though the early history is obscure and contentious) increased the workload without any guarantee
of a proportionate increase in earnings. Growing alienation within the profession produced spasms of militant
trade union activity among performers in the 1870s and
1880s. The unions proposed to by-pass the much detested
agent (another product of the commercialisation of entertainment), end the turn system, control entry to the profession and, in one case, open their own co-operative
music hall. But these occasional essays at organisation
and protest left the exploitative grip of management un-
shaken. (12)

The increased scale of operations and the pervasiveness
of market values under the authoritarian control of the
caterers affected in turn the nature of the entertainment
offered by the halls. As the simple platform of the
singing saloons was gradually superseded by the full
theatrical apparatus of a stage and proscenium arch, the
big halls were encouraged to introduce greater show and
theatricality into their programmes - lavish tableaux of
famous battle scenes, hundred-strong corps de ballet,
troupes of Can-Can dancers from Paris and Blondin cooking
omelettes on the high wire. The 'Music Halls' Gazette',
29 August 1868, detected 'a feverish excitement abroad ...
which sacrifices everything to sensation, a constant
hankering after something, not only novel but more or less
terrible', conditions bred by the hectic pace of change in
modern city life; Louis Blanc, in less charitable mood,
implied that dangerous trapeze acts met an English taste
for violence which could no longer be satisfied with blood
sports. (13) Whatever the source of the audiences' ap-
parent needs, the caterers, by their increasing use of
publicity and show business hyperbole, sharpened the
demand for spectacle and novelty.

This manipulation was applied not only in production
techniques but in the making of the stars. The distancing
of the performer from the audience, one of the essential
conditions of star appeal, began with the introduction of
the formal stage at the Canterbury. The turn system
further removed the performer from his original place

among the audience for, with the need to keep to a strict
schedule, there was no time to spend hob-nobbing with the
groundlings by the singers' table (a hangover from the
singing saloons which, together with the office of
chairman, gradually disappeared from the halls). (14)
Morton began the projection of the star performer as
something larger than life with his promotion of the
Great Mackney.   Another leading London proprietor, William
'Billy' Holland, the 'People's Caterer', took the process
a step further and persuaded the star to live the role he
had created on stage.   Thus he insisted that George
Leybourne ride everywhere in his personal brougham, dis-
playing his fur-collared coat, a fistful of gold rings and
a glad hand with the drinks, as befitted the style of
'Champagne Charlie'. (15)   As a star, the performer became
more important than his material;   he was the agent who
transformed the dross of a prolific cheap sheet-music
market into gold for, as the 'Music Halls' Gazette', 27
June 1868, advised, 'a good song must be written, not for
its own sale, but for that of the singer....   It must
simply be a vehicle.'   Moreover, once the leading performers took care to copyright hit songs under their name,
and the Performing Rights Society proved capable of prose-
cuting infringers among even the minor professionals in
the back rooms of pubs, songs ceased to be common property
and the star's position was reinforced. (16)   At the same
time the spread of the railways and the cheap press opened
up the provinces to the touring London star and company.
There was still a distinctive topography of regional,
indeed parochial, taste in entertainment (which comedians,
in particular, could ignore only at their peril), but much
of the style and content of music hall performance was
becoming standardised across the country.

III

The modernisation of popular entertainment taking place
in the music halls in this period was remarkable;   yet
just as remarkable was the extent to which the gregarious
congeniality inherited from the antecedent singing saloons
remained unimpaired.   Only gradually did fixed seating
facing the stage become the norm, and many halls continued
to seat their public at rows of tables which allowed easy
access for waiters and customers alike;   thus for many
audiences the music hall remained a face-to-face encounter
- drinking, smoking, eating and general good fellowship
went on unabated during the performances.   As the comedian
Arthur Roberts recalled, 'It was all uproar whether they

liked you or not.' (17) Moreover, only in a few of the
very largest halls such as the Alhambra could spectacle
eclipse the appeal of the individual artist as the staple
attraction; all the accretions of the new show business
mystique had not yet removed even the most exalted of
these from active contact with their public, for the
essence of music hall entertainment remained the dialogue
between performer and audience. Several middle-class
visitors noted this, for it stood in marked contrast to
the conventions of the legitimate theatre. At a Bradford
music hall, the northern writer James Burnley was struck
by the way artists would single out individuals in the
crowd for particular attention, and was critical because
they played so directly to the audience, 'instead of
trying to be natural'. An American, Daniel Kirwan, reported that everyone in the audience at London's Royal
Victoria 'seemed to be on speaking terms with each and
all of the performers'. (18) The dialogue was robust, as
Edgar Jepson recalled: (19)

> The old music hall was a place of freedom and ease, and
> I have heard a soprano, when her accompaniment was
> bungled, pause in her song to curse the conductor, the
> orchestra, the manager, the proprietor and his hall,
> and the audience, with a brilliance of invective never
> attained on the legitimate stage.

In similar fashion the stars themselves were not immune
to the traditional sanctions of a dissatisfied audience.
Charles Coborn muttered darkly about certain halls in
Liverpool where 'the customers were as rough as the furniture.' At Glasgow the locals dispatched the Great Vance
from the stage by hurling handfuls of rivets; at
Harwood's in London's East End - 'the Sods' Opera' - the
favoured missiles were trotter bones. Popular control did
not stop short with the performers - at Chester Music Hall
in the 1870s, the audience proceeded to dismantle all the
stage machinery when a dioramic entertainment of the Zulu
War failed to please and they were refused a refund of
their admission money. Audiences could of course be extremely generous in their attentions, cheering the
favoured artist on into innumerable encores, and in some
halls the performers were wired in to prevent the audience
from jumping on stage and dancing with them. (20)

The point in any performance at which the audience asserted its presence came with the chorus singing. Then
the songs of the music hall would be reclaimed as common
property; often the audience would alter the words to
their own liking and the revised version would supersede
the original. One common type of song demanded audience
response: the Great Vance enjoyed considerable success

with his number 'Is He Guilty?' into which he would introduce topical events and personalities, and refer such
subjects to the cheers or hisses of popular judgment.
Stephen Fiske recorded this phenomenon in the 1860s: (21)

> at a music hall the singer turns the news of the week
> into rhyme. Nowhere can you hear the Duke of Edinburgh
> more heartily cheered, the opinion of the people in
> regard to the disestablishment of the Irish Church more
> frankly expressed, the bills before Parliament more
> freely criticised, the general national feeling more
> truly manifested, than at the music halls. Public
> sentiment is often better represented there than in the
> newspaper. The applause and hisses are surer criteria
> of popular favour or disfavour than the cheers of
> packed meetings, or the groans of suborned disturbers
> of the peace. Disraeli, Gladstone, Bright and Beales
> go for precisely what they are worth at these places
> of amusement.

A modern student of music hall entertainment has argued in
persuasive fashion that there was little in the way of
active political conviction in the crowd's response. We
may allow that this ritual antiphony is unreliable as an
accurate register of popular political opinion, but it
undoubtedly met the expressive needs of an audience for
whom demonstrative involvement in the performance was a
fundamental and powerful attraction. Recalling the halls
before they succumbed to the respectable programming of
the 1880s and 1890s, one music hall regular put the matter
succinctly: 'We went there not as spectators, but as performers.' (22)

Despite some contemporary contentions to the contrary,
the music hall public remained predominantly working and
lower middle class. Addressing the audience at his annual
benefit night - reported in the 'Era', 23 March 1862 -
John Wilton, proprietor of Wilton's Music Hall in
Whitechapel, apostrophised on the great social and moral
improvement that the halls had wrought among the working
classes, 'for it is the working classes alone', he concluded, 'who are the great support of them.' A decade or
so later, in a novel by Walter Besant, Emmanuel Leweson,
owner and manager of the North London Palace itemised his
clientèle thus:

> City clerks, dressed a la mode, young shopmen, making
> half-a-crown purchase nearly as much dissipation as a
> sovereign will buy in the West; with a good sprinkling
> of honest citizens, fond of an evening out, neither
> they nor their wives averse to the smell of tobacco
> and the taste of beer.

The weight of other evidence confirms this picture of an

audience largely comprised of the better-off artisans and
tradesmen, together with the sprigs of clerkdom from
office and shop; in the provinces we can note more of
the same. (23) Women were in a minority; the number of
wives was relatively small, though the complement of
single working girls in the cheaper upper reaches of the
hall could be considerable and was probably increasing.
Particular note should be taken of the gallery - 'the top
shelf' - for in this period few observers paid it a visit.
The composition of its audience comes to us via the
casualty lists of music hall fires and crowd disasters:
of twenty killed in a crush at Dundee in 1865, the greater
number were male and female factory hands between twelve
and eighteen years of age; of twenty-three killed in a
fire panic among a similar audience at the Victoria Music
Hall, Manchester three years later, few were more than
twenty years old. (24) The frequency of attendance is
difficult to assess. Admission prices were comparatively
low, the most commonly quoted ranging from 6d for the main
body of the hall to 3d or less for the more cramped and
distant accommodation. Thomas Wright complained in the
late 1860s that 'vampirish' waiters who pushed the drink
could drive up the cost of an evening's amusement, and
critics pointed out how the lure of the halls drew in
those who could ill afford it in the first place, but the
logic of the market operation seems to have kept the basic
cost of the entertainment within fairly regular and
manageable reach of a substantial number of working
people. (25)

The major caterers did strive to draw in a higher class
audience. Morton had intended that the superior amenities
of the Canterbury would lure the fashionable supper-room
set from the Strand across the river to Lambeth. The
price differential at the Oxford advertised his continuing
bid for the quality, and the newly emerged music hall
press of the 1860s regularly trumpeted the halls'
breakthrough to respectability - 'audiences', announced
the 'Music Halls' Gazette' in 1868, 'are in the main
formed of the middle-class members of society.' (26)
These claims were a public relations fiction. The
novelist James Greenwood saw through the caterers' myth
on a visit to the 'Oxbridge' in 1868. He concluded, (27)

The bulk of the people there were mostly people not
accustomed to music halls, and only induced to pay them
a visit on account of the highly respectable character
the halls are in the habit of giving themselves in
their placards and in their newspapers.

Fifteen years later 'The Times' remarked that no gentleman
would wish to patronise the music halls by choice; a

cartoon of this time showed a middle-class couple deciding
to risk a visit, but only after the close of the London
season, when none of their friends would be in town to
catch them slumming. In the suburbs large new halls began
to provide proper resort for the respectable bourgeois and
his family, but not much before the 1890s. (28)

The halls in the big city centres had always attracted
certain fringe elements from the middle class and above -
journalists, bohemians, officer cadets, undergraduates,
medical students, foreign tourists, sprigs of the nobility
- and in London the West End halls such as the Empire came
eventually to cater predominantly for this clientèle, but
in general it was the working class whose presence set the
common tone of the halls, not the glamorous interlopers.
At the Oxbridge, Greenwood noted the stalls full of cham-
pagne-swilling men about town and their painted ladies,
but awarded greater significance to the more numerous
complement of workingmen and their families in the 6d
seats in the body of the hall: (29)

> Not but that the frequenters of the sixpenny part are
> very useful; indeed, to speak the truth, the Oxbridge
> could not get on well without them. They keep up ap-
> pearances, and present a substantial contradiction to
> the accusation that the music hall is nothing better
> than a haunt for drunkenness and debauchery.

The smaller halls were often well meshed into the fabric
of the local working-class community. Artists who worked
the provinces in the 1860s and 1870s reported sharing the
bill with tests of local skills: a bootmaking contest in
Northampton, netmaking in Grimsby. Prizes were practical
- blankets, bags of flour, buckets of coal - and often
constituted thinly disguised hand-outs to the needy; in
the same spirit, benefit nights brought in cash for local
families hit by death or injury. (30) Some music hall
managers in the East End gave workingmen's trade and
philanthropic societies special rates for their meetings,
and Crowder of the Paragon in the Mile End Road received
a special presentation from the unions for allowing them
free use of his premises during trade disputes in the
1880s. (31)

Even if they chose not to visit them, the inhabitants
of the Victorian town or city could hardly have remained
unaware of the music halls and their popularity. Built
on the main thoroughfares and emblazoned with posters,
they ranked second only to the new town halls in size and
capacity as places of indoor assembly. Music hall advertising was ubiquitous - Morton even succeeded in placing
copy with 'The Times' - and the barrel organ and the
whistling errand boy brought the hit songs out on to the

streets. Those with first-hand acquaintance of working-
class taste knew well the extent of the music halls'
appeal: 'One place of its kind', reported a rueful James
Hole from Leeds in the early 1860s, 'has a larger nightly
attendance than the evening classes of all its seventeen
Mechanics' Institutes put together.' (32) The report of
the select committee of 1866 made the statistics of
success better known, and received considerable attention
in the press. (33) (Most periodicals of the period, whatever their leanings, carried occasional reports from
correspondents who had seen the inside of a music hall
and lived.) Fires, accidents to trapeze artists and the
patronage of the Prince of Wales kept the halls in the
news, and the mounting hostility of reform interests
captured wide public attention in the mid-1880s with the
cluster of demonstrations and court actions which the
press declared the 'Battle of the Music Halls'.

IV

Though the most publicised reaction, hostility was far
from being the sole or necessarily the commonest response
to the rise of the halls. The magistrates, for example,
when not under immediate pressure from reform lobbies,
were generally tolerant. In the mid-1850s, the 'Era'
reported: 'The magistracy of the metropolis and districts
have relaxed their former stringency in respect to the
music licensing system and, with a liberality highly to be
appreciated, regranted all the old licences and acceded to
new applications.' William Lovett, whose Chartist National Hall in Holborn had been repeatedly denied a licence
for music and dancing, noted that the local publican who
evicted him and opened Weston's Music Hall on the premises
met with no licensing problems; in Lovett's opinion the
bench was facilitating the spread of cheap entertainment
as an antidote to political excitement. (34) Further
evidence from Liverpool in the 1850s suggests that magis-
strates were also becoming aware of the efficacy of the
halls as a brake upon intemperance. This estimation
certainly confirmed itself to the chief magistrate at Bow
Street, who told the 1866 committee that he received
'scarcely ever a case of drunkenness from any of the music
halls'. Similarly, chief constables had few complaints
about the conduct of the halls, and caterers could often
be sure of police testimony to the good order of their
establishments when their licence was challenged. (35)
    Some observers saw more of value in the music hall
experience than the negative controls discerned by the

harder-headed members of society - they saw the halls as
valuable new socialising agencies for the city dwellers.
In the first place, they accepted that the logic of an
industrial society honouring free trade principles meant
that entertainment, like any other commodity, was subject
to the dictates of a self-operating market. Accordingly,
the halls were a legitimate operation, sanctioned by
popular demand. What was encouraging was not just the
good order and temperate thirst which marked these mass
assemblies, but the flux of direct and open social intercourse maintained within them. Furthermore, the halls
were not exclusively male territory, as the pubs and clubs
tended to be; some workingmen went there with their
wives, and sometimes families, and as the journalist
Matthew Browne remarked, 'with wives there come the first
lessons in courtesy.' (36) Might not the halls serve as
a milieu for repairing the estrangement of the classes
and the isolation of the individual which disfigured
modern city life?

The proposition appealed to the Christian Socialist
leader, the Reverend Stewart Headlam, who attempted to
convert churchmen from their general abhorrence of the
stage, and sought to encourage the attendance of clergy
and the respectable classes at the theatre and the music
hall. Headlam founded the Church and Stage Guild in
London in 1879 and lectured regularly on this theme,
drawing upon the evidence of his own frequent visits to
popular entertainments, where he met and talked with
artists and managers. He was dismissed from his curacy
for publishing his lectures, and the Guild was never a
very effective body, but Headlam continued as an outspoken
defender of the halls, and in this role he became one of
the few clerical speakers welcome to the East End radical
Working Men's Clubs. For Headlam, the music halls brought
pleasure into a brutal industrial society: 'Those who
work on the music hall stage are', he contended, 'genuine
servants of humanity.' (37)

Stewart Headlam was no doubt exceptional in the intensity of his support, but there was a sizeable body
of opinion which was generally sympathetic to the music
halls, yet found certain features of their operation disturbing. The principal misgiving was that the halls were
being run primarily as speculative ventures by men whose
avarice led them to corrupt the popular taste. Headlam
himself was disquieted on this point, and attacked what
he called 'the plutocratic evil - the power which money
had in comparison with worth and talent'. (38) Similarly,
Hodgson Pratt, among others, complained that the halls
had 'been started and managed by men who cared only for

bringing money into the till': 'They have only thought of
what would "take", whether it was bad or good, false or
true in taste, refined or coarse; idiotic or indecent
stuff.' (39) The caterer was cast as the villain of the
piece, a gross and insidious mutation of the publican.
Distaste for this despicable new archetype of capitalism
was combined with another, older prejudice in the picture
which Walter Besant drew of Emmanuel Leweson, music hall
proprietor, in the early 1870s: (40)

> He was gorgeously attired in a brown velvet coat and
> white waistcoat, with a great profusion of gold chain
> and studs.... His features were highly Jewish.... His
> hair, thick and black, lay in massive rolls.... In his
> hand, big in proportion, was a tumbler of iced soda and
> brandy.

Leweson supervised performances from the wings, 'contemplating his patrons with an air of undisguised contempt'.

Disclosing the cynical manipulations of the caterer
could not, however, explain away completely what seemed to
many to be the lamentably low nature of music hall entertainment. Most disquieting were the frequent charges that
much of it was morally offensive. Observers objected to
the semi-nude tableaux or 'poses plastiques', and the
'indecent elevation of the leg' in the Can-Can; there
was, reported one witness, 'a predominance of "fleshings"
and female shamelessness'. (41) It is less easy to discover the specific offence in other features of the entertainment for, though many writers did their duty under
fire by recording the alleged indecencies on the halls,
they were seldom explicit. Characteristically, Henry
Mayhew contained his distaste long enough to record a
song sung in a London penny gaff, (42)

> the whole point of which consisted in the mere utter-
> ance of some filthy word at the end of each stanza -
> 'Pineapple Rock' was the grand treat of the night and
> offered greater scope to the rhyming powers of the
> author than any of the others.

There were other occasions for vulgarities, as had once
been explained to a parliamentary committee: 'There are
certain things which, in technical phraseology, are called
"gags", and in which there are often vulgarisms and lewd
expressions.' A later committee risked defilement and
asked for an example; E.T.Smith, the unlikely son of an
admiral, and a music hall proprietor who had once fitted
his barmaids out in the unholy bloomers, obliged: (43)

> Perhaps a man comes on stage, and he has a clock under
> his arm, and he says 'This is the way I wind the old
> woman up on Saturday nights', and all kinds of
> allusions and bestialities in a mild way. Sometimes
> they have an organ, and make the same remarks.

Given the low threshold of moral indignation which obtained among the Victorian bourgeoisie, such repartee must
clearly have put the halls beyond the pale for the respectable middle-class family. It was this failure of
propriety which 'The Times', 15 October 1883, identified
as a kind of class discrimination in reverse, when it
charged that the halls 'intensify the tendency of the
nation to become two'.

Almost as affronting to the well-disposed outsider was
the inanity of many music hall songs. Middle-class
critics applied their own standards of literary judgment
in separating the song from its performance, and the
unadorned lyrics were dismissed with disdain in the periodical press - 'arrant nonsense', was the verdict of the
'Saturday Review', which otherwise looked kindly if conde-
scendingly on the halls. Working-class writers who
thought the halls represented some advancement in popular
manners were embarrassed by the low intellectual content
of the entertainment, (44) and respectable opinion in
general was discouraged by the halls' unedifying repertoire - all the more so because the Victorians believed
music to be the least corruptible and most civilising of
all arts. An article in the 'Dublin University Magazine'
of 1874 expresses the disillusionment with the halls in
this respect:

At the time when Music Halls were first started, high
expectations were formed of their capabilities in this
direction. It was thought that, by coming within the
reach of the general public, instead of being a luxury
confined to the favoured few, good music and true art
would flourish more widely and beneficially than ever
they had done before. Literature, which has on the
whole done such immense good by becoming cheap and
universal, afforded a parallel instance, giving substantial grounds for this hope.... We cannot but
lament especially the disappointment of the expectations that were once entertained of the Music Halls
as means of elevating recreation for the people.

Thus were erstwhile friends of the halls reduced to ac-
cepting them on sufferance.

Declared friends of the halls were fewer in number and
quieter of voice than the root and branch men of the
religious and temperance groups to whom the halls were
anathema. Their principal objection to the music hall
was the sale of strong drink. The association of drink
and public entertainment confirmed the publican as the
controlling interest and, it was claimed, fatally sapped
the work of moral improvement. Songs which extolled the
attractions of drink, and the extravagant wages paid to

those who sang them, encouraged prodigality in the
audience. On this point, we may recall the indignation of
Ewing Ritchie (an inveterate music hall hater) at what he
considered the excessive expenditure of an East End
working-class audience, 'when people in the middle ranks
of life are in despair at the hard prospect before them.'
(45) Opponents of the halls were particularly worried by
the susceptibility of shopmen and clerks to the tem-
tations of the fast life as extolled by the star in his
recurrent role of the Swell. Contemplating the rootless
army of young lodgers who aped the manners and style of
Champagne Charlie, one critic fulminated against the halls
for promoting 'a sham gentility among the striplings of
the uneducated classes'. They should, he recommended, 'be
stripped of the sham finery and sham jewelry they wear on
their indifferently cleaned fingers.... and sent to serve
a couple of years before the mast'. (46) Predictably
offensive were the sexual innuendoes of music hall entertainment, which were alleged to corrupt working-class
girls and make them easy prey for prowling roués; the
enemies of the halls were generally convinced that, in
the words of one of their number, they were mostly 'ante-
rooms to the brothels'. (47)

The opposition drew little comfort from evidence of
good order and incipient respectability. A Liverpool
vicar confronted by singing saloons in which all was
drunken confusion, found such scenes 'too disgusting to
be very dangerous', maintaining that 'the best conducted
of the rooms I fear the most ... where there is more attention to appearances, and a thin gauze of propriety is
thrown over all.' Another reformer, who recorded an
increase in the number of respectably dressed women going
in to the halls, found this disturbing testimony to the
latter's ingenuity in the refinement of old temptations,
rather than evidence of real improvement upon the gin
shop. This witness drew his conclusions from vigils
passed outside the music halls. Few reformers felt the
need to go inside in order to prove their case; as one
of them remarked: 'One does not want to taste poison to
know that it exists in a chemist's shop.' Prejudice
against the halls was served by imaginations well
practised in discerning the worst - reviewing hostile
evidence to the 1866 select committee, Browne remarked
shrewdly: 'Good people have too often an exaggerating
pruriency of their own.' (48)

The major strategy of the reform lobbies was to contest
the annual renewal of music hall licences on the grounds
of the moral dereliction of the proprietor. The strategy
grew more menacing as the number and scope of licensing

regulations increased. Before the 1850s it had been only
in London and the area within a twenty-mile radius of its
centre that a music and dancing licence had been required
in addition to a liquor licence. In 1851 Birmingham
introduced music licences, and the rest of the country
gradually followed suit. Bolton's magistrates received
the new licensing powers in 1872 as a result of a Corporation Improvement Bill. Faced with a petition from the
town's Sunday school leaders they refused a music licence
to the Museum Music Hall, the descendant of the famous
Star, and thus reactivated the controversy which had split
Bolton twenty years earlier. The magistrates recanted in
the face of public protest meetings, but imposed a form of
censorship on all music hall entertainment in the town.
(49) Proprietors who learned to negotiate the hazards of
the magistrates' sessions faced new difficulties as the
administration of music licences passed to elective town
and county councils which were more sensitive to organised
public opinion. (50) The London County Council in particular won itself a reputation for the stringency of its
licensing committee; it had a further powerful sanction
to hand in its fire and safety regulations which, as noted
previously, caused the closure of many smaller halls
unable to afford the alterations necessary to meet them.
    In London in the 1880s certain reformers went further
than petitioning licensing authorities. For Frederick
Charrington, scion of the famous brewing family and
convert to Temperance, the road to Damascus lay past the
door of his own pubs; shouting 'This way to Hell', he
carried out a personal campaign of picketing East End
music halls. Hired mobs pelted him with salvoes of flour
and pease pudding, but he stood his ground, and was
eventually taken to court by one proprietor for injuring
his trade. Though found guilty of libel Charrington was
undeterred, and his concern to mount a sustained offensive
on the halls found ready support from the 'Methodist
Times', which called on the LCC for a general purge of the
halls as part of the programme of a new Social Purity
movement. Stewart Headlam mounted a counter-attack with
some support from the Working Men's Clubs. This was the
Battle of the Music Halls (which opened well in advance of
Mrs Chant's more famous attack upon the Leicester Square
Empire in the following decade). (51)
    Frontal assault did not, however, recommend itself to
all reformers, and the same decade witnessed an attempt to
defeat the halls by providing rival entertainment of an
improved nature. In 1880 the Coffee Music Hall Company
was founded in London, as an extension of the Temperance-
based coffee public house movement. (52) A company circu-

lar explained its intentions to provide several large
music halls in various parts of London to which
workingmen could take their wives and children 'without
shaming or harming them'. No intoxicant drinks were to
be sold. The company's first (and only) venture was to
rent the famous south London theatre, the Royal Victoria,
which after extensive redecoration and heavy advertising
opened as the first Coffee Music Hall in December 1880.
The company was meant to pay its own way, but within seven
months it was badly in debt, and the counter music hall
only survived through the generous subventions of Samuel
Morley.

The faltering career of the Victoria Coffee Music Hall
illustrates the growing difficulty of effective direct
competition with an institution as commercialised as the
regular music hall; it demonstrates too how authentic
reproduction of a vigorous popular ritual eluded outsiders
whose principal concern was control and dilution. 'In the
first place', to quote one of the post mortems of the
Coffee Music Hall's initial collapse, 'there was an evident want of real, bona fide commercial energy in the
management.' The promoters shied away from engaging professional expertise; John Hollingshead, a respected
theatre manager with considerable knowledge of the music
hall business, was approached for his advice, but was
obliged to stay in the background because of doubts about
the 'safeness' of his associations. The promoters claimed
that they were unable to afford top artists because,
unlike the regular halls, they did not enjoy the substantial additional revenue which came from drink sales.
This claim, and the assertion that managements elsewhere
were warning their artists off the Royal Victoria, may
have been true, but it is at least as likely that the
coffeemen refused to pay what they condemned as 'reckless
wages' on principle (Arthur Roberts, the comedian, recalled how he got 1s 6d, a cup of coffee and a piece of
cake for performing at a Temperance music hall, compared
to the half a guinea he had made as a beginner on the
regular halls). (53)

The entertainment was as unsatisfactory as the management, and attendances were often poor. Friendly critics
pointed to one familiar failing: 'There was an air of
patronage about the place, which the Briton, even in his
most unpolished condition, will at once detect; and woe
then to success!' Then too, the Temperance propaganda
which alternated with the regular acts was too obtrusive:
'At the Victoria', said one complainant, 'you were likely
to get, not art, but a huge illuminated diagram of the
liver of a Drunkard.' (54) In the further interests of

improvement, the artists were obliged to submit to censorship of their material by rehearsing their acts in private
for the manager. On stage restraints vanished, and the
popular voice broke through: (55)

> Yet, in spite of all these precautions, let there come
> a chance such as an encore verse, such as some slip or
> stoppage in the stage machinery, and out will come
> something, not in the programme and never heard or seen
> before, which will bring down a thunder of enjoyment
> from the audience, and at the same time fill the
> manager's box with sorrow and humiliation.

Audience and performers were never completely tamed,
but the music halls were reformed none the less; the
industry had little to fear from the inept experiments of
the Royal Victoria, but it did respond to the pressures of
hostile opposition as the caterers discovered that improvement made for better business as well as sound defence.

V

Music hall interests had from the outset sought to disarm
their critics by advertising the moral superiority of
their operations to the older tavern entertainments. The
'Era' became well practised in defending the licensed
trade's new offspring, declaring in effect 'We are all
Improvers now.' Speaking up for Sharples against the opponents of the Bolton Star in the 1850s, the paper argued:
'Public amusements must be left to individual knowledge
and private enterprise, where they will be well directed
and controlled by wholesome competition and authoritative
public opinion.' Stewardship was safe in the hands of the
responsible publican like Sharples because of his proven
competence in a field best left to professionals. 'Public
amusement', continued the 'Era', 'is a trade and a mystery
and requires to be learned like any other trade.... no
amateur ever ventured into it without damaging its character and injuring its professors.' (56) Charles Morton had
been the prime example of the modern reconstructed publican. Although an inveterate gambler, he maintained an
impressively respectable front. As one music hall habitué
recalled: 'No man was ever half so respectable as Charles
Morton looked - his sense of decorum would have done
credit to a churchwarden.' (57)

But this kind of protective colouring was poor defence
against the intensified attacks of reformers. Alarmed at
the threat to their licences and livelihoods, the major
London proprietors reconstituted their Protection Associ-

ation in 1876, and memorialised the Home Secretary with a
scheme for an official censor for the halls. At the same
time the proprietors asked again to be allowed to play the
legitimate drama so that they might introduce dramatic
(and improving) sketches. This concession, so it was
claimed, would lessen their dependence on the comic
singers, who could not be effectively controlled under
the current state of the law. (58) When the project collapsed, the proprietors cast themselves as moral vigi-
lantes. House rules of the 1880s warned 'Any artiste
giving expression to any vulgarity, in words or actions,
when on stage, will be subject to instant dismissal, and
shall forfeit any salary that may be due for the current
week', and programmes on sale in the halls invited the
public to inform the manager of any suggestive or offensive word or action that might have escaped his notice.
The 'Era', 28 November 1885, lent its weight to the internal improvement campaign with a progressive editorial
which identified a further matter for reform:

It is one of the greatest nuisances possible to sensible people who go to places of amusement to divert
their minds from politics and business alike to have
the opinions of the daily papers reproduced in verse
and flung at their heads by a music hall singer....
persons who go to a place of amusement to be amused,
and these we believe, form the steadily paying class,
are too sensible to care to proclaim their private
opinions by applauding senseless rubbish with a political meaning. Proprietors who cater (as it is in
their interest to do) for the tastes of the general
public would do well to keep the political song
nuisance decidedly in abeyance, and we do not despair
of the day when such allusions shall be as severely
reprobated as, from the manifesto now so often to be
read on music hall programmes, we see that impropriety
is.

Such proscriptions were soon in practice. At the New
Sebright Wholesome Amusements Temple in London, artists
were warned to observe the following house rules: (59)

No offensive allusions to be made to any Member of the
Royal Family; Members of Parliament, German Princes,
police authorities, or any member thereof, the London
County Council, or any member of that body; no
allusion whatever to religion, or any religious sect;
no allusion to the administration of the law of the
country.

The give and take between the performer and his public
continued to pose a challenge to house discipline. Some
managements obliged artists to sign contracts forbidding

them to 'address the audience'. Just as the entertainers
and the entertainment had been censored, so too did the
audiences themselves eventually come under restraint:
encores were limited, chorus singing was discouraged and
uniformed commissionaires policed the auditorium. Will
Thorne recalled proprietors in Birmingham who refused
entry to any man not wearing a collar, and the Order and
Decorum which became the cliché of every music hall advertisement were so rigidly enforced in Collins Music Hall
in Islington that it became known locally as the Chapel.
(60)

   Despite this conspicuous concern for respectability,
the music hall proprietor still remained vulnerable in
his role as drink seller. Although, from the 1850s,
entertainment had revealed itself as a potentially market-
able commodity in its own right, drink seemed essential to
the commercial success of the halls. At the Canterbury,
Morton had kept a sharp eye on the flow of 'wet money';
when the volume of female attendance (another much advertised guarantee of respectability) had seemed to inhibit
the sale of drink, he had been quite ready to turn the
ladies away. The trade claimed that ginger beer sold
better than the intoxicants, and that door rather than
bar receipts provided the greater part of their revenue,
(61) but it was not until the 1880s that music hall
managements began to phase out the sale and consumption
of strong drink in the auditorium. By then, changes in
the domestic economy were affecting traditional consumption habits in such a way as to displace strong drink
as the prime commodity of working-class leisure time, and
the modest but significant increment of a more respectable
clientèle also seemed to allow a safe retreat from the
previously considerable reliance on liquor sales. As the
solicitor for the London proprietors' association explained: 'Every year we find that so soon as we raise
our prices and increase our better class accommodation,
so soon does the drinking go down.' (62) Thus the phasing
out of drink in the auditorium is not to be solely explained as a nervous reaction to the increased militancy
of reformers.

   The caterer's concern to qualify the music halls as a
rational recreation was variously motivated. He was, it
is true, anxious to disarm his reform opponents, and the
protestations of respectability can be interpreted most
obviously as a defensive response. Some of these protestations were undoubtedly disingenuous and misleading, of
a piece with the hyperbole of showmanship - on this count
we may adduce the trade papers' unsubstantiated claims for
extensive middle-class patronage in the 1860s - yet, for

the most part, the caterer was a man of honourable
intention in his courtship of respectability. Despite
his frequent occupational posture of man of the people
(an initially valuable role which he derived from his
antecedent office of publican) he was pricked by bourgeois
ambition and keen aspirations to gentility, and respectability was a necessary condition for their achievement.
(63) That the caterer's affirmations of respectability
involved the enforcement of operational controls of the
music hall more far-reaching and stringent than either the
threat or calibre of the reform opposition necessarily
justified or the traditions of its antecedent institutions
sanctioned, gives the measure of the caterer's maturation
as dynamic entrepreneur. Respectability served as a
defensive umbrella for the music hall industry and a
status lever for its tycoons, but its practice also made
for the more efficient and profitable management which was
necessary to realise the spectacular new growth opportunities of the mid-1880s.

Applying the disciplines of respectability to audience
and performer was part of a general rationalisation of
music hall operation. Banishing drinking from the auditorium - 'Abandon hops, all ye who enter here' was the
wag's lament - made it less visible and therefore less
offensive, (64) but it also facilitated the replacement of
free-standing tables and chairs with fixed stall seating
facing the stage which made for more efficient logistics:
stall seating brought higher audience capacities, allowed
for more effective price differentials, encouraged the
habit of seat reservation and simplified the running of
twice nightly houses. Diminishing the flow of drink may
also have had some effect in controlling the volatility
of the audience and its random interruptions of the performance. Censoring the artist and restraining the audience was meant to purge the halls of vulgarity, but in
cutting down ad libs and encores it also helped ensure
the predictable time-tabling of acts. This was important,
for the development of the turns system and twice-nightly
and matinée performances indicated a managerial concern
for the maximum exploitation of time and resources which
demanded their efficient scheduling and co-ordination.
Eschewing the controversial as well as the vulgar also
affirmed the respectability of the reformed music hall
(or variety theatre as it was now styled), but it marked,
too, the entrepreneurs' bid for the patronage of 'the
general public', a clientèle more passive, more predictable and more numerous than that defined by the categories
of class. (65)

The credo of the new regime was put by John Hollings-

head, dramatic critic, author and sometime music hall
manager, in contemplating the formation of the Moss
Empires music hall syndicate in 1900 with a capitalisation
approaching £2 million: (66)

> This interest has been created by commercial instinct
> for the supply of wholesome amusement for the people.
> Its work, without any false veneer, is entirely com-
> mercial. Its first duty, which it strictly observes,
> is to conduct its business according to the rules of
> good citizenship; and its second duty, which it
> performs to the best of its ability, is to earn a
> satisfactory dividend for its shareholders.

Thus by the late Victorian period it could be claimed
that the music hall had been assimilated to the cultural
apparatus of a capitalist society. In reality the conversion was far from complete. The particular chemistry
of artist and audience which characterised the essential
music hall experience was, for example, not easily extinguished, and the greatest of all music hall stars,
Marie Lloyd, derived no little of her popular success in
these years through flouting the new proprieties, and
maintaining the traditional flow of ribaldry. (67) But
many knowledgeable contemporaries recorded distinct
changes in tone as well as those of scale and lay-out in
the music hall of the 1880s and 1890s. (68) Managements
had succeeded in impressing something of a more compliant
manner upon the members of this robust institution. In a
sense, big business had succeeded where the social reformers of recreation had failed. The improvements fell
far short of the grand designs of the reformers, and
proceeded from motives less scrupulously high-minded than
theirs, but the manipulations of the music hall entrepreneur manifested a potential for defining and enforcing
socially appropriate behaviour - 'the rules of good
citizenship' - which identify the emergent mass entertainment industry as a conscious and effective agency of
rational recreation. Addressing the Public Morals Conference in London in 1910, the Reverend Thomas Phillips remarked, without flippancy, 'If you bring a puritan saint
and a music hall manager into contact, it is wonderful how
well they get on together.' (69)

Conclusions

The control of leisure was a serious matter. Not everyone would have followed Bishop Fraser in adjudging it 'the great question of the day', but the debate it generated, if not the actual support it won, testified to a general acknowledgment of its importance to social reform in Victorian England. Traditionally, a nation's recreations were taken as a test of its people's character: 'when we follow men into their retirements', pronounced Joseph Strutt in 1801, 'we are most likely to see them in their true state, and may judge of their natural dispositions.' (1) Most observers who applied this test in the 1830s and 1840s found the recreations of the working people in a general state of physical and moral degeneracy. This state of affairs reflected poorly not only on the natural dispositions of working people, but on the general ability of the nation to match its astonishing material advances with commensurate social improvements. In repairing popular recreations, therefore, reformers were engaged in the responsible tasks of servicing national self-respect and demonstrating the efficacy of human agency in broadening and accelerating progress.

Contributing to the renovation of society was an exciting undertaking which encouraged, and indeed demanded, bold and sanguine expectations; yet it was characteristic of the propaganda of rational recreation that it produced no extensive scenarios of the future society that would reap the benefit of its endeavours. Visionary indulgence was limited to the occasional invocation of a bowdlerised Merrie England. We can understand why the reform literature produced no new Cockaigne, but why, from among ruling classes raised on a classical education, were there so few glimpses of the Good Life, of any modern equivalent of the 'otium cum dignitate' of antiquity? This deficiency (for which, for example, one could not chide free

169

traders) suggests how strongly the prospect of an increasingly leisured society was a matter of disquiet
rather than gratification.

In the bourgeois ideology of the reformers, leisure was
less the bountiful territory in which to site Utopia, than
some dangerous frontier zone beyond the law and order of
respectable society. Traditionally it dispensed its own
licence, and it was its abuse which had imprinted itself
most deeply in middle-class consciousness; in a work-
oriented culture it represented an invitation to idleness
and dissolution - the weakness of an ill-disciplined
working class, the badge of an unduly privileged aristocracy. The prospect of leisure in abundance was
therefore alarming, for it promised to extend a domain
of free choice wherein the customary restraints of morality were more honoured in the breach than the observance,
at a time when traditional primary and community controls
were being atrophied by the strains of industrialisation
and urban growth. The corruptions of leisure threatened
to undo the painstakingly fashioned bonds of a new work
discipline in the labour force, and its blandishments
seriously unsettled the internal disciplines of the
middle-class world.

Rational recreation was an attempt to forge more effective behavioural constraints in leisure. Popular
recreations were to be improved, not through repression,
but through the operation of superior counter-attractions.
Within the new controlled environments, reformers would
instruct workingmen in the elementary accomplishments of
social economy - time-budgeting and money management - and
introduce them to the satisfactions of mental recreation,
thus immunising them against the contagion of the pub and
the publican, and the animal regression of 'sensuality'.
Building the new play discipline depended upon motivating
the resources of self-help, but reformers recognised the
need to provide some collective reinforcement for individual initiative in the fluid and open milieu of leisure.
From the mid-1860s occasional voices could be heard
canvassing for State direction and subsidy for certain
popular pastimes, (2) but in general reformers put their
faith in the voluntary and fraternal association of the
classes as a more appropriate and effective instrument of
rational recreation. The middle classes were to be the
superintendents of the reformation, taking the lead in
providing new amenities, and ensuring by their presence
the display and projection of approved standards of
leisure conduct to their inferiors; in the enaction of
the superior example, the middle classes would be reminded
of their own moral responsibilities. The taking of recre-

ation in common would, it was claimed, assuage the hostilities of capital and labour, and restore a sense of community between the classes.

Conceived as a measure of humanitarian relief and an antidote to political subversion in the Chartist era, rational recreation became more than an exercise in repair or pacification: it became part of the ongoing and fundamental re-socialisation of the working classes. For Henry Solly, it was one of the three vital fronts upon which working-class improvement had to proceed. Recreation, Temperance and Education, he claimed, were like a three-legged stool - remove one and the whole project collapsed. To the reformer, Francis Fuller, the question of popular recreations went 'to the root of the social tree - to the deepest foundation of the political fabric'. (3)

Implementing the new regimen of rational recreation was a difficult business. The reformer's counter-attractions had to supersede those of a powerful rival. With his manoeuvrability along the margins of the class line, his commercial expertise and his historical capital of social skills, the publican still enjoyed the strategic advantage in the expanding world of popular leisure. The history of the music hall shows how well some men in the trade seized the new market opportunities, transforming the recreational function of the publican from obliging pedlar of popular merry-making to large-scale manager and entrepreneur. The reformers were unable to attract capable management for schemes like the coffee taverns and palaces, which anticipated later successful enterprises by commercial interests, but which could not survive as essentially amateur ventures in the competitive retail sector which formed a growing adjunct to the leisure market. (4) It was difficult too, to supplant the public house in the affections and habits of the workingman. Despite legislative curtailment and the loss of some of its functions to more specialised institutions, the pub continued to offer the irreducible attractions of drink and good fellowship which still qualified it, in Brian Harrison's phrase, as 'the working man's voluntary association'. Some club promoters tried to encourage new loyalties by urging members to regard their club 'as a schoolboy regards his school, or the university man his college', but even with the allowance of beer, the Club movement found it hard to approximate the comforting rituals and ambience of the public house and the traditional mediations of its steward. (5) Because many institutions of rational recreation duplicated the material apparatus of the pub with considerable authenticity, the shortcomings in social warmth were all the more obvious.

A major impediment to the achievement of sociability in rational recreation was the heavy prescriptive burden that the reform experiments were obliged to bear. Although the formula of the Club movement represented a tactical modification of the didactic design, much of CIU literature, in general with that of other reform sources, is like an admonitory finger held under the reader's nose. Coffee taverns which provided refreshment and entertainment put across their fundamental raison d'être in the friezes of improving tracts which covered their walls. Striking a balance between easy congeniality and earnest improvement – 'How to steer between weak tea and good behaviour and a rollicking free and easy' – was a social exercise for which the bourgeois philanthropist was ill equipped. (6)

A further problem in achieving a fruitful modus vivendi in a reform setting sprang from the reformer's impatience with the culture he sought to reform. The working classes were credited with the fundamental potential which allowed of their ultimate perfectibility, but this acknowledgment was often compounded by an insistent note of moral censure at their current delinquency. Henry Solly could discern the angel in marble, the new Greeks among the roughs and toughs of Victorian London, but realisation of the ideal was slow and frustrating. Thus Samuel Greg could talk in one breath of 'gently leading' his workmen, in the next of 'breaking them into my system'. In promoting reform through voluntary association, the reformers settled for a normative authority which provided few effective sanctions, certainly nothing like the statutory power of Temperance and education legislation or the coercive power implicit in the semi-custodial institutions of factory villages or board schools. In their concern to expedite improvement, reformers frequently rejected the osmosis of example-setting and adopted an autocratic manner which alienated workingmen. Obtrusive patronage evidenced the best intentions perhaps, but it was also symptomatic of a social distance between the classes which disallowed of any easy informality of address. Autocracy was the mode which sat most comfortably with an upper bourgeoisie that saw itself as a new urban gentry, but manifestly lacked the traditional common touch. As Canon Barnett remarked of a later generation of reform endeavour, what was offered was 'machine hospitality'. (7)

The middle classes in general failed to answer the reformers' call to community. A good deal of the debate on recreation in middle-class family periodicals was concerned only to legitimise bourgeois leisure, and while the middle classes acknowledged the need for improved and expanded amenities for working people, they refused the

role of superintendent. Whatever assurances reformers
gave to the contrary, popular recreation seemed unlikely
ground whereon to preserve one's own respectability, let
alone impress it successfully upon the strident mob that
was Matthew Arnold's populace:

> that vast portion ... of the working class which, raw
> and half-developed, has long lain half-hidden amidst
> its poverty and squalor, and is now issuing from its
> hiding-place to assert an Englishman's heaven-born
> privilege of doing as he likes, and is beginning to
> perplex us by marching where it likes, meeting where
> it likes, bawling what it likes, breaking what it
> likes.

Popular recreations were viewed by middle-class opinion
as a series of nuisances. If the commonest bourgeois
experience was that of being jostled by rowdies on the
promenade or offered contumely by the loafers in the
street, one can understand the distaste for joining in
what Matthew Browne described - accurately enough, but
to the detriment of his case - as 'monstrous symposia of
the people'. Indeed one recurrent argument on this
question relieved respectable citizens of any responsibility for reforming popular assemblies by their presence
by suggesting that such places were better left unreformed. The delinquencies of popular recreation could
never be completely extinguished, so it was claimed, but
they could none the less be contained and isolated if some
natural law of quarantine was left to operate - 'Let the
vices that cannot be suppressed by law collect in their
own haunts, and thus relieve other places of their
loathsome presence.' (8)

It was no recommendation that recreational improvement
promised to remake the workingman in the image of his
master. Encouraging working people to 'ape their
betters', as Stanley Jevons proposed, was acceptable
where it fostered moral rectitude, but not where it produced the 'sham gentility' that 'Tinsley's Magazine' noted
among the music hall crowds. Here, emulation parodied the
status insignia of the superior classes, threatening class
and status differentials that the latter were trying
anxiously to reinforce. Defending social frontiers became
increasingly important as the economic and political
primacy of the middle classes seemed jeopardised by
business uncertainties and the extension of the franchise
- 'The destruction of a political privilege', said the
'Saturday Review', 'is tacitly compensated by an increase
of social exclusiveness.' Leisure in particular represented an area where social distinctions were vulnerable.
It was here, in 1860, that 'The Times' had discerned the

makings of 'a great revolution ... great displacement of
masses, momentous changes of level'. (9) The defence of
the reformed athletic sports against infiltration from
below is a good example of middle-class determination to
maintain existing levels. Thus the bourgeoisie refused
to indulge in 'workingman worship', and withheld their
active support from a reform programme which appeared as
much a social solvent as a social anodyne.

Despite the many difficulties which dogged reformers,
popular recreations had much improved by the mid-1880s,
and afforded one of the major proofs of national progress
in the Jubilee year. (10) The irregular and spasmodic
flux of pre-industrial leisure was now contained in the
standardised instalments that came with the routine of
the modern working week and year. With certain gross
exceptions drink was becoming more of an incidental social
lubricant and less of a total experience. Though it was
true that, as Chesterton later remarked, the Englishman
was more interested in the inequality of horses than the
equality of man, some areas of popular sport had been
purged of gambling under the new reformed codes. Bolton's
butcher boys no longer undertook bizarre eating contests,
and no latter-day Ben Hart emptied the mills in working
hours; if there were still loungers in the street,
passers-by were no longer 'slutched and stoned by wild
natives', as one of the town's chroniclers had recorded
in the 1830s. In Bolton, as in England, popular recreations had undergone a considerable transformation - 'From
the Roaring Boys to the Boys' Brigade', as the social
anthropologist Geoffrey Gorer has neatly put it. (11)

What had the various campaigns for rational recreation
contributed to this? The Club movement and innumerable
individual and municipal benefices were owed to reforming
zeal, and in their conception, if not always their propa-
gation, the new sporting codes can be credited to rational
recreation. It would, however, be impossible to arrive at
a precise balance sheet, for reformers were only one
element in a broader process of social change. The continued tightening of discipline that came with increasing
mechanisation, the further sub-division of labour and the
spread of scientific management in the workplace; the
development of major institutionalised agencies of social
control in state education and modern policing; the more
pervasive and effective jurisdiction of local government;
improvements in working-class purchasing power and the
increasing availability and more forceful marketing of
cheap consumer goods; perhaps too the habits that came
with the routine use of trains and trams - all contributed
to the house-training of the English proletariat in this

period, and the rationing and rationalisation of its
leisure. As we have seen, there were many times when the
prescriptions of rational recreation seemed counter-
productive; certainly, reformers did not achieve the
moral monopoly of working-class recreation that they had
hoped for and, on the face of it, they had little success
in effecting a fraternal association of the classes in
play. Yet, if rational recreation failed to achieve
regular occasions of social community, it was likely to
have played an important part in the dissemination of
those middle-class values of discipline and conformity
which allegedly linked the upper sections of the working
classes to the bourgeoisie in a common vertical allegiance
to the tenets of respectability. Thus if the practice of
leisure was still compartmentalised according to class, it
may none the less have answered to the authority of a
shared ideology which cut across class lines.

In seeking to explain what it was that gave mid-
Victorian England its relative cohesion and stability, a
number of recent students of the period have identified
respectability as a key factor. Drawing upon one of the
commonplaces of contemporary social observation, they have
confirmed to their own satisfaction a basic division in
society between respectables and non-respectables. Essentially a secular distillation of evangelical disciplines enjoining moral rectitude and economic self-
sufficiency, respectability is represented as a pervasive
value system that exerted, in Geoffrey Best's words, 'a
socially-soothing tendency, by assimilating the most
widely separated groups (separated socially or geographi-
cally) to a common cult'. 'Here', he maintains, 'was the
sharpest of all lines of social division, between those
who were and those who were not respectable: a sharper
line by far than that between rich and poor, employer and
employee, or capitalist and proletarian.' The spread of
respectability, it is argued, secured social compliance
of the upper strata of the working classes, and opened up
a gulf between them - the respectable poor - and their
inferior brethren - the roughs. The gulf was particularly
noticeable, according to Brian Harrison, in the public
conduct of recreation. Harrison argues that the Temperance movement, with its strong presence in rational recreation, consolidated bonds between middle and working-class
respectables, who then worked in concert to improve the
remainder. (12) Other researchers have identified
distinct Temperance communities in working-class areas
which preserved a complete sub-culture of respectability
over several decades. (13)

Schemes of rational recreation outside the sphere of

the major Temperance organisations recruited from the
'respectable' working class. Henry Solly, though not
always discriminatory on this count, appealed to 'the
more prudent, worthier members of the working class' to
seek refuge in the clubs, away from 'their reckless,
drinking, cowardly or dishonest neighbours', and a guest
MP at the CIU's first annual meeting distinguished between
'Thinkers and Drinkers' among the Union's prospective
clientèle. (14) The enforcement of standards of dress,
cleanliness and previous good conduct as conditions of
membership in certain schemes, while perhaps designed to
encourage a wholesale improvement in manners, seems aimed
at recruiting those workingmen who had made some important
elementary accommodations to respectability. The specific
social and occupational membership of the institutions of
rational recreation requires further research, but we may
assume that except in the case of casual or itinerant
working-class custom, such as that drawn to the coffee
taverns, the clientèle was self-selective, comprising the
superior workingmen who actively sought improvement. The
fragmentary evidence of the composition of committees and
teams in workingmen's social and sports clubs suggests the
dominance of the artisanat or labour aristocracy, the
element in the working classes supposedly most susceptible
to the embraces of respectability.

Thus far, we may allow that rational recreation assisted in extending and reinforcing the constituency of
respectables: what is much less certain is the degree to
which the respectability of workingmen represented a
stable and consistent pattern of behaviour and belief
denoting real attachment to bourgeois values. The new
scholarly emphasis on the normative power of respectability carries with it some acknowledgment of the variations
and ambiguities that attended its operation. Significantly here, those historians who have tested the embour-
geoisement thesis against detailed reconstructions of the
social and material culture of the labour aristocracy in
specific localities have suggested that workingmen generated their own kind of respectability; in important
respects they reformulated its conventional values and
preserved a distinctive working-class identity in its
practice. (15) In demonstrating the complex nature of
respectability in working-class sub-cultures, these
studies also emphasise that its ideals were expressed in
terms of style and appearance as much as in a set of
beliefs and attitudes. A fuller study of respectability
as a behavioural mode may enable historians to understand
more clearly the nature and implications of its operation,
particularly in inter-class relationships. To do this

properly, however, we need a more realistic and conceptu-
ally apposite appreciation of the urban context. Certainly we need to guard ourselves against the tendency to
represent working-class respectability, whether primarily
emulative or indigenous, as a cultural absolute in the
lives of its practitioners – once a respectable, always a
respectable – for this is to adopt Victorian presumptions
of behavioural consistency that ignore the changes wrought
in personal behaviour patterns by the new circumstances of
modern city life. It may be more fruitful if for the
moment we disregard respectability as the manifestation of
a generalised social code or ideology, and consider its
incidence in the more limited and situational sense as the
performance of a particular role.

The combination of elementary role analysis and a
simple ecological model of the urban process suggests a
further modification of the respectability thesis. The
expansion of the urban population and the development of
a society ordered by the priorities of industrial growth
fragmented social interaction, and the coherent and
readily comprehensible pattern of social life shared
within the small-scale traditional community was increasingly supplanted by a pattern of life notable for
its discontinuities of experience in terms of time, space
and personnel. In the city, residential segregation and
the establishment of new work routines compartmentalised
social classes and the basic activities of work, leisure
and home life to such a degree that man the social actor
was obliged to play out his encounters in an ever greater
number of discrete situational settings. As personal
behaviour became increasingly segmentalised, so did those
units of responsive conduct that sociology identifies as
roles become more insulated from the continuous observation of others. (16) Insulation was most pronounced in
inter-class relationships, for here physical discontinuities were compounded by the bourgeois concern to maintain
social distance. However, although middle-class commentators frequently acknowledged how little they really knew
of the world of working people – it was, in a much used
phrase, 'terra incognita' – they had a rudimentary map of
the territory; this they peopled with stereotypes con-
structed from the imaginary projections of the role-
specific behaviour met with in the intermittent social
exchanges of real life. Only rarely were they confronted
with evidence which revealed their mistake in presuming
upon a consistency in role progression that duplicated
the conventional uniformity of their own lives. The
Birmingham manufacturer, William Sargant, who is quoted
in chapter 2, realised as much when he discovered by

accident that one of his steadiest and, as he had thought,
most temperate workmen was a heavy drinker away from the
workshop. Sargant's bewilderment on being met with the
evidence of this aberration suggests how little cognisant
of role discontinuities contemporaries could be, particularly in inter-class relationships. The role progression
of Bill Banks on his day off is germane here too, for it
suggests how readily a workingman could move in and out
of respectability as a succession of situations dictated.
In his social classification of 'The Nether World', George
Gissing offered that the broad distinction lay between two
great sections of workingmen: 'those who do, and those
who do not, wear collars'. (17) It is plausible that respectability was assumed or discarded, like a collar, as
the situation demanded.

If we approach respectability as a role rather than as
an ideology or a uniform life-style the nature of class
relationships in leisure takes on a new light. Thus
working-class membership of church football teams can be
seen as a purely instrumental attachment, calculated to
extract certain benefits often unobtainable from the resources of working-class life. In this case, working-
class behaviour which might have appeared as deferential
mimesis from above, functioned as a kind of exploitation
in reverse for its actors, who assumed respectability to
meet the role demands of their class superiors. (18)
Given the episodic and otherwise limited nature of most
class exchanges, respectability was an undemanding role
to play for workingmen who possessed the minimal apparatus
of dress, speech and demeanour required to match its
standardised public image. It may be too, that the middle
class were particularly susceptible to calculative or
instrumental adoptions of respectability by working-class
men, because of the bourgeois need to believe in the
existence of a regiment of working-class respectables
recruited from the denizens of Victorian England's terra
incognita. To the middle-class outsider, the myth of
substantial working-class respectability was a necessary
prop to the self-esteem of his own class, proof of the
middle-class capacity to remake society in its own image,
a preservative of the flattering fiction of an open
society and, not least, a source of reassurance in a
period whose conventional appellation as an age of equipoise obscures the extent to which the bourgeoisie were
still mindful of the social and political combustibility
of the urban masses. (19) At the same time, it is possible that the unease of the bourgeois patron in the company
of workingmen derived in part from his vague perception of
the latter's capacity for dissembling; in CIU official

reports, the emphasis placed on the well-mannered behaviour of club audiences at lectures and the respect
accorded visiting middle-class speakers suggests a need
for reassurance that all was truly what it seemed, and
indicates a certain apprehension at the tenuous hold of
the normative sanctions of respectability in the relatively unstructured territory of modern leisure.

Obviously not all respectable behaviour was superficial
and calculative, but the degree to which some or other
variant of respectability operated as a consistent or
exclusive imperative in working-class life must not be
exaggerated. The elevation of respectability as a key
concept in the ordering of our understanding of mid-
nineteenth century England reflects the current scholarly
concern to acknowledge and explain major determinants of
group behaviour other than simply class. But in the more
sophisticated social map of Victorian society that is
emerging, class will not go away, and in the world of
recreation its differentials are more striking than those
of other significant social categories that have recently
been explored.

Popular recreations in the latter years of the period
under consideration were marked by a strong class character; though they conformed to certain features of the
reform design, the marks of rationalisation and respectability which they bore were no proof of cultural embour-
geoisement. In part, the rationalisation which overtook
working-class recreation - the regular programming of
sport, for example, and the stabilising of the weekend
break - represented an internal adjustment to the irre-
versible pressures on time, space and energy brought by
a modern industrial society. In part, rationalisation
was an extension of existing disciplines in working-class
life, an amplification of the rules and regulations that
had long ordered the good fellowship of the friendly
societies. Within these constraints the working classes
maintained a considerable autonomy of style and jurisdiction. Thus the early clubmen secured important modifi-
cations of Solly's original prescription, and in the 1880s
a later generation won democratic control of the CIU administration. In the same decade working-class enthusiasm
brought professionalism to association football, and
infused the game with an atavistic tribalism which put it
beyond the reach of middle-class tolerance or understanding. At the same time the beleaguered music halls
continued to nourish a vigorous popular sub-culture that
celebrated life with such unabashed vulgarity that the
halls were accused of practising inverted class discrimination. In his investigation of the remaking of working-

class culture in London in the last thirty years of the
century, Stedman Jones suggests that an increasing ad-
diction to the consolations of a new leisure world contributed significantly to the dilution of any widespread
class combativity among workers. Here, so we are told,
was a distinctive new way of life (in essence duplicated
among the English working class as a whole) which remained
impervious to middle-class attempts to determine its
character or direction, yet in the manner of its resistance was 'no longer threatening or subversive, but
conservative and defensive'. Much of the evidence from
recreational life that I have drawn upon reinforces this
impression of the impermeability of working-class culture,
yet there seems to be more here than simply the refusal to
comply. The cultural politics of the 1880s indicate a
capacity for collective assertiveness among working people
that goes beyond the simply conservative and defensive.
Moreover, as I have suggested, there is a case to be made
that in various leisure time transactions with their class
superiors workers were capable of manipulating the social
order to their own advantage; this can be seen as a form
of class-based combativity, albeit more piecemeal and less
demonstrative than a formally organised and overtly political mode of opposition. (20)
    There is obviously a great deal more to be learned of
the place and function of leisure in working-class culture
in this period. Its significance for the understanding of
the dialectic of social class is clearly considerable, but
there are other questions to be asked. What, for example,
were the nature and extent of its satisfactions? Leisure
is more than the simple conjunction of time and activity
in whatever areas of life we conventionally designate as
'free'. In today's world leisure, to be authentic, must
be felt to be free, and in many people's minds it is
closely associated with a positive sense of enjoyment and
the opportunity for self-expression and growth. Though
the historian can by several criteria identify a phenomenon called modern leisure in Victorian society he cannot
therefore assume that it was fully perceived as such by
any but a small and socially sensitive minority. Yet
working people throughout this period did articulate a
high regard for leisure as freedom. This regard was most
commonly expressed in what Robert Baker, the factory inspector, called 'Labour's great motto' - 'The master's
right in the master's time, and the workman's right in
his own time', a sentiment echoed from the floor at more
than one annual conference of the CIU. (21) It may be
objected that any freedom that is bought by a surrender
in the workplace must be fatally flawed, and there is

considerable evidence of the contamination of modern
leisure by the long shadow of alienated labour; in this
respect free leisure may have been as dubious a gain as
the free labour market. This consideration cannot be
ignored, but there is more to understanding leisure than
locking it into some work-leisure dichotomy and there is
an affirmative quality to popular recreation in these
years which disallows the reduction of its gratifications
to those of simple compensation for the frustrations of
work.

Yet if we are to understand the satisfactions of popular leisure we must take into account the frustrations
that impinged upon them, and these were undoubtedly considerable. Leisure could rarely have been a constant in
the lives of working people. In the course of industrialisation the ample resources of time and space that were
the sureties of much traditional recreation were expropri-
ated, and the modern worker was in large part obliged to
pay for their retrieval, as well as for much else that
made leisure palatable. Though there was an overall
improvement in working-class income in the second half of
the century, this relative affluence was acutely vulnerable to short-term fluctuations in trade, changes in
family size and the vagaries of money management in the
working-class home. There were, it was true, always some
pleasures to be had very cheaply or for free, but as the
cycle of poverty turned so the good things of modern
leisure must have continually advanced then receded,
moving within then beyond the reach of individual men
and women for whom such a pattern was now likely to be
perceived less as part of some eternal order of things,
than as one of the major and demoralising inequities of
relative deprivation. Bites at the cherry were in any
case fewer for the women in working-class life; many of
its leisure institutions were predominantly masculine and
what evidence there is suggests that married men often
persisted in funding their own pleasures at the expense
of their dependants. (22) These were some of the problems
of leisure for working people that their betters ignored;
but they were none the less real, and the advent of
leisure for the masses may have intensified rather than
ameliorated the endemic social and psychological anxieties
of life in a modern urban industrial society in a way that
reduces the much advertised agonies of the bourgeois
conscience and the conventional 'problem of leisure' to
the level of a moral charade.

Yet amid its contradictions, leisure served as an
important milieu for preserving the identity of a working
class which offered substantial resistance to the cultural

hegemony of its superiors. Contemplating the question
'How to win our workers?', the 'Saturday Review', 5 July
1862 recognised the stubborn reality that confronted all
campaigns to change their social life:

> As classes rise in social importance (as our working
> classes undoubtedly do), as they acquire a position and
> make a law and society for themselves, they almost
> necessarily become more inaccessible to external
> influence. They grow in a sense more sufficient for
> themselves, and the sympathy implied by mixing of
> classes becomes more difficult. We suspect the great
> working classes as a body become every day a firmer
> phalanx, not really impressible or subject to change -
> or rather, only to be changed through causes which go
> deeper than their 'betters' can easily get at.

In the last two decades of the century the broadening
impact of technology and the quickening of commercialisation constituted the forces that were to impress themselves more deeply on leisure and popular culture than any
social reform campaign. Though the debate on leisure was
far from extinguished, society was coming to terms with
its modern role. Leisure was now less to be explained
than exploited, and the eventual success of the reformed
music halls in turning its customers into disciplined
consumers adumbrated a new formula for capitalist growth
that was to make the mass leisure industries of the
present century more formidable agents of social control
than anything experienced in Victorian society. (23) In
this sense, the contest for the hearts, minds and pockets
of the new leisure class had only just begun.

Abbreviations

'BC'	'Bolton Chronicle'
BM	British Museum
BRL	Bolton Reference Library
'Bull.SSLH'	'Bulletin of the Society for the Study of Labour History'
'CIJ'	'Club and Institute Journal'
PP(HC)	Parliamentary Papers (House of Commons)
PP(HL)	Parliamentary Papers (House of Lords)
RC	Royal Commission
SC	Select Committee
'SR'	'Saturday Review'
'Trans.NAPSS'	'Transactions of the National Association for the Promotion of Social Science'

Notes

INTRODUCTION

1   For the dark age, see Working-class culture: confer-
    ence report, 'Bull.SSLH', 9 (1964), p.6; Work and
    leisure in industrial society: conference report,
    'Past and Present', 30 (1965), pp.96-103. Cf. J.L.
    and B.Hammond, 'The Age of the Chartists, 1832-1854:
    A Study of Discontent' (1930). For the emergence of
    the new 'traditional' culture, see E.J.Hobsbawm,
    'Industry and Empire' (1968), pp.135-7. For the final
    stage, see A.Briggs, 'Mass Entertainment: The Origins
    of a Modern Industry' (Adelaide, 1960). More recent
    work is noted below.
2   R.W.Malcolmson, 'Popular Recreations in English
    Society, 1700-1850' (Cambridge, 1973). Also useful
    for reconstructing the world of pre-industrial recre-
    ations are K.Thomas, Work and leisure in pre-
    industrial society, 'Past and Present', 29 (1964),
    pp.50-62; E.P.Thompson, 'The Making of the English
    Working Class' (New York, 1963), passim, esp. pp.402-
    12; idem, Time, work-discipline, and industrial
    capitalism, 'Past and Present', 38 (1967), pp.56-97;
    idem, Patrician society, plebeian culture, 'Journal of
    Social History', vii (1974), pp.382-405.
3   For an impression of the nature and extent of current
    research, see The working class and leisure-class
    expression and/or social control: conference report,
    'Bull.SSLH', 32 (1976), pp.5-18. Of the more than
    twenty papers presented to the conference at the
    University of Sussex, 29 November 1975, the majority
    dealt with the nineteenth century; copies of the
    papers can be consulted in the university library and
    Brighton Public Library. For the general structural
    transformation of leisure in the period, see S. de

184

Grazia, 'Of Time, Work and Leisure' (New York, 1964),
pp.181-95; J.Dumazedier, 'Toward a Society of
Leisure' (New York, 1967), pp.33-41; T.Burns, Leisure
in industrial society, in M.A.Smith, S.Parker and C.S.
Smith, eds, 'Leisure and Society in Britain' (1973),
pp.40-55. For the historian's appreciation, see M.R.
Marrus, 'The Rise of Leisure in Industrial Society'
(St Charles, Mo., 1974); J.Myerscough, The recent
history of the use of leisure time, in I.Appleton,
ed., 'Leisure Research and Policy' (Edinburgh, 1974),
pp.3-16. The latter provides a useful brief survey of
the period as a whole.
4 W.C.Lake, Leisure time, in J.E.Kempe, ed., 'The Use
and Abuse of the World', 3 vols (1873-5), i, pp.39-56.
5 The best recent text for the field in general is S.
Parker, 'The Sociology of Leisure' (1976). For the
problems of definition, see S.Parker, 'The Future of
Work and Leisure' (1971), pp.20-5; J.Dumazedier,
'Sociology of Leisure' (Amsterdam, 1974), pp.67-76;
B.M.Berger, The sociology of leisure: some sug-
gestions, 'Industrial Relations', i (1962), pp.31-45.
For the neo-classicists, see de Grazia, op.cit., and
W.R.Torbert and M.P.Rogers, 'Being for the Most Part
Puppets: Interactions among Men's Labor, Leisure and
Politics' (Cambridge, Mass., 1973).

CHAPTER 1   POPULAR RECREATION IN THE EARLY VICTORIAN TOWN

1 J.L. and B.Hammond, 'The Skilled Labourer' (1920),
p.7. The pessimistic view finds contemporary support
in P.Gaskell, 'The Manufacturing Population of
England' (1833), p.24, and F.Engels, 'The Condition of
the Working Class in England' (Pan edn, 1969), pp.56,
128,156-8. There is no adequate modern treatment of
popular recreation in these years. R.W.Malcolmson,
'Popular Recreations in English Society, 1700-1850'
(Cambridge, 1973), affords an excellent introduction
to the subject, but his treatment of the early
Victorian period is concerned primarily with the
growing hostility to popular recreation rather than a
continuing study of the recreation itself, and he
concentrates on the village, not the town. Two
dissertations offer some help: K.Allan, 'Recreations
and Amusements of the Industrial Working Class in the
Second Quarter of the Nineteenth Century, with special
reference to Lancashire', University of Manchester MA
thesis, 1947; M.B.Smith, 'The Growth and Development
of Popular Entertainments and Pastimes in the

Lancashire Cotton Towns, 1830-1870', University of
Lancaster MLitt. thesis, 1970.

2 M.Shearman, 'Athletics and Football' (1889), p.269;
L.Faucher, 'Manchester in 1844: Its Present Condition
and Future Prospects' (Manchester, 1844), pp.83-4;
F.Place, 'The Improvement of the People' (1834), pp.
12-15; J.M.Ludlow and Lloyd Jones, 'The Progress of
the Working Class, 1832-67' (1867), p.18.

3 J.Lawson, 'Letters to the Young on Progress in Pudsey'
(Stanninglen, 1887), p.58.

4 Bolton's history in the nineteenth century can be
studied from C.H.Saxelby, 'Bolton Survey' (1953);
H.Hamer, 'Bolton, 1838-1938' (Bolton, 1938); J.C.
Scholes, 'History of Bolton' (1892); W.Brimelow,
'Political and Parliamentary History of Bolton'
(Bolton, 1888). J.Clegg, 'Annals of Bolton' (Bolton,
1888), is useful for chronology. The course of urban
development is covered in A.Dingsdale, 'Bolton: A
Study in Urban Geography, 1793-1910', University of
Durham BA Hons thesis, 1967. For a very useful
bibliography, see A.Sparke, 'Bibliographia Boltoniensis' (Manchester, 1913). Of Bolton's press I have
most frequently used the 'Bolton Chronicle', the
longest surviving newspaper in continuous existence
in the period 1830-85.

5 SC further report on the licensing of places of public
entertainment, PP(HC) 1854, xii, qq.195-6, 3175.
Sources for the study of the public house are many and
diverse. Brian Harrison offers a selection in Drink
and sobriety in England, 1815-1872, 'International
Review of Social History', xii (1967), pp.204-76, and
provides an admirable review of the various functions
of the pub and the role of strong drink in society in
the 1820s in 'Drink and the Victorians: The Temperance Question, 1815-1872' (1971), pp.37-63. See also
Brian Harrison, Pubs, in H.J.Dyos and M.Wolff, 'The
Victorian City', 2 vols (1973), i, pp.161-90; B.
Spiller, 'Victorian Public Houses' (Newton Abbot,
1972). M.Girouard, 'Victorian Pubs' (1975), is a
social as well as an architectural history, and very
good on both counts, though mainly confined to London.

6 For the general prominence of the societies in
working-class life, particularly in Lancashire, see
J.H.Clapham, 'An Economic History of Modern Britain',
3 vols (Cambridge, 1932), ii, pp.471-3; P.H.J.H.
Gosden, 'The Friendly Societies in England, 1815-1875'
(Manchester, 1961), pp.62-6,115-27. For Bolton's
societies, see BRL, 'Grand Lodge Circular', 115 vols
(1831-1959), and B.T.Barton, 'Historical Gleanings of

Bolton and District' (Bolton, 1881), pp.11-13 for the
women's societies which also flourished in the 1840s.
'BC', 17 August 1850 has a useful list of club anni-
versaries.

7 W.L.Sargant, 'Economy of the Labouring Classes'
(1857), p.352.

8 J.W.Hudson, 'The History of Adult Education' (1851),
pp.148,211; 'BC', 7 March 1857; Faucher, op.cit.,
pp.49-53. For pub debates in Birmingham, see B.H.
Harrison, 'Drink and the Victorians', pp.337-8; for
working-class music-making in industrial Staffordshire, see R.Nettel, 'Music in the Five Towns, 1840-
1914: A Study in the Social Influence of Music in an
Industrial District' (Oxford, 1944), pp.7-9.

9 V.E.Chancellor, ed., 'Master and Artisan in Victorian
England: The Diary of William Andrews and the Autobiography of Joseph Gutteridge' (New York, 1969), pp.
84-7; C.M.Smith, 'The Working Man's Way in the World'
(1853), pp.259-60.

10 S.Bamford, 'Walks in South Lancashire' (Blackley,
1844), pp.13-14. See also E.P.Thompson's claim, 'The
Making of the English Working Class' (New York edn,
1963), p.831, that 'This was, perhaps, the most
distinguished popular culture England has known.'

11 E.P.Thompson, Time, work-discipline, and industrial
capitalism, 'Past and Present', 38 (1967), pp.56-97.
For the general question of working hours, see M.A.
Bienefeld, 'Working Hours in British Industry: An
Economic History' (1972).

12 SC on the operation of the Factory Act, PP(HC) 1840,
x, qq. 1602-6; J.Fielden, 'The Curse of the Factory
System' (1836), p.30.

13 SC on public institutions, PP(HC) 1860, xvi, qq.444,
1484. John Ruskin defended the Sunday lie-in before
the same committee, q.1693.

14 W.R.Smee, 'National Holidays' (1871), pp.2-4; J.A.R.
Pimlott, 'The Englishman's Holiday: A Social History'
(1947), p.81. For early examples of employers'
restrictions on traditional holidays, see S.Pollard,
'The Genesis of Modern Management' (1968), pp.214-15.

15 B.Disraeli, 'Sybil, or the Two Nations' (Brimley
Johnson edn, 1904), p.217. But St Monday was not
always spent on, or recovering from, the bottle. In
a valuable article on Birmingham workers, Douglas Reid
shows that many took the opportunity to attend exhibitions, visit the local botanical gardens and
organise rail excursions. The decline of Saint
Monday, 1766-1876, 'Past and Present', 71 (1976),
pp.76-101.

16   SC on the operation of the Factory Act, qq.370-85;
     'BC', 4 October, 15 November 1834, 22 May, 18 Sep-
     tember 1841;   RC Children's Employment, PP 1842, xv,
     pp.134-7.
17   'Morning Chronicle', 12 April 1828, in Place col-
     lection of newspaper cuttings, xli, Manners and
     morals, p.43, BM;   E.P.Thompson quotes 'The Times' in
     'The Making of the English Working Class' (Penguin
     edn, 1968), pp.935-6. All other references to this
     work are to the American edition.
18   SC further report on licensing, qq.259-61. Evidence
     of Rev.J.J.Baylee, secretary of the Lord's Day
     Observance Society.
19   R.Rooney, 'The Story of My Life' (Bury, 1947), pp.
     28-9.
20   Allan, op.cit., pp.22-5;   J.Lilwall, 'The Half-Holiday
     Question Considered' (1856), p.25;   Bienefeld, op.
     cit., pp.47,79.
21   Reports of the assistant hand-loom weavers commission-
     ers, PP(HC) 1840, xxiv, pp.315-16;   'BC', 2 October
     1852.
22   W.Wroth, 'Cremorne and the Later London Gardens'
     (1907), pp.11,44-5.
23   'BC', 22 June 1850. On footpaths, see W.Cooke Taylor,
     'Notes of a Tour in the Manufacturing Districts of
     Lancashire' (Manchester, 1842), p.136;   E.Chadwick,
     'Report on the Sanitary Condition of the Labouring
     Population of Great Britain' (1842, ed. M.W.Flinn,
     1965), p.337.
24   C.Dickens, 'Sketches by Boz', 2 vols (1836), i, pp.
     314-30. There is a particularly good account of
     Bolton's New Year Fair in 'BC', 13 January 1872.
     Representative reports on Halshaw Moor Wakes, Deane
     Church Wakes and the historic Turton Fair are to be
     found in 'BC', 5 October 1833, 13 September 1834, 13
     and 27 September 1851, respectively. See also S.
     Alexander, 'St Giles' Fair, 1830-1914: Popular
     Culture and the Industrial Revolution in Nineteenth
     Century Oxford' (Oxford, 1970) and, for recollections
     of boisterous times at Lansdown Fair in Bath, 'Lord'
     George Sanger, 'Seventy Years a Showman' (1910), pp.
     86-7. For fairs and wakes in general, see Thompson,
     'The Making of the English Working Class', pp.403-7;
     Malcolmson, op.cit., pp.16-33.
25   Henry Mayhew records the exodus of London's street
     children to the Derby;   some appeared at other race
     meetings as far afield as Wolverhampton. 'London
     Labour and the London Poor', 4 vols (Frank Cass edn,
     1967), i, pp.166,265,478. For Manchester, see C.

Aspin, 'Lancashire, The First Industrial Society' (Helmshore, 1969), pp.165-9.

26   SC on the observation of the sabbath, PP(HC) 1831-2, vii, p.247; 'Era', 28 July 1850; H.Shimmin, 'Town Life' (Liverpool, 1858), pp.163-70; SC on the operation of the Factory Act, qq.4047-54.

27   Mayhew, op.cit., is the most obvious source for the study of street life. See also, for the young, J.Gillis, 'Youth and History' (New York, 1974), p.62. For the point about the Whit walks, see S.G.Checkland's conference comment in H.J.Dyos, ed., 'The Study of Urban History' (1968), pp.337-42.

28   SC on drunkenness, PP(HC) 1834, viii, qq.3327-33.

29   For contemporary descriptions of the gin palace, see Dickens, op.cit., i, pp.276-87; Faucher, op.cit., p.49. For the new-style publican and the barmaid as glamour object, see SC on drunkenness, q.3270; 'Town', 22 July 1837; J.C.Coyne, The barmaid, in A.Smith, ed., 'Sketches of London Life and Character' (1859), pp.142-8. For changes in the operation and logistics of the pub, see M.Gorham and H.M.Dunnett, 'Inside the Pub' (1950), pp.26,64-5,94-113; Girouard, op.cit., pp.23-53.

30   Public amusements, 'Colburn's Monthly Magazine', lvi (1838), p.300; The age before the music halls, 'All The Year Round', xi (December 1873), pp.175-80. Note should be made too, of the proliferation of penny theatres or 'gaffs' which provided cheap entertainment, mainly for youths and children. Here again, any available space was pressed into service - empty shop premises, stables, etc. Mayhew, op.cit., i, pp. 18,40-2, stumbled upon scores of these dens in his perambulations.

31   'The Times', 18 October 1834.

32   S.Pollard, Factory discipline in the industrial revolution, 'Economic History Review', xvi (1963), pp. 254-91. Malcolmson provides the fullest treatment on the general assault on popular recreations, op.cit., pp.89-107.

33   Public amusements: the pretensions of the Evangelical class, 'Edinburgh Review', liv (1831), pp.100-14. For the Methodists, see RC on children's employment, PP 1843, xiii, p.527.

34   For Bishop Blomfield and the new regime, see R.A. Solloway, 'Prelates and People: Ecclesiastical Social Thought in England, 1783-1852' (1969), pp.150,219,240, 319-30. The old-style sporting parson was however far from extinct: clergymen were noted among the crowd at the famous Sayers-Heenan prize fight in 1860, and

there was consternation in church circles in 1874 when
it was discovered that the winner of the St Leger was
owned by a vicar in Lincolnshire, see 'The Times', 12
October 1874.

35 For these various reform movements, see B.H.Harrison,
Religion and recreation in nineteenth century England,
'Past and Present', 38 (1968), pp.98-125. For
Stamford, see Malcolmson, op.cit., pp.130-3.

36 Representative debates can be found in 'Hansard',
xxiii, 21 May 1835 (when the volume of petitions was
remarked); xxxiii, 21 April 1836; lv, 14 July 1840.

37 The history and ramifications of the Temperance
movement are examined at length in B.H.Harrison,
'Drink and the Victorians'. The constructive role of
the movement in recreation is considered below, ch.2.

38 For the controversy over the Star, see 'BC', 14
August-9 October 1852, and 'Era', 29 August-9 October
1852. As a prominent local Tory (like most publicans)
Sharples was obviously unlikely to attract the sympa-
thies of a predominantly Liberal bench; significantly, the magistrates had refused his invitation to
visit the Star, though JPs from other towns had accepted.

39 SC on public houses and places of public entertainment, PP(HC) 1852-3, xxxvii, q.870; SC on gaming,
PP(HC) 1844, vi, p.iii; SC on the observance of the
sabbath, p.176.

40 T.Frost, 'The Old Showmen and the Old London Fairs'
(1874), pp.337-56.

41 'Hansard', lvii, 22 March 1841.

42 W.Howitt, 'The Country Year Book' (New York, 1850),
p.263; W.E.Adams, 'Memoirs of a Social Atom', 2 vols
(1903), i, p.54; reports of James Fogg, 'BC', 30
November 1850, 17 May 1851.

43 Sanger, op.cit., pp.37-41,178; F.Place, 'Autobiography' (ed. M.Thale, Cambridge, 1972), pp.65-7,77; 'A
Working Man', 'Scenes from My Life' (1858), pp.30-1;
R.D.Storch, The plague of blue locusts: police reform
and popular resistance in northern England, 1840-57,
'International Review of Social History', xx (1975),
pp.61-90.

44 E.G. 'BC', 24 April, 1 May 1841; 7 May 1842; 29 September 1849.

45 G.Godwin, 'Town Swamps and Social Bridges' (1859),
pp.94-5, also records a police campaign against the
penny gaffs.

46 S.Dyson, 'Local Notes and Reminiscences of Farnworth'
(Farnworth, Lancs, 1894), pp.39-42, typescript in
Farnworth Central Library; and his Recollections of
rural Congregationalism, 'BC', 29 April 1882.

47 As Max Gluckman observes in his study of the licence in ritual in certain African societies, rituals which allow people to behave in normally prohibited ways can only be tolerated where all parties agree to the normal rightness of a particular kind of social order: once the social order is questioned (as was clearly the case in the 1830s and 1840s) such rituals become inappropriate. 'Custom and Conflict in Africa' (Oxford, 1956), pp.109-37.

48 Diary of Henry Richard, 22 March 1853, National Library of Wales, MS 10199B. I owe this reference to Dr Eric Sager. In previous times householders had been glad to invite the pace-eggers into their houses; by the 1850s the term had become synonymous with disturber of the peace in local reports of any kind of disorder. For Ashton, see W.E.Axon, 'The Black Knight of Ashton' (Manchester, 1870).

49 SC on the laws governing gaming, PP(HL) 1844, xii, pp.v-vii,78; H.Custance, 'Riding Recollections and Turf Stories' (1894), pp.23,40-41; R.Mortimer, 'The Jockey Club' (1958), p.69. For a useful history of the sport in the nineteenth century, see W.Vamplew, 'The Turf: A Social and Economic History of Horse Racing' (1976).

50 Doncaster races, 'Bentley's Miscellany', xxxi (1851), pp.116-22; SC on the laws governing gaming, p.95; J.Ashton, 'History of Gambling in England' (1898).

51 Pam's part in the 1853 bill is described in 'Era', 1 January 1854. For the rest, see SC on the suppression of betting houses, PP(HC) 1852-3, i; 'Hansard', cxxix, 11 July 1853.

52 C.Dickens, 'The Uncommercial Traveller' (1861), p.139; Mayhew, op.cit., i, pp.11-16; Shimmin, op.cit., pp. 59-71. Modern accounts include J.C.Reid, 'Bucks and Bruisers: Pierce Egan and Regency England' (1971), and J.Ford, 'Prizefighting' (1971).

53 The decline of the Ring, 'Tinsley's Magazine', iv (1869), pp.552-8; H.Hawkins, 'Reminiscences', 2 vols (1904), p.58.

54 H.D.Miles, ed., 'Tom Sayers, His Life and Pugilistic Career' (1866). The fight ended in a draw; among other things, Sayers was rewarded with a public subscription and a reception at the Stock Exchange. The Queensberry Rules were introduced in the same year.

55 SC on the observation of the sabbath, p.24; 'Era', 8 September 1850.

56 Storch, op.cit., p.79; SC on the education of the poorer classes, PP(HC) 1838, vii, p.96; Malcolmson, op.cit., pp.126-33. The Stamford bull-running was

however still being celebrated by an annual dinner in
1850, see 'Era', 17 November 1850.
57 W.Andrews, 'Bygone England' (1892), pp.179-80; P.H.
Ditchfield and W.Page, eds, 'The Victoria History of
Berkshire', 3 vols (1907), ii, p.296. One bull could
provide up to six days' sport.
58 Dyson, op.cit., pp.39-42. BRL, T.Hampson, 'Horwich:
Its History, Legends and Church' (Wigan, 1883), pp.
229-35; S.Rothwell, 'Local Reminiscences' (Bolton,
1899), p.6.
59 BRL, R.S.Hilton, T.Grimshaw and W.Witherington,
'Sunday Closing' (Bolton, 1853); 'BC', 4,11 June
1853; B.H.Harrison, The Sunday trading riots of 1855,
'Historical Journal', viii (1965), pp.219-45.
60 The story appears in A.L.Crauford, 'Sam and Sallie:
A Romance of the Stage' (1933), pp.145-55, a respectable piece of theatre history recording the careers of
the Lane family who ran the Britannia in Hoxton.
There are allusions to such an incident in other
sources. See also C.Barker, A theatre for the people,
in K.Richards and P.Thomson, eds, 'Essays on
Nineteenth Century British Theatre' (Manchester,
1971), pp.1-17.
61 BM, 'A Fellow Workman', 'The Races Defended as an
Amusement' (Newcastle, 1853). The writer was careful
to dissociate himself from the drink interest.
62 G.J.Holyoake, 'The Rich Man's Six and the Poor Man's
One Day: A Letter to Lord Palmerston' (1856). See
also the observations of the old Chartist, R.J.
Richardson, before SC further report on licensing,
1854, q.3589.
63 'Bolton Free Press', 16 September 1843. (The 'Press'
provided - intermittently - a Liberal voice to counter
the Tory and Anglican bias of the 'Chronicle'.) The
history of the publican is in large part the history
of the pub, but there is certainly room for a study of
the publican per se.
64 'Era', 28 July 1850, 12 September 1852. A national
trade paper of the licensed victuallers, the 'Era' is
an excellent source for the study of popular recreation throughout most of the nineteenth century.
65 The early history of licensing, in Report on the
supply of beer, Monopolies Commission, Sessional
Papers (HC) 1969, ccxvi, app.8, pp.153-8; B.H.
Harrison, 'Drink and the Victorians', pp.73-4.
66 SC on the observation of the sabbath, pp.254-5;
'Town', 21 July 1838. In Birmingham, the publican and
later music hall impresario, James Day, was organising
canal and railway excursions in 1841. For the

obituary of this unsung Thomas Cook, see 'Era', 27
February 1876.

67 Dickens, 'The Uncommercial Traveller', pp.63-6.

68 J.Macmillan, 'Description of the Checks issued by
Birmingham Concert Halls, 1850-1920', MS 1924 in
Birmingham Central Reference Library. The young
patrons of penny gaffs bought entrance with an empty
bottle or a scrap of food.

69 SC further report on licensing, qq.3175-6; SC on
public houses and places of public entertainment, q.
3964.

70 J.Adams, 'A Letter to the Justices of the Peace of
the County of Middlesex, on the subject of Licences
for Public Music and Dancing' (1850); 'Town', 18
August 1838.

71 SC on drunkenness, qq.571,4297-9; Hudson, op.cit.,
p.157; W.Dodd, 'The Factory System Illustrated in a
Series of Letters to Lord Ashley' (1842), pp.182-3.
See also Disraeli's entertaining description of a
singing saloon in the factory town of Mowbray (perhaps
based on Dodd), op.cit., pp.105-16.

72 'BC', 17 July 1852 provided a history and description
of the Star on the famous occasion of its destruction
by fire. See also BRL, Star Music Hall account book,
1847-50, xerox copy from the original in the
possession of Mrs D.Scholefield, St Mary's Cray, Kent.
For Gray's evidence, see SC report on licensing, qq.
7715-16,7653,7789, where there is further material on
the number and composition of northern audiences.
Bolton's population was then about 60,000.

73 There is an interesting analysis of theatre and saloon
entertainments in Manchester, 1837-54, by R.J.
Richardson in SC further report on licensing, qq.
3621-3. A major limitation on saloon repertoire
followed from the 1843 Theatre Act which virtually
prohibited the staging of legitimate drama where there
was smoking or the sale of intoxicants in the auditorium; this ruling did much to determine the unique
character of saloon, and later, music hall entertainment, though opposed by music hall interests
throughout the century. The main quotation is from
The amusements of the mob, 'Chambers's Edinburgh
Journal', xxvi (1856), pp.225,281.

74 Taylor, op.cit., p.136; SC on public houses and
places of public entertainment, qq.3927-31.

75 'Bowtun Luminary', 13 January 1855; 'BC', 18 September 1852.

76 (J.Clay), 'Chaplain's Report on the Preston House of
Correction' (Preston, 1841), p.6.

77 Hudson, op.cit., p.140; J.Hole, 'An Essay on the
    History and Management of Literary, Scientific, and
    Mechanics' Institutes' (1853), pp.74-5.

CHAPTER 2 RATIONAL RECREATION: VOICES OF IMPROVEMENT

1 For the state of society and the idea of improvement
   in this period, see A.Briggs, 'The Age of Improvement,
   1783-1867' (1959); J.F.C.Harrison, 'The Early
   Victorians, 1832-51' (Panther edn, 1973), pp.162-73.
2 E.Bulwer Lytton, 'England and the English', 2 vols
   (1833), i, pp.35-8. See also T.Arnold, 'Thirteen
   Letters on our Social Condition' (Sheffield, 1832),
   pp.29-31.
3 'Hansard', xv (1833), cols 1049-59; R.A.Slaney, 'A
   Plea for the Working Classes' (1847), pp.134-43.
4 E.Chadwick, 'Report on the Sanitary Condition of the
   Labouring Population of Great Britain' (1842, ed.
   M.W.Flinn, 1965), pp.337-8; B.Heywood, 'Addresses
   delivered at the Manchester Mechanics' Institute'
   (Manchester, 1843), p.120; J.C.Symons, 'Tactics for
   the Times' (1849).
5 Report of the commission on the state of the population in mining districts, PP 1850, xxiii, pp.578-87.
6 W.Cooke Taylor, 'Notes of a Tour in the Manufacturing
   Districts of Lancashire' (Manchester, 1842), pp.132-6.
7 J.P.Kay-Shuttleworth, 'The Moral and Physical Condition of the Working Classes' (1832), pp.61-3, quoted
   in R.Johnson, Educational policy and social control in
   early Victorian England, 'Past and Present', 49
   (1970), pp.101-2.
8 W.Howitt, 'The Rural Life of England', 2 vols (1838),
   ii, pp.142-3,272-3.
9 SC on drunkenness, p.viii.
10 'Hansard', xxxvii, 9 March 1837, 23 April 1839; SC on
    public walks, PP(HC) 1833, xv, pp.54-5,57; Second
    report of the commission for enquiring into the state
    of large towns and populous districts, PP 1845, xviii,
    pp.73-4; 'The Times', 26 March 1845. The C in C of
    the Army, Lord Hill, issued an order in 1841 providing
    for cricket grounds to be made near every barrack
    station in the kingdom, but I do not know whether they
    were to be open to the public or how many were actual-
    ly completed under this directive.
11 Quoted in W.A.Munford, 'Penny Rate: Aspects of
    British Public Library History, 1850-1950' (1951),
    pp.14-15.
12 'Hansard', xxvii, 2 May 1835; xxxv, 11,12 July 1836;

lxxi, 15 August 1843;   SC on public houses and places of public entertainment, PP(HC) 1852-3, xxxvii, q. 4486. The tag regarding opinions and manners is attributed to Bulwer-Lytton by C.S.Peel in G.M.Young, ed., 'Early Victorian England, 1830-65', 2 vols (Oxford, 1934), i, p.30.

13   'Hansard', xxiii, 15 May 1834;   'BC', 25 September 1852.

14   SC on the observation of the sabbath, p.242.

15   J.Manners, 'A Plea for National Holydays' (1843). See also A.Chandler, 'A Dream of Order: The Medieval Ideal in Nineteenth Century Literature' (Lincoln, Nebr., 1970), pp.157-83. Cobden's concern is noted in J.A.Nicholls, 'Collected Letters' (Manchester, 1862), p.8.

16   B.H.Harrison, Two roads to social reform: Francis Place and the 'Drunken Committee' of 1834, 'Historical Journal', ix (1968), p.296; S.G.Green, 'The Working Classes of Great Britain: Consideration of the Means for their Improvement and Elevation' (Leeds, 1850), pp.47-8.

17   W.Lovett, 'The Life and Struggles of William Lovett' (1876), pp.287-8,372-5; W.Blott, 'A Chronicle of Blemundsbury' (South Norwood, 1892), pp.204-6.

18   SC on public walks, p.9.

19   S.Greg, 'Two Letters to Leonard Horner on the Capabilities of the Factory System' (Manchester, 1840), p.12; Report of inspectors of factories, PP 1856, xviii, p.87.

20   Greg, op.cit., pp.21-3; 'Dictionary of National Biography'.

21   J.F.C.Harrison, 'Robert Owen and the Owenites in Britain and America' (1969), p.223; R.Boyson, 'The Ashworth Cotton Enterprise: The Rise and Fall of a Family Firm, 1818-80' (Oxford, 1970); App. to First report of the commission on children's employment, PP 1842, xiii, p.201. For other examples of recreational provision by employers, see R.S.Fitton and A.P. Wadsworth, 'The Strutts and Arkwrights, 1758-1830' (1958), pp.258-60; A.Raistrick, 'Two Centuries of Industrial Welfare' (1938), p.71.

22   'Spectator', 22,29 October 1842; A.Ure, 'The Philosophy of Manufacturers' (1835), p.349. See also W.Ashworth, British industrial villages in the nineteenth century, 'Economic History Review', iii (1950), p.378; S.Pollard, Factory villages in the industrial revolution, ibid., lxxix (1964), pp.513-31.

23   Report of the commissioner on the population of mining districts, PP 1845, xxviii, pp.219-20; 1847, xvi, p.425; 1849, xxii, p.395.

24 App. to first report on children's employment, p.381.
    See also Leonard Horner's remarks in Factory in-
    spectors' reports, PP 1846, xx, p.576.
25 See Horner again in Factory inspectors' reports, PP
    1849, xxii, pp.148-55. Cf. J.Glyde, 'The Moral,
    Social and Religious Condition of Ipswich' (Ipswich,
    1850), p.64; P.A.Whittle, 'Blackburn As It Is'
    (Preston, 1852), pp.154,159-60.
26 J.W.Hudson, 'The History of Adult Education' (1851),
    p.v (his emphasis). Potter is quoted in Munford, op.
    cit., p.60; cf. 'Manchester and Manchester People ...
    by a Citizen of the World' (Manchester, 1843), p.19.
    Factory inspectors' reports, PP 1849, xxii, pp.148-55.
27 There is a considerable literature on the Mechanics'
    Institutes. Hudson provides the best contemporary
    account and notes the various expedients to which some
    institutes resorted in 'straining for popularity' in
    the 1840s. Their manipulation by the middle class and
    the difficulties of attracting a working-class member-
    ship are dealt with in M.Tylecote, 'Mechanics' Insti-
    tutes of Lancashire and Yorkshire before 1851'
    (Manchester, 1957); J.F.C.Harrison, 'Learning and
    Living, 1790-1960: A Study in the History of the
    English Adult Education Movement' (1961); B.Simon,
    'Studies in the History of Education, 1780-1870'
    (1960).
28 T.Heywood, 'A Memoir of Sir Benjamin Heywood'
    (Manchester, 1863), p.201; Hudson, op.cit., pp.137,
    140.
29 BRL, J.Johnston, 'Mawdsley Street Congregational
    Chapel, 1808-1908' (Bolton, 1908), p.127. By 1837
    the weekly attendance at Bolton's Sunday schools was
    estimated at close to 10,000, of which number the
    Anglican churches claimed a quarter, the Methodists a
    half, the balance being shared by other denominations.
    Later reports recorded continuing growth in at-
    tendance. J.Black, 'A Medico-Topographical, Geologi-
    cal and Statistical Sketch of Bolton and its
    Neighbourhood' (Bolton, 1837), p.70; P.A.Whittle,
    'A History of Bolton' (Bolton, 1855), p.151. For the
    anti-singing saloon association, see 'BC', 28 August
    1852.
30 SC on the education of the poorer classes, PP(HC)
    1838, vii, pp.19,123-4.
31 Johnson, op.cit., p.110; E.D.Mackerness, 'A Social
    History of English Music' (1964), pp.154-65.
32 SC on drunkenness, p.viii, qq.1067-73.
33 J.S.Pudney, 'The Thomas Cook Story' (1953), p.59;
    R.Marchant, Early excursion trains, 'Railway Maga-
    zine', c (1954), pp.426-9. Cf. above, ch.1, n.66.

34 L.L.Shiman, The Band of Hope movement: respectable
    recreation for working-class children, 'Victorian
    Studies', xviii (1973), pp.49-74; B.H.Harrison,
    Liberalism and the English Temperance press, 1830-72,
    ibid. (1969), pp.126-58; 'People's Journal', 4 July
    1846; W.Howitt, 'The Country Year Book' (New York,
    1850), p.227. For digest histories of Bolton's
    Temperance movement by contemporaries, see 'BC', 15
    March 1862, 11 March 1882.
35 J.G.Rule, 'The Labouring Miner in Cornwall, c.1740-
    1870: A Study in Social History', University of
    Warwick PhD thesis, 1971, p.316; B.H.Harrison, Two
    roads to social reform.
36 Lovett, op.cit., p.311; 'Address and Rules of the
    Workingmen's Association' (n.d.); W.Lovett and J.
    Collins, 'Chartism: A New Organisation for the
    People' (1841), pp.33,46,60-1; SC on public
    libraries, PP(HC) 1849, xi, p.vii, qq.2759-803.
    T.Cooper, 'Letters to the Young Men of the Working
    Classes' (1851), p.9.
37 E.Yeo, Robert Owen and radical culture, in S.Pollard
    and J.Salt, eds, 'Robert Owen, Prophet of the Poor'
    (Lewisburg, Pa, 1971), pp.84-114. See also the evi-
    dence of John Finch to SC on drunkenness, qq.3814-30.
38 C.Thomson, 'The Autobiography of an Artisan' (1847),
    pp.345-71. This little-known but useful title
    deserves a reprint.
39 'BC', 20 September 1850.
40 For the 1840s, see 'BC', 7 December 1844; 'Bolton
    Free Press', 30 November, 14 December 1844; W.E.
    Brown, 'Robert Heywood of Bolton' (Wakefield, 1970).
    Then, 'BC', 18 November 1854, 31 October 1857.
41 App. to first report on children's employment, pp.
    201-2; Factory inspectors' reports, PP 1846, xx,
    p.576; E.Waugh, 'Sketches of Lancashire Life' (1855),
    p.8; 'The Times', 22 April 1841; 'Hansard', lxxvii,
    8 June 1846.
42 The printer was C.M.Smith, 'The Working Man's Way in
    the World', p.304. See also Report of the commission-
    er on the mining districts, PP 1850, xxiii, p.520;
    'The Times', 24 September 1844.
43 The history of the park scheme was reviewed in 'BC',
    26 May 1866, on its opening. For the controversy over
    funding, see 'BC', February 1851 to September 1852.
44 'BC', 4 June 1853.
45 'BC', 17 March 1860.
46 W.L.Sargant, 'Economy of the Labouring Classes'
    (1857), p.390. For the rest, see E.P.Thompson,
    Patrician society, plebeian culture, 'Journal of

Social History', vii (1974), pp.382-405; SC on public
libraries, p.vii; SC on public walks, p.66.
47 'BC', 31 May 1851, 5 October 1850.
48 H.Mayhew, 'London Labour and the London Poor', 4 vols
(Frank Cass edn, 1967), i, p.42.
49 Report on mining districts, 1850, pp.578-87. Cf. G.R.
Porter, 'The Progress of the Nation' (1847), pp.680-8;
Howitt, 'The Rural Life of England', ii, p.257.

CHAPTER 3   THE NEW LEISURE WORLD OF THE MID-VICTORIANS:
THE EXPANSION OF MIDDLE-CLASS RECREATION, ITS
PRACTICE AND PROBLEMS

1   For a further discussion of the middle-class leisure
experience, see Peter Bailey, 'A mingled mass of
perfectly legitimate pleasures': The Victorian middle
class and the problem of leisure, 'Victorian Studies',
xxi (1977). For a valuable survey of leisure at all
levels of society in this period, see G.Best, 'Mid-
Victorian Britain, 1851-75' (1971), pp.197-227.
2   J.H.Plumb, The public, literature, and the arts in the
eighteenth century, in P.Fritz and D.Williams, eds,
'The Triumph of Culture: Eighteenth Century Perspectives' (Toronto, 1972), pp.27-48; H.Perkin, 'The
Origins of Modern British Society, 1780-1880' (1969),
pp.69-70; S.Bamford, 'Walks in South Lancashire'
(Blackley, 1844), p.13; J.Clegg, ed., 'Autobiography
of a Lancashire Lawyer' (Bolton, 1883), pp.23-125;
W.Besant, The amusements of the people, 'Contemporary
Review', xlv (1884), pp.342-53.
3   General improvements in the middle-class standard of
living and the increasing range of satisfactions it
allowed are charted in J.A.Banks, 'Prosperity and
Parenthood: A Study of Family Planning among the
Victorian Middle Classes' (1954). For the economic
background, see S.G.Checkland, 'The Rise of an
Industrial Society in England, 1815-1885' (1964), pp.
35-60,296-301. R.Boyson, 'The Ashworth Cotton Enterprise' (Oxford, 1970), p.39.
4   Mind and muscle, 'SR', 21 April 1860. The 'Saturday
Review' was primarily a literary weekly, but it
provides a valuable running commentary on bourgeois
mores; its reputation for arrogance was due as much
to the accuracy of its perceptions as to the abrasive
nature of its style, see R.G.Cox, The reviews and
magazines, in B.Ford, ed., 'Pelican Guide to English
Literature: From Dickens to Hardy' (1964), pp.197-8.
5   (T.H.Escott), 'A Foreign Resident', 'Society in

London' (1886), pp.166-7; H.Mayhew, The Cockaynes in
Paris, in 'Shops and Companies of London, and the
Trades and Manufactories of Great Britain' (1865),
pp.81-4.

6   R.H.Mottram, 'Portrait of an Unknown Victorian'
(1936), pp.120-5; The rising generation, 'SR', 26
March 1864; E.Hodder, 'Life of Samuel Morley' (1887),
pp.430-43; 'Daily Telegraph', 8-21 January 1869. See
also Banks, op.cit., pp.195-6.

7   T.H.S.Escott, 'Social Transformations of the Victorian
Age' (1897), p.14; (P.W.Clayden), Off for the
holidays: the rationale of recreation, 'Cornhill
Magazine', xvi (1867), pp.315-22.

8   Evening amusements, 'SR', 4 January 1862. For
domestic games, see F.Bellew, 'The Art of Amusing'
(1866), the serial publication 'Games for Quartets'
(1857-63) and the monthly recreation supplement in
'Gentleman's Journal and Youth's Miscellany' (November
1869-September 1872).

9   B.S.Frankle, 'The Genteel Family: High Victorian
Conceptions of Domesticity and Good Behaviour',
University of Wisconsin PhD thesis, 1969. For
croquet, see E.L.Woodward, 'The Age of Reform, 1815-
70' (Oxford, 1938), p.627; for tennis, J.M.Heathcote,
'Tennis' (1890) and below.

10 W.F.Rae, 'The Business of Travel' (1891); Mind and
muscle, 'SR', 21 April 1860.

11 S.M.Ellis, ed., 'Letters and Memoirs of Sir William
Hardman, a Mid-Victorian Pepys' (1923), p.26.

12 Major foundations included the Football Association,
1863; Amateur Athletic Club, 1866; English Rugby
Union, 1871. The county championship in cricket dates
from 1873, by which time international matches between
the home countries were a fairly common feature of
most other organised games. For the Volunteers, see
H.Cunningham, 'The Volunteer Force: A Social and
Political History, 1859-1908' (1975). The quotation
is from A.Wynter, Our sports and pastimes, 'Once a
Week', v (1861), pp.151-3.

13 S.Fiske, 'English Photographs by an American' (1869),
pp.127-8. For other reactions to the English Sunday,
see E.Smith, 'Foreign Visitors in England and What
They Have Thought of Us' (1889), p.151f.

14 C.Dickens, 'Hard Times' (New York, Signet edn, 1961),
pp.30-3 and his 'The Uncommercial Traveller', pp.
170-85; An Australian's impression of England,
'Cornhill Magazine', xiii (1866), pp.110-20.

15 Cf. R.H.Mottram, Town life and London, and J.H. and
M.H.Clapham, Life in the new towns, in G.M.Young, ed.,

'Early Victorian England, 1830-65' 2 vols (1934), i,
pp.153-224,225-44. See also, Provincial amusements,
'SR', 11 October 1862.

16   T.Frost, 'Forty Years' Recollections, Literary and
Political' (1880), pp.349-61.

17   'BC', 13 June, 31 October, 28 November 1857; 6 June
1868; 29 January 1875. Clegg, op.cit., pp.122-5;
W.E.Brown, 'Robert Heywood of Bolton', pp.12-13;
J.Holden, 'Autobiography of Joseph Holden of Bolton'
(Bolton, 1872), p.9, BRL.

18   A.Trollope, 'The New Zealander' (Oxford, 1972), pp.
150-70; M.Arnold, My countrymen, 'Cornhill Magazine',
xiii (1866), pp.153-72.

19   'The Times', 8 October 1861; Holiday plans, 'SR',
16 June 1866.

20   Clayden, loc.cit; 'Daily Telegraph', 12 January 1869.

21   G.J.Romanes, Recreation, 'Nineteenth Century', vi
(1879), pp.401-24; (W.H.Miller), 'The Culture of
Pleasure' (1872), pp.64-5; J.Morley, 'Studies in
Conduct' (1867), pp.1-10.

22   Quoted in K.Inglis, 'The Churches and the Working
Classes in Victorian England' (1963), p.74, concerning
the middle class. See also Exeter Hall on popular
amusements, 'SR', 21 March 1857.

23   H.R.Haweis, 'Thoughts for the Times' (1872), p.288.

24   J.B.Brown, 'The Gregarious Follies of Fashion: An
Address to the Younger Generation' (1876).

25   G.J.Chester, 'The Young Man at Rest and at Play'
(Sheffield, 1860); S.Earnshaw, 'The Tradition of the
Elders' (Sheffield, 1860). See also E.R.Wickham,
'Church and People in an Industrial City' (Lutter-
worth, 1957), p.153.

26   What attitude should Christian churches take in
relation to amusements?, 'Congregationalist', viii
(1879), pp.543-56,650-65.

27   Popular recreations and their moral influence, 'Dublin
Review', xlii (1857), pp.271-93; Miller, op.cit., pp.
67-8; J.Kay, 'The Church and Popular Recreations'
(Edinburgh, 1883), p.17.

28   W.Thomson, W.C.Lake in J.E.Kempe, ed., 'The Use and
Abuse of the World' 3 vols (1873-5), i, pp.57-74,
39-56. See also the report of an Anglican conference
in Amusements, 'All The Year Round', xvi (1876), pp.
133-6.

29   'BC', 26 December 1868, 18 May 1872; R.Fitzsimmons,
'The Baron of Piccadilly: The Travels and Enter-
tainments of Albert Smith, 1816-60' (1967); J.Ella,
'Musical Sketches' (1878), p.149, quoted in E.D.
Mackerness, 'A Social History of English Music'
(1964), p.186.

30   F.E.Kingsley, ed., 'Charles Kingsley: His Letters and
     Memories of his Life', 2 vols (1877), ii, p.2; E.F.
     Johns, ed., 'Words of Advice to Schoolboys by Charles
     Kingsley' (1912), p.6; C.Kingsley, 'Health and Edu-
     cation' (1874), pp.2-17; H.Spencer, 'Education,
     Intellectual, Moral and Physical' (1861), pp.146,173.
31   Mind and muscle, 'SR', 21 April 1860; 'The Times',
     2 March 1869.
32   C.Box, 'Musings for Athletes: Twelve Philosophical
     Essays' (1888); D.Newsome, 'Godliness and Good
     Learning: Four Studies on a Victorian Ideal' (1961),
     pp.196-239.
33   E.C.Mack and W.H.G.Armytage, 'Thomas Hughes' (1952);
     T.Hughes, 'The Manliness of Christ' (1894), pp.232,
     252.
34   'The Times', 21 June 1871; Haweis, op.cit., p.300.
     At the Hurlingham live birds were sprung from traps
     to provide relatively easy targets for sportsmen who
     wished to avoid the discomfiture and higher standards
     of marksmanship which prevailed in the field. The
     unusually high bag and the presence of fashionable
     ladies added to public disquiet; there was, however,
     considerably less condemnation of the pigeon-shooting
     organised by London publicans. There was a further
     outcry against the sport in 1883-4 though proscriptive
     legislation failed to pass a second reading in the
     Commons, see 'Hansard', cclxxvi (1883), 7 March 1883.
     For a contemporary debate on cruelty in field sports,
     see the exchanges between the historian E.A.Freeman
     and Anthony Trollope in 'Fortnightly Review', xii
     (1869), pp.353,616; xiii (1869), p.63; xiv (1870),
     p.674. See also E.S.Turner, 'All Heaven in a Rage'
     (1964), pp.174-87.
35   Sports versus studies, 'SR', 30 August 1873; J.A.
     Hobson, 'Confessions of an Economic Heretic' (1938),
     pp.31-2. See also R.Wilkinson, 'The Prefects:
     British Leadership and the Public School Tradition'
     (Oxford, 1964), ch.3; D.C.Coleman, Gentlemen and
     players, 'Economic History Review', xxvi (1973), pp.
     96-8.
36   Opinions of the press, in W.Wingfield, 'The Game of
     Sphairistike' (1874). The Greek name that Wingfield
     coined for his brainchild understandably never caught
     on.
37   'Porcupine' (Liverpool), 10 February 1866.
38   Escott, 'Society in London', p.163, and 'Social
     Transformations', p.195. The progress of the briefly
     fashionable sport of indoor ice-skating can be studied
     in the periodical 'Rink' (1876) and J.A.Harwood,
     'Rinks and Rollers' (1876).

39 J.E.Ritchie, 'The Night Side of London' (1857), pp. 132-8.
40 A.Esquiros, 'The English at Home', 4 vols (1861-3), ii, pp.52-63. For the voluntary association as social fortress and quasi-kinship system, see also L. Davidoff, 'The Best Circles: Women and Society in Victorian England' (Totowa, N.J., 1973), p.24, and H.McLeod, 'Class and Religion in the Late Victorian City' (Hamden, Conn., 1974), pp.134-5.
41 'BC', 28 November 1857, 19 August 1865, 20 January 1872, 3 July 1875 and passim.

CHAPTER 4 DISPENSING RECREATION TO THE MASSES IN THE NEW LEISURE WORLD

1 M.A.Bienefeld, 'Working Hours in British Industry' (1972), ch.4. The famous strike for the nine-hour day among Newcastle engineers in 1871 provided a rallying cry for several trade groups in Bolton, including miners, joiners, shop assistants and clerks. The comment on the half-holiday came from John Heap, secretary of the Sunday League, to SC on public institutions, PP(HC) 1860, xvi, qq.1109-10, and his suspicions are confirmed by D.Reid, The decline of Saint Monday, 1776-1876, 'Past and Present', 71 (1976), p.89.
2 'The Times', 14 April 1873; SC on bank holidays, PP (HC) 1867-8, vii, qq.825,960; P.S.Bagwell, 'Railwaymen' (1963), p.66, cited in J.A.R.Pimlott, 'Recreations' (1968), p.68n.
3 R.J.Morris, Leeds and the Crystal Palace, 'Victorian Studies', xiii (1970), pp.283-300; J.A.R.Pimlott, 'The Englishman's Holiday' (1947), pp.96-115. For the Boltonians' trip to Paris, see J.T.Staton, 'The Visit t' Paris Eggsibish' (Bolton, 1867), BRL, and for the venturesome Londoner, 'A Journeyman' (C.F. Blackburn), 'A Continental Tour of Eight Days for Forty Shillings' (1878).
4 Factory inspectors' reports, PP 1875, xvi, p.135.
5 W.A.Abram, The social condition and political prospects of the Lancashire workmen, 'Fortnightly Review', iv (1868), pp.426-41. For some figures on the proportions of open space to population size, see M.J.Vernon, Public parks and gardens, 'Trans.NAPSS' (1867), p.471; (1877), p.498. See also H.E.Meller, Cultural provisions for the working classes in urban Britain in the second half of the nineteenth century, 'Bull.SSLH', 17 (1968), pp.18-19.

6   B.H.Harrison, Religion and recreation, 'Past and
    Present', 38 (1968), p.111; 'BC', 8,13 June 1867,
    15 May 1869. 'BC', 31 August 1867 remarked on the
    continued aversion of the bench to granting new
    licences in the face of organised opposition. The
    licence for the Museum Music Hall was granted only
    after a public protest meeting, at which there were
    many references to previous wranglings over the Star,
    'BC', 18 January-22 February 1873.

7   'BC', 17 March 1866. Will Thorne records how the
    police in Birmingham in the 1870s interfered with his
    athletic training, carried out perforce in the
    streets, 'My Life's Battles' (1925), pp.26-7.

8   See the letter to the 'BC', 18 March 1871, on the
    morality of the streets, and R.D.Storch, The policeman
    as domestic missionary: urban discipline and popular
    culture in northern England, 1850-1880, 'Journal of
    Social History', ix (1976), pp.481-509.

9   A.E.Dingle, Drink and working-class living standards
    in Britain, 1870-1914, 'Economic History Review', xxv
    (1972), pp.608-22.

10 J.Spencer Curwen, The progress of popular music,
    'Contemporary Review', lii (1887), pp.236-48; H.
    Cunningham, 'The Volunteer Force' (1975), pp.18-32,
    154.

11 (T.Wright), 'Some Habits and Customs of the Working
    Classes by a Journeyman Engineer' (1867), pp.184-248.

12 T.Barclay, 'Memoirs and Medleys: The Autobiography
    of a Bottle Washer' (Leicester, 1934). Baker appears
    in F.Rogers, 'Labour, Life and Literature: Some
    Movements of Sixty Years' (1913), p.27. The Leeds
    report is in 'Beehive', 27 August 1870 - I owe this
    and most subsequent references from the paper to Eric
    Sager. See also A.Esquiros, 'The English at Home',
    4 vols (1861-3), i, pp.344-7.

13 Racing and counter-attractions, SR, 31 July 1869;
    S.Alexander, 'St Giles' Fair, 1830-1914' (Oxford,
    1970); 'BC', 11 January 1872 offers a lengthy report
    on the New Year's Fair by a clergyman investigating
    the condition of Bolton's masses.

14 A.Wynter, Our sports and pastimes, 'Once a Week', v
    (1861), pp.151-3; The suburban race nuisance, 'SR',
    17 May 1879. W.Vamplew, 'The Turf: A Social and
    Economic History of Horse Racing' (1976) details the
    modernisation of the sport. For a vignette of the
    bookmaker and his cronies, see H.Shimmin, 'Liverpool
    Life, Its Pleasures, Practises and Pastimes'
    (Liverpool, 1856), pp.96-123. The earliest cheap
    daily racing sheet I have found is the 'Bradford

Chronicle and Mail Sporting Echo', first published
in 1877.

15 See, e.g., G.S.R.Kitson Clark, 'The Making of
Victorian England' (1962), p.62; G.Best, 'Mid-
Victorian Britain, 1851-75' (1971), p.203.

16 R.H.Dana, 'Hospitable England in the Eighteen
Seventies: The Diary of a Young American, 1875-76'
(1921), pp.294-9, is the Anglophile. The comment is
from Paul Blouet, French master at a London boys'
school in the 1870s, see 'Max O'Rell', 'John Bull and
his Island' (1883), p.114. See also T.Wright, 'Our
New Masters' (1873), p.70; H.Taine, 'Notes on
England' (1872), pp.37-44.

17 Dingle, op.cit.; B.H.Harrison, Pubs, in H.J.Dyos and
M.Wolff, 'The Victorian City', 2 vols (1973), i,
pp.170-1; M.Girouard, 'Victorian Pubs' (1975), pp.34,
54-73,93. Cf. M.R.Marrus, Social drinking in the
belle époque, 'Journal of Social History', vii (1974),
pp.115-41.

18 The quote is from Esquiros, op.cit., i, p.269. See
also T.Coleman, 'The Railway Navvies' (1965).

19 'BC', 14 July 1866; 26 May 1877. A contemporary
estimate suggests that over half of Bolton's male
labour force were members of friendly societies, 'BC',
8 November 1877. For the weekly routine of club life
in the 1860s and 1870s, see A.Bennett, 'Clayhanger'
(Methuen edn, 1947), pp.76-86, and (a more critical
treatment) Wright, 'Some Habits and Customs', pp.
67-82.

20 T.Wright, in A.Halliday, ed., 'The Savage Club Papers'
(1868), pp.214-30.

21 S.W.Jevons, Methods of social reform: amusements of
the people, 'Contemporary Review', xxxiii (1878), pp.
499-513; 'Working Men's College Magazine', 1 March,
1 November 1859.

22 T.Cooper, 'The Life of Thomas Cooper' (1872), p.393
and 'Thoughts at Fourscore' (1885), pp.31-2.

23 K.Inglis, 'Churches and the Working Classes in
Victorian England' (1963), p.267; B.H.Harrison,
'Drink and the Victorians' (1971), pp.267-89.

24 J.L.Clifford-Smith, 'The National Association and its
Twenty Fifth Anniversary: A Manual and a Narrative'
(1882); O.R.McGregor, Social research and social
policy in the nineteenth century, 'British Journal of
Sociology', viii (1957), pp.146-57.

25 C.Kingsley, 'Sanitary and Social Essays' (1880), pp.
207-10; B.G.Orchard, 'The Clerks of Liverpool'
(1871), pp.3-4; H.Shimmin, 'Town Life' (Liverpool,
1858), p.139.

26   The genesis of the cad, 'Tinsley's Magazine', iv
     (1869), pp.178-81.
27   Quote from Rev. E.Corderoy, Popular amusements,
     'Lectures to the YMCA' (1857), pp.45-6. See also
     C.Binfield, 'George Williams and the YMCA: A Study
     in Victorian Social Attitudes' (1973), pp.296-315,
     and for a similar though secular rescue operation,
     C.Kent, The Whittington Club: a bohemian experiment
     in middle-class social reform, 'Victorian Studies',
     xviii (1974), pp.31-55.
28   Rev. J.E.Clarke, 'Plain Papers on the Social Economy
     of the People' (1858), p.7; The philosophy of
     amusement, 'Meliora: A Quarterly Review of Social
     Science', vi (1864), pp.193-210; Rev. H.S.Brown,
     'Lectures to Working Men' (1870), p.11. Unless
     otherwise stated the emphasis is in the original.
29   'Working Men's College Magazine', 1 January 1861.
30   'The Times', 11 October 1872.
31   J.Belford, 'The Saturday Half-Holiday: Its Bearing
     on the Due Observance of the Sabbath' (Glasgow, 1867);
     'Quarterly Messenger of the YMCA', October 1864;
     Corderoy, loc.cit.
32   M.Browne, 'Views and Opinions' (1866), p.253;
     Spottiswoode to Horner, Factory inspectors' reports,
     PP 1857, xvi, p.37; (W.R.Greg), The proletariat on
     a false scent, 'Quarterly Review', cxxiii (1872), pp.
     251-94.
33   G.Smith, The labour movement, 'Contemporary Review',
     xxi (1873), pp.226-51; W.Rathbone, 'The Increased
     Earnings of the Working Classes and their Effect on
     Themselves and on the Future of England' (Liverpool,
     1877).
34   Labour and recreation: a plea for a mens sana,
     'Tinsley's Magazine', xiv (1874), pp.424-31.
35   R.B.Litchfield, The social economy of a working men's
     college, 'Trans.NAPSS' (1862), pp.787-93. For the
     fear of social disintegration as a motive for reform,
     see G.Stedman Jones, 'Outcast London: A Study in the
     Relationship between Classes in Victorian Society'
     (Oxford, 1971), pp.241-61.
36   'BC', 3 June 1882.
37   R.K.Dewhirst, Saltaire, 'Town Planning Review', xxxi
     (1960), pp.135-44. Cf. J.N.Tarn, The model village
     at Bromborough Pool, ibid., xxxv (1965), pp.329-36.
38   The claims of home life were a recurrent theme in the
     evangelical paper 'After Work: A Magazine for
     Workmen's Homes', published 1874-87. See also W.G.
     Blaikie, 'Better Days for Working People' (1863), pp.
     243-5.

39 W.T.Marriott, 'Some Real Wants of the Working Classes'
    (Manchester, 1860), pp.12-13; Shimmin, 'Liverpool
    Life', pp.2-3.
40 Muir's improvements in public houses and taverns,
    'Licensed Victuallers' Gazette', 24 February 1866, and
    the proposals of Liverpool philanthropist William
    Rathbone, in M.B.Simey, 'Charitable Effort in
    Liverpool in the Nineteenth Century' (Liverpool,
    1951), p.55.
41 See E.H.Currie, 'Appeal for a People's Palace' (1886)
    and Thomas Brassey's enthusiasm for the 'social
    palace' of the French industrialist and philanthropist
    Godin in 'Lectures on the Labour Question' (1878), pp.
    150-2.
42 For a convert from sabbatarianism who became vice-
    president of the National Sunday League which cam-
    paigned for the opening of museums and galleries, see
    M.L.Bruce, 'Anna Swanwick: Memoir and Recollections'
    (1903), pp.32-3. For a counterpart working-class
    movement, see the evidence of R.M.Morrell of the
    Recreative Religionists to SC on the sale of liquors
    on Sunday, PP(HC) 1867-8, xiv, qq.6318-26. For the
    People's Garden Company, see 'Beehive', 3 September
    1870, and for correspondence on the squares, see 'The
    Times', 14, 17 July 1871.
43 Report of Dr Lyon Playfair on the London Mechanics'
    Institution, PP 1857-8, xlviii, p.327.
44 'Working Men's College Magazine', 1 February 1861;
    'Quarterly Messenger of the YMCA', July 1864. Charles
    Coborn recalled that Temperance societies recruited
    music hall acts on the understanding that any refer-
    ence to drink must be deprecatory, 'The Man Who Broke
    The Bank: Memories of Stage and Music Halls' (1928),
    pp.139-40.
45 E.H.Hall, 'Coffee Taverns, Cocoa Houses and Coffee
    Palaces: Their Rise, Progress and Prospects' (1878)
    is the best source for these related movements,
    together with the files of the 'Coffee Public House
    News', and the later 'Refreshment News'. There are
    reports on the dry pubs in 'Trans.NAPSS' (1871), pp.
    591-2, and the other societies are noted in 'Time',
    July 1879 and 'Work and Leisure', June 1880.
46 J.Macmillan, 'Description of Checks issued by
    Birmingham Concert Halls, 1850-1920', MS in Birmingham
    Central Reference Library. See also The Coffee Tavern
    Company, 'Practical Hints for the Management of Coffee
    Taverns' (1878).
47 J.Hole, 'The History and Management of Literary,
    Scientific and Mechanics' Institutes' (1853), pp.74-6.

48   Shimmin, 'Liverpool Life', pp.2-3.
49   'Trans.NAPSS' (1865), p.7;   ibid. (1866), p.792.
50   W.Besant, Amusements of the people, 'Contemporary
     Review', xlv (1884), p.342.
51   Reports on Church Congresses at Sheffield, 'The
     Times', 4 October 1878, and Wakefield, ibid., 8 Oc-
     tober 1886. A progressive figure in the Church's
     approach to social reform, Fraser was speaking in
     Bolton on recreation for workers, 'BC', 4 September
     1875. See also P.d'A.Jones, 'The Christian Socialist
     Revival, 1877-1914: Religion, Class and Social
     Conscience in Late-Victorian England' (Princeton,
     N.J., 1968);   Rev. T.Hancock, The church and the pub,
     'Church Reformer', May 1888.
52   'BC', 29 January 1876, 29 May 1875.
53   'Trans.NAPSS' (1865), p.7.
54   'BC', 26 May 1866;   'The Times', 14 November 1865.
55   'BC', 29 January, 4 September 1875. See also the
     dialect letter from an artisan, 'Dicky Drawfoile',
     ibid., 21 August 1875.
56   There were some obvious exceptions, but it should be
     noted that improving employers could meet with con-
     siderable hostility from their peers, see, for
     example, the case of Hugh Mason in W.M.Bowman,
     'England in Ashton under Lyne' (Altrincham, 1960),
     pp.461-2.
57   (Jane) E.Hopkins, 'Work Amongst Working Men' (1879),
     p.131.
58   'The Times', 14 April 1873;   The workingman, 'SR',
     22 February 1873. See also, On strike and on spree,
     'Meliora', ix (1866), pp.323-33.
59   Behind the scenes, 'Daily News', 18 December 1868;
     J.E.Ritchie, 'Days and Nights in London' (1880), pp.
     49-50. For middle-class finances, see J.A.Banks,
     'Prosperity and Parenthood: A Study of Family
     Planning among the Victorian Middle Classes' (1954),
     pp.129-38;   S.G.Checkland, 'The Rise of an Industrial
     Society in England, 1815-1885' (1964), pp.35-60.
60   Reproduced in J.F.Sullivan, 'The British Workingman
     by One Who Does Not Believe in Him' (1878), p.86
     ('Fun' was an imitation of 'Punch'). Ritchie, op.
     cit., pp.182-95;   Ouida (M. de la Ramée), 'Views and
     Opinions' (1895), pp.333-4,340. The image of vomiting
     was common to the latter kind of commentary. See also
     George Gissing's distressed account of an August Bank
     Holiday outing in his novel of the 1880s, 'The Nether
     World' (John Murray edn, 1903), pp.104-13.
61   M.Browne, op.cit., p.280;   J.K.Cook, The labourer's
     leisure, 'Dublin University Magazine', xc (1877), pp.

174-92; W.Besant, The People's Palace (1887), in 'As We Are and As We May Be' (1903), p.55.

CHAPTER 5   RATIONAL RECREATION IN OPERATION: THE WORKING MEN'S CLUB MOVEMENT

1 Materials for the study of the club movement are to be found in the seventeen vols of the Solly Collection of cuttings and manuscripts, assembled by Henry Solly, founder of the CIU, British Library of Political and Economic Science, London School of Economics, Misc. MSS 154. There is a typescript index but the collection is often difficult to use and generally disappointing in content. The first official history, 'Our Fifty Years: The Story of the Working Men's Club and Institute Union' (1912), by B.T.Hall, secretary of the Union in the early years of this century, is still useful, as is his edited collection of Solly's pamphlets, 'Working Men's Social Clubs and Educational Institutes' (1904). Solly's autobiography, 'These Eighty Years', 2 vols (1893) is also helpful. A centenary history of the movement, G.Tremlett, 'The First Century' (1962), adds little of substance for the Victorian period. Several periodicals which served intermittently as the house organ of the CIU and provide an entrée to club life itself are referred to below. I know of only three surviving examples of individual club minute books from the period and these are also referred to more precisely below.
   Until recently historians have neglected the clubs beyond a few simple gleanings from B.T.Hall and Solly, e.g. G.D.H.Cole and R.Postgate, 'The Common People' (second edn, 1961), pp.378-9, but the quickening interest in popular culture has lately produced some good original work, see two Ruskin History Workshop pamphlets, S.Shipley, 'Club Life and Socialism in Mid-Victorian London' (Oxford, 1971) and J.Taylor, 'From Self-Help to Glamour: The Working Man's Club, 1860-1972' (Oxford, 1972). The findings of my own independent research accord most closely with the valuable work of Richard Price, see his The working men's club movement and Victorian social reform ideology, 'Victorian Studies', xv (1971), pp.117-47 and 'An Imperial War and the British Working Class' (1972), pp.47-67. Other scholars have been luckier, but I was refused access to such papers as the present Union possesses, though this may be no great disadvantage since Hall mentions that many early minute books were lost by the time he was writing.

2 C.Knight, 'Passages of a Working Life', 3 vols (1873),
   iii, pp.84-6; S.A.Brooke, 'Life and Letters of F.W.
   Robertson' (1865), pp.131-51. The designation is
   Price's, The working men's club movement and Victorian
   social reform ideology, p.119.

3 S.G.Osborne, The beer shop evil, in C.J.C.Talbot, ed.,
   'Meliora, or Better Times to Come' (1852), pp.1-11;
   T.H.Bastard, The Charlton club for labourers, 'Trans.
   NAPSS' (1863), pp.685-6; Rev. J.E.Clarke, Labourers'
   clubs and working men's refreshment rooms, 'Church of
   England Monthly Review', January 1859; (C.Dickens),
   The poor man and his beer, 'All the Year Round', i
   (1859), pp.126-31; J.E.Clarke, 'Plain Papers on the
   Social Economy of the People' (1858), pp.14-27. See
   also the list of early clubs in 'Occasional Papers of
   the Working Men's Club and Institute Union', no.1
   (March 1863).

4 M.Bayly, 'Ragged Homes and How to Mend Them' (1860);
   F.M.Gladstone, 'Notting Hill in Bygone Days' (1924),
   pp.146-7.

5 Solly to Brougham, 9, 24 August 1861, Brougham MSS,
   University College Library, London; Solly, 'These
   Eighty Years', ii, pp.159-60. See also the exchange
   of letters on the difficulties of running Adeline
   Cooper's club in Duck Lane, Westminster, 'The Times',
   9, 11 January 1862.

6 Solly, 'Social Clubs and Institutes', pp.28-9; 'These
   Eighty Years', ii, pp.189-93; Solly to Brougham, 13
   December 1862, Brougham MSS.

7 H.Solly, 'James Sandford, Carpenter and Chartist', 2
   vols (1883). See also R.V.Holt, 'The Unitarian
   Contribution to Human Progress' (1948).

8 Solly, draft for pamphlet, 'The Rich and the Poor',
   n.d. Solly Coll. xii, probably from the mid-1860s;
   Working men's clubs and institutes in relation to the
   upper classes and to national progress, 'Trans.NAPSS'
   (1866), p.791, in which Solly declares the aristocracy
   'with a few notable exceptions' enfeebled; 'How to
   Deal with the Unemployed Poor of London and with its
   Roughs and Criminal Classes?' (1868). For the
   background of insecurity in the capital, see G.Stedman
   Jones, 'Outcast London' (Oxford, 1971), pp.241-3.

9 Address to TUC in 1871, recorded in 'Occasional
   Papers', no.20 (January 1872); Solly, 'Social Clubs
   and Institutes', p.57; Knight, op.cit., iii, pp.
   220-1.

10 Solly, 'Social Clubs and Institutes', p.57; E.V.
    Neale, 'True Refinement: Address to Rochdale WMC'
    (Manchester, 1876). See also Taylor, op.cit., pp.
    10-11.

11   B.T.Hall, op.cit., pp.20-1; Lyttelton to Brougham,
     30 August 1864, 22 February 1865, Brougham MSS;
     Lyttelton to Solly, 29 July 1871, Solly Coll. xvi.
     A list of vice-presidents for 1874-5 is given in
     Taylor, op.cit., pp.3-5. At one time or another
     almost every member of the familiar cast of mid-
     Victorian friends of the working classes appeared on
     the list - F.D.Maurice, Thomas Hughes, Samuel Smiles,
     Samuel Morley et al.

12   The dispute centred on Solly's refusal to co-operate
     with other officers of the Union, particularly
     Paterson, whom he accused of leading intrigues against
     him. See, inter alia, Solly to Lichfield, 27 June
     1868; Solly to Pratt, 3 July 1870; Lyttelton to
     Solly, 10 November 1871; Hole to Solly, 5 July 1872,
     Solly Coll. xvi. For Paterson, see the introduction
     by his wife in his 'New Method of Mental Science'
     (1886), pp. i-viii. He was a cabinetmaker, secretary
     of the Clerkenwell WMC and active in the Workmen's
     Peace Association, but his obvious credentials as a
     self-improving artisan failed to recommend him to
     Solly - perhaps he lacked the deference of James
     Sandford, alias Bainbridge.

13   Adam Weiler, prominent in London working-class associ-
     ations in the 1870s, quoted in Price, The club
     movement and social reform, p.131n. Solly's claims
     for travelling expenses was one of the points at issue
     in the office politics of the Union.

14   H.Solly, 'Hints and Suggestions for the Formation and
     Management of Working Men's Clubs and Institutes'
     (1862).

15   Pratt to 'The Times', 5 January 1872. A prematurely
     retired civil servant, Pratt became a member of the
     Union council in 1864, secretary in 1874 and president
     in 1883. His interest in the condition of the working
     classes derived from boyhood memories of the Chartist
     movement in Bristol and he was active in several
     reform causes. Less assertive in manner than Solly,
     and decidedly secularist in intention, Pratt helped
     turn away the charge of 'parsondom' which had dogged
     the Union under his predecessor. 'Dictionary of
     National Biography'; J.J.Dent, 'Hodgson Pratt,
     Reformer: An Outline of his Work' (1932).

16   Lyttelton to 'The Times', 13 July 1863.

17   'The Times', 11 May 1864; 'Occasional Papers', no.10,
     1867, no.20, 1869. For a later round of discussions,
     see 'Workmen's Club Journal', 29 April, 20 May 1876.

18   Pratt to 'The Times', 13 January 1872; Solly, The
     growing importance of working men's clubs, 'Trans.

NAPSS' (1871), p.592;   SC on intemperance, PP(HL) 1877, xi, p.171;   Shaen to Solly, 23 July 1869, Solly Coll. xiv.

19   'The Times', 20 July 1875.   His son later recalled how Rosebery's gift of £180 on debenture had seen the Union through a sticky patch.

20   B.T.Hall, op.cit., pp.24-5;   'The Times', 9 January 1872;   Solly, 'Social Clubs and Institutes', pp.7, 56-7.

21   Working men's clubs, 'Meliora', v (1863), pp.259-66.

22   'BC', 2 April 1864.   The Bolton club was one of the casualties of the difficult early years of the Union; its demise was attributed to bad management and restrictive supervision which forbade, among other things, all political discussion.   The club was wound up in 1869 though a fresh start was made in the 1870s.

23   B.T.Hall, op.cit., p.35.

24   Censorship had its farcical side - a music hall artist performing at a Sunday concert in a club in Burnley discovered that members were forbidden to applaud on the sabbath, but were allowed to show their appreciation by raising their hands.   W.H. Boardman, 'Vaudeville Days' (1935), p.201.

25   'The Times', 15 April 1863;   R.Harrison, 'Before the Socialists: Studies in Labour and Politics, 1861-81' (1965), pp.226-8;   Solly, quoted in 'Wisbech Advertiser', 2 February 1887, cutting in Solly Coll. xv.

26   'CIJ', 7 December 1883;   'Common Good', 15 January 1881.   There are few reliable figures for the growth of the Club movement in these years, but there were over 800 clubs known to the Union by the early 1880s. It is difficult to know what passed as a 'political' club, but we may allow that it was the independent Radical clubs that offended Solly and the Union oligarchy rather than those formed under the auspices of the two political parties (whose history remains to be written).

27   'List of Clubs Known to the Union', November 1869, May 1871, CIU pamphlets;   H.Pratt, 'Notes of a Tour among Workmen's Clubs' (1870);   F.J.Gardiner, 'The Eightieth Birthday of a Model Institution: An Account of the Origin and Development of Wisbech WMC and Institute' (Wisbech, 1914).   The only big city club to win an honourable mention in Pratt's tour was one in Liverpool.

28   'Occasional Papers', no.5, May 1864;   'The Times', 11 July 1866.

29   'The Times', 29 February 1864;   copy of the 11th Annual Report in Solly Coll. xvi;   'BC', 24 April 1869.

30   J.Hollingshead, 'Today: Essays and Miscellanies',
     2 vols (1865), i, pp.171-7. See also Taylor, op.
     cit., pp.18-20.
31   'Workman's Magazine', no.6, June 1873. See also the
     history of the Cobden Club in Westbourne Park, London,
     recalled in 'CIJ', 4 July 1884, and the report of a
     club conference in Manchester, 'BC', 20 January 1872.
32   There is an interesting commentary on the course of
     this campaign in London in the 'Beehive', 24 June-22
     July 1871; for later developments see Marriott in
     'CIJ', 6 July 1883.
33   E.T.Hall, 'Coffee Taverns, Cocoa Houses and Coffee
     Palaces' (1878); Pratt in 'CIJ', 6 July 1883. See
     also evidence of Solly and Pratt in Fourth report of
     commissioners inquiring into friendly and benefit
     building societies, PP 1874, xxiii, pp.614-6.
34   The official view of the defection of the London clubs
     can be found in 'House and Home', 11 December 1880,
     and Solly's report in 'Trans.NAPSS' (1880), pp.504-5.
     For the conference itself see 'CIJ', 16, 23 November
     1883; for subsequent deliberations in committee,
     'CIJ', 18 January 1884 and Price, 'An Imperial War',
     pp.56-8.
35   'CIJ', 21 November 1884; 'The Times', 26 May 1884.
36   H.Mayhew, 'Report of the Trade and Hours of Closing
     at Workingmen's Clubs' (1871) - a piece of detective
     work for the licensed victuallers; 'The Times', 8,
     9 January 1872, 15 April 1863; unidentified cutting
     re Leeds WMC, August 1873, Solly Coll. xv. The
     surviving minute books of the Newcastle WMC for
     1865-6, 1870-3 are bound in two volumes in the
     Newcastle Central Reference Library. The club seems
     to have been self-managed and the committee in 1865-6
     comprised joiners, cabinetmakers, whitesmiths and a
     tailor. The only other extant material of this kind
     relates to village clubs, viz. Horringer and Ickworth
     Village Club minute books, mostly intact from 1877
     onwards, together with the club accounts, held by
     Mrs Z.Ward of Horringer, Suffolk, the grand-daughter
     of one of the founder members; the minute book of
     the Romsley WMC in Worcestershire for 1879, deposited
     with the Marcy Hemingway papers, bundle 486, in the
     County Record Office. The Horringer club was started
     by Lord John Hervey for his estate workers; Romsley
     was similarly a proprietary club, patronised by Lord
     Lyttelton, president of the CIU. I have not consulted
     the Romsley material.
37   'Occasional Papers', no.7, December 1865; 'Workmen's
     Club Journal', 10 July 1875, 29 July 1876.

38 'The Common Good', 15 January 1881; 'CIJ', 5 December 1884; F.Rogers, 'Labour, Life and Literature: Some Movements of Sixty Years' (1913), pp.73,96-7.

39 'CIJ', 1 August 1884; RC on the companies of the City of London, PP 1884, xxxix, pp.115-17.

40 See the comments of Shaw and William Morris on lecturing engagements in the clubs, quoted in Taylor, op.cit., p.59.

41 Newcastle WMC minute book, 1866; R.Harrison, op.cit., p.227; 'Beehive', 14 April 1875. The Kingsland Club in Stoke Newington, London had a political council of twelve elected annually 'to watch over social and political events, and to give their support to measures calculated to advance the interest of the masses. It shall report to the club before it pledges the club to any policy in any election contest.' From club by-laws for 1876, copy in Solly Coll. xv, item 27.

42 Club members at Tower Hamlets Radical Club and Institute recalled how they were hounded from tavern to tavern by the police until the opening of their club in 1874, 'CIJ', 26 September 1884.

43 W.Besant, 'All Sorts and Conditions of Men', 2 vols (1882), ii, pp.206-36; Solly, 'Social Club and Institutes', p.71.

44 Rogers, op.cit., p.68. Brian Jackson has an interesting account of modern club life in his 'Working Class Community' (1968), pp.39-68, which shows how these qualities still mark the character of club leadership.

45 B.T.Hall, op.cit., p.176.

CHAPTER 6   RATIONAL RECREATION AND THE NEW ATHLETICISM

1 W.E.Gladstone, Locksley Hall and the Jubilee, 'Nineteenth Century', xxi (1887), pp.1-18.

2 R.C.K.Ensor, 'England, 1870-1914' (1936), p.164. Salvador de Madariaga's epigram is at once less congratulatory and ominously more specific: 'One Englishman, a fool; two Englishmen, a football match; three Englishmen, the British Empire.' Quoted in J.L. and B.Hammond, 'The Growth of Common Enjoyment' (Oxford, 1933), p.9.

3 E.g. G.Magnane, 'Sociologie du sport' (1947), p.43: 'Sport is the chief pole of attraction toward approved activities: licit, consciously social and, in the broadest sense of the term, docile.' Quoted in E.Weber, Gymnastics and sports in fin de siècle France: opium of the classes?, 'American Historical

Review', lxxvi (1971), p.91. See also 'Sport and the
Community: Report of the Wolfenden Committee on Sport
for the Central Council of Physical Recreation'
(1960), p.6: 'Sportsmanship ... in its deeper (and
usually inarticulate) significance ... still provides
something like the foundations of an ethical standard
... in hard practice it is no bad elementary guide to
decent living together in society.' For a practical
discussion of this contemporary orthodoxy, see E.
Dunning, ed., 'Sport: Readings from a Sociological
Perspective' (Toronto, 1972), pp.233-78.

4   W.Collins, 'Man and Wife', 3 vols (1870), i, pp.viii-
xi; B.Haley, Sports and the Victorian world, 'Western
Humanities Review', xxii (1968), pp.115-25.

5   M.Shearman, 'Athletics and Football' (1889), p.241.
This is one of the Badminton series of handbooks which
provides a useful introduction to Victorian sport.
Contemporary material is too diffuse to admit of a
meaningful select bibliography here. The first-fruits
of modern scholarly research are noted below.

6   J.S.Smith, 'Social Aspects' (1850), pp.1,43; Physical
puritanism, 'Westminster Review', i, new series
(1852), pp.405-42.

7   Physical strength, 'SR', 10 December 1859; J.Hulley's
address to the Athletic Society of Great Britain,
'Athletic Review and Journal of Physical Education',
2 July 1867.

8   L.Stephen, Athletic sports and university studies,
'Fraser's Magazine', ii, new series (1870), pp.691-
704; J.Morley, 'Studies in Conduct' (1867), pp.
256-65.

9   'The Times', 5 August 1858, and a debate by correspondence during the Crimean War, recalled by L.Blanc,
'Letters on England', 4 vols (1866-7), i, pp.32-5;
F.Gale, 'Modern English Sports: Their Use and Abuse'
(1885), p.60.

10 W.Hardwicke, Recreation for the working classes?,
'Trans.NAPSS' (1867), pp.471-7,552-7; Lord Brabazon,
The decay of bodily strength in towns, 'Nineteenth
Century', xxi (1887), pp.673-6 and his 'Social Arrows'
(1886). Lord Elcho had tried, unsuccessfully, to pass
a bill through the Commons in 1862 to organise a
national programme of gymnastic training. The big
railway companies instituted physical tests for job
applicants in the mid-1870s and reported a large
number of rejects.

11 C.Kingsley, 'Health and Education' (1874), pp.2-17;
H.Spencer, 'Education, Intellectual, Moral and
Physical' (1861), pp.146,173. For Darwinism in

medical terms, see H.W.Acland, 'National Health:
Health, Work and Play' (1871); for popular Darwinism,
G.J.Romanes, Recreation, 'Nineteenth Century', vi
(1879), pp.401-24.

12   C.Dukes, 'Health at School' (third edn, 1894), p.284.

13   J.Kay, 'The Church and Popular Recreations'
(Edinburgh, 1883), p.10.

14   W.H.G.Armytage, Thomas Arnold's views on physical
education, 'Journal of Physical Education', xlvii
(1955), pp.27-44; Dunning, Development of modern
football, in idem, op.cit., pp.133-51.

15   E.Lyttelton, Athletics in public school, 'Nineteenth
Century', vii (1880), pp.43-57. Educators also
recommended games as a counter to 'unnatural lusts'
prevalent in public schools. See (Thomas Markby),
Athletics, 'Contemporary Review', iii (1866), pp.
374-91; 'The Science of Life: A Pamphlet addressed
to All Members of the Universities of Oxford and
Cambridge and to All Who Are, or Who Will Be Teachers,
Clergymen, or Fathers' (1877).

16   N.L.Jackson, 'Sporting Days and Sporting Ways' (1932),
pp.9-10; C.Box, 'Musings for Athletes' (1888), p.167.
See also T.Cook, 'Character and Sportsmanship' (1927);
Dunning, loc.cit.

17   H.B.Philpott, 'London at School: the Story of the
School Board' (1904), p.127. I owe this reference to
Raphael Samuel.

18   G.J.Cayley, 'The Working Classes: Their Interest in
Reform' (1858). Cricket had in fact been criticised
in its early years for mixing inferiors and superiors,
see J.Strutt, 'The Sports and Pastimes of the People
of England' (Methuen reprint edn, 1903), p.102. For
its mythical qualities, see, e.g., T.Sparks (C.
Dickens), 'Sunday Under Three Heads' (1836), pp.
39-44.

19   J.Lawson, 'Letters to the Young on the Progress in
Pudsey' (Stanninglen, 1887), p.63. The claims made
for cricket were many and remarkable, but one in
particular I find irresistible; it comes from Thomas
Hughes, reporting a letter from an officer in the
engineers before Sebastopol: 'The round shot which
were ever coming at him were very much like cricket
balls from a moderately swift bowler; he could judge
them quite as accurately, and by just turning round
when the gun which bore on him was fired, and marking
the first pitch of the shot, he could tell whether to
move or not, and so got on with his work very comfortably.' Physical education, 'Working Men's College
Magazine', May 1859.

20   'Hansard', ccxxv, 1 July 1875;   Shearman, op.cit.,
     pp.226-7.
21   'The Times', 13 September 1861;   T.Okey, 'A Basketful
     of Memories' (1930), pp.22-3;   Philpott, op.cit., pp.
     115-33.   Official obstacles were not removed until
     the introduction of a new elementary school code in
     1890.
22   P.C.McIntosh, 'Physical Education in England since
     1800' (second edn, 1968), pp.11-14,50;   Copy of papers
     submitted to the education committee by Mr Chadwick,
     PP 1862, xlii, pp.1-88;   Stan Shipley, School board
     drill, paper delivered at the History Workshop on
     education, Ruskin College, Oxford, 7 May 1972.   The
     quotations are from F.H.Spencer, 'An Inspector's
     Testament' (1938), pp.63-5;   W.McLaren in the preface
     to A.McLaren, 'Physical Education' (1895), p.vi,
     quoted in McIntosh, op.cit., p.120.
23   H.F.Wilkinson, ed., 'The Athletic Almanack' (1868);
     Shearman, op.cit., pp.48-53.   The 'Almanack' for 1872
     provides a useful list of clubs registered with AAC.
24   Rye Collection of press cuttings, Guildhall Library,
     London, pp.189-90.
25   The contemporary press provides the major source for
     the study of pedestrianism.   For its leading per-
     formers, see P.Lovesey, 'Kings of Distance' (1968),
     pp.15-40, and for Scotland, D.A.Jamieson, 'Powderhall
     and Pedestrianism: The History of a Famous Sports
     Enclosure, 1870-1943' (Edinburgh, 1943).   A brief
     biography of Richard Manks, the 'Warwickshire Ante-
     lope', in 'Era', 2 March 1862 provides a picture of
     pedestrianism among its lesser luminaries, and A.R.
     Downer, 'Running Recollections and How to Train'
     (1908) reveals the sharp practices which attended it.
26   C.Hole, 'English Sports and Pastimes' (1949), pp.24-5.
27   A.Wynter, Our sports and pastimes, 'Once a Week', v
     (1861), pp.151-3.   See also Dickens's amiable dis-
     section of the sporting press in The roughs' guide,
     'All the Year Round', 16 December 1865.
28   H.Ellington, Athletes of the present and past,
     'Nineteenth Century', xxi (1887), pp.517-29.
29   H.Jones, Recreation, 'Good Words', xxii (1881), pp.
     43-9.
30   Questionable amusements, 'Young Men of Great
     Britain', 25 August 1868.
31   Gale, op.cit., pp.43-6.   A good account of contempo-
     rary gambling is provided in A.Esquiros, 'The English
     at Home' 4 vols (1861-3), ii, pp.388-413.
32   'All-England Cricket and Football Journal'
     (Sheffield), March 1879.

33   W.Rye, 'An Autobiography of an Ancient Athlete and
     Antiquarian' (Norwich, 1916),pp.31-2. A young
     solicitor in the City in the 1860s, and a member of
     the London Athletic Club, Rye left a useful collection
     of materials to the Guildhall Library. A.Trollope,
     'British Sports and Pastimes' (1868), pp.1-7.
34   Such a case, involving 'the second rate professionals'
     of the Prince of Wales and White Star clubs (obviously
     pub-based) in London, is reported in the 'Athletic
     Record and Monthly Journal of Amateur Amusements',
     September 1876.
35   Rye Coll.; The athletic sports at Beaufort House,
     'SR', 20 April 1867.
36   Letter to 'Athletic Record and Monthly Journal', June
     1876, emphasis in original.
37   S.Smiles, 'Self-Help' (1859), pp.241-6; W.Lovett,
     'Elementary Anatomy and Physiology' (1851), pp.129-52.
     See also B.H.Harrison's comments in Work and leisure
     in industrial society: conference report, 'Past and
     Present', 30 (1965), pp.96-103 and W.H.G.Armytage,
     Care of the shape: changing views in the nineteenth
     century, 'Journal of Physical Education', xlvii
     (1955), pp.71-4.
38   C.E.Maurice, ed., 'Life and Letters of Octavia Hill'
     (1913), pp.317-8; J.Johnston, 'Parks and Playgrounds
     for the People' (1885); C.L.Lewes, How to ensure
     breathing space, 'Nineteenth Century', xxi (1887),
     pp.677-82.
39   For sports propaganda in the Anglican Church, see
     Canon Money at the Croydon Church Congress, 'The
     Times', 11 October 1877, Rev. H.C.Shuttleworth at the
     Leicester Congress, ibid., 2 October 1880. See also
     Dickens's parody of Canon Septimus Crisparkle in
     'Edwin Drood' (1870), pp.9, 62-3; (W.L.Collins), Our
     amusements, 'Blackwood's Magazine', c (1866), pp.
     698-712.
40   M.H.Elsworth, 'The Provision for Physical Recreation
     in Bolton in the Nineteenth Century', Dissertation for
     the Diploma in the Advanced Study in Education,
     University of Manchester, 1972, p.48; P.Scott,
     Cricket and the religious world in the Victorian
     period, 'Church Quarterly', iii (1970), pp.134-44.
41   Quote from P.M.Young, 'A History of British Football'
     (1968), p.111; D.D.Molyneux, 'The Development of
     Physical Recreation in the Birmingham District',
     University of Birmingham MA thesis, 1957, pp.39-42.
     The most recent student of the game, J.Walvin, 'The
     People's Game: A Social History of British Football'
     (1975), pp.56-7 notes a similar pattern in Liverpool
     and other big cities.

42 'BC', 24 July 1875. Bolton's Peel Park charged a rent
    for pitches, which discouraged workingmen's teams.
43 W.T.Marriott, 'Some Real Wants of the Working Classes'
    (Manchester, 1860), p.29; Dean of York speaking to
    Church Congress at Derby, 'The Times', 6 October 1882
    and the Dean of Buxton to the same body at Wakefield,
    ibid., 7 October 1886.
44 Jackson, op.cit., pp.21-3; Elsworth, op.cit., p.48;
    E.L.Levy, 'History of the Birmingham Athletic Club,
    1866-98' (Birmingham, 1898), p.25.
45 See the recollections of working-class boyhood in F.H.
    Spencer, op.cit., pp.31,85; H.Snell, 'Men, Movements
    and Myself' (1936), p.15; and R.Roberts, 'The Classic
    Slum' (Manchester, 1971), p.127, who describes his
    bewilderment at the conflicting claims of the moral
    codes of Greyfriars and Salford.
46 The rise and progress of the Aston Villa Club,
    'Birmingham Mail', 24 October 1883, in the Osborne
    collection of cuttings, Birmingham Central Reference
    Library; P.M.Young, 'The Wolves' (1959), pp.23-31;
    idem, 'Bolton Wanderers' (1961), p.19; G.W.Simmons,
    'Tottenham Hotspur Football Club' (1947), pp.15-16.
47 W.Thorne, 'My Life's Battles' (1925), p.25.
48 'Athlete', March 1871.
49 The controversy can best be followed in 'Athletic
    News', a Manchester paper which emerged from the ruck
    of lesser rivals as the most influential provincial
    sports weekly, see ibid., 11 June, 9 July, 1 October,
    3 December 1879. See also Shearman, op.cit., pp.
    216-21. The Bicycle Union dropped the mechanics
    clause two years previously, 'Wheel World', May-
    September 1878.
50 Professional pedestrianism survived longer in
    Scotland, see Jamieson, op.cit., who also gives
    examples of the scandals and riots which accelerated
    its decline in England, pp.46,63-5.
51 G.Green, J.R.Witty and H.V.Usill, 'The History of the
    Football Association' (1953), pp.19-33.
52 McIntosh, op.cit., p.25; P.M.Young, 'Football in
    Sheffield' (1962), pp.16,43; F.Wall, 'Fifty Years of
    Football' (1935), p.2.
53 Walvin, op.cit., chs 3,4. See also W.F.Mandle, Games
    people played: cricket and football in England and
    Victoria, 'Historical Studies', xv (1973), pp.511-35.
54 'BC', 11, 18, 25 October 1884. The first protest
    meeting was held in Bolton.
55 Ibid., 22 November 1884.
56 'Athletic News', 29 November, 6 December 1884.
57 Green et al., op.cit., pp.95-109.

58 C.E.Sutcliffe and F.Hargreaves, 'History of the
    Lancashire Football Association, 1878-1928'
    (Blackburn, 1928), pp.147-51.
59 Villa Incorporated, 'Birmingham Gazette', 9 January
    1888, Osborne Coll.
60 J.A.H.Catton, 'Wickets and Goals' (1943), p.135;
    Young, 'A History of British Football', pp.123-6;
    idem, 'Manchester United' (1960), pp.41-4.
61 E.Ensor, The football madness, 'Contemporary Review',
    lxxiv (1898), 751-60; 'Creston', Football,
    'Fortnightly Review', lv (1894), pp.24-38; C.
    Edwardes, The new football mania, 'Nineteenth
    Century', xxxii (1892), pp.622-31. For the dis-
    tinction between soccer and rugby football, one need
    only repeat the old adage: 'Soccer is a game for
    gentlemen, played by hooligans; rugger is a game for
    hooligans, played by gentlemen.'
62 H.Spencer, 'Facts and Comments' (1902), pp.128-9.
63 For soccer as a sub-culture which preserved a signifi-
    cant continuity in working-class life, see I.R.Taylor,
    Soccer consciousness and soccer hooliganism, in
    S.Cohen, ed., 'Images of Deviance' (1971), pp.134-64.
64 W.F.Mandle, The professional cricketer in England in
    the nineteenth century, 'Labour History', xxiii
    (1972), pp.1-16; R.Bowen, 'Cricket: A History of its
    Growth and Development' (1970), pp.116,144-5.
65 Professionals, 'SR', 14 July 1883; R.G.Barlow, 'Forty
    Seasons of First Class Cricket' (Manchester, 1908),
    p.2; O.F.Christie, 'The Transition from Aristocracy,
    1832-67' (1927), p.115.

CHAPTER 7 RATIONAL RECREATION AND THE ENTERTAINMENT
           INDUSTRY: THE CASE OF THE VICTORIAN MUSIC
           HALLS

1 This chapter is derived from my long essay, Profit and
   morality in a nineteenth-century entertainment
   industry: the case of the Victorian music halls,
   undertaken for publication in a forthcoming volume on
   popular culture in the History Workshop series
   (Routledge & Kegan Paul), ed. R.Samuel, and I would
   like to thank Raphael Samuel for his kind and informed
   encouragement of my research in this field.
      Though material for the study of the halls is
   abundant, most secondary work has until recently been
   disappointing. The best point of departure is C.D.
   Stuart and A.J.Park, 'The Variety Stage: A History of
   the Music Halls from the Earliest Period to the

Present Time' (1895). To a great extent subsequent
historians have merely reworked their material, but
H.Scott, 'The Early Doors: Origins of the English
Music Hall' (1946) and R.Mander and J.Mitchenson, 'The
British Music Hall' (1965) are honourable exceptions.
A valuable tool for the research student is D.Howard,
'London Theatres and Music Halls, 1850-1950' (1970),
which provides a comprehensive listing for the capital
and an excellent bibliography; other recent scholarly
work is noted below.

2   SC on public houses and places of public entertainment, PP(HC) 1852-3, xxxvii, p.4198.

3   C.M.Smith, 'Curiosities of London Life' (1853), pp.
166-7; J.Rivière, 'My Musical Life' (1893), p.133;
Renton 'Baron' Nicholson, 'Autobiography of a Fast
Man' (1863), pp.284-7.

4   Though important, Morton was not the solitary pioneer
that music hall mythology has made him out to be. He
acceded to the title of Father of the Halls in the
1890s by the happy contrivance of outliving his
rivals; apotheosis was completed in W.H.Morton and
H.C.Newton, 'Sixty Years' Stage Service: The Life of
Charles Morton' (1905). Scott, op.cit., pp.131-41
gives a more realistic appreciation. For details of
the Canterbury and Oxford, see D.F.Cheshire, 'Music
Hall in Britain' (Newton Abbot, 1974), pp.26-8.

5   W.White, 'Illustrated Handbook of the Royal Alhambra
Palace' (1869).

6   Stuart and Park, op.cit., pp.86-92; SC on theatrical
licences and regulations, PP(HC) 1866, xvi, app. 3,
p.313.

7   S.Fiske, 'English Photographs by an American' (1869),
p.130; Dion Boucicault to the 'Era', 5 October, 21
December 1862. Music halls outnumbered theatres of
all descriptions by eight to one in London by the
1880s, but the popular theatre often interspersed
music hall acts with the straight drama, and it
retained considerable working-class support.

8   Stuart and Park, op.cit., pp.86-92; The cost of
amusing the public, 'London Society', i (1862), pp.
193-8; 'Era Almanack' (1868). G.J.Mellor, 'The
Northern Music Hall: A Century of Popular Entertainment' (Newcastle upon Tyne, 1971) makes a start
on the history of the provincial halls, though it is
a loose and indiscriminate compilation. M.Vicinus,
'The Industrial Muse: A Study of Nineteenth Century
British Working-Class Literature' (1974), pp.238-85
is good on the north-east, as well as the general
development of the halls. See also Bailey, Profit
and morality.

9   'Era', 7 September 1856;   SC on theatrical licences,
    1866, q.1006;   SC on theatres and places of enter-
    tainment, PP(HC), xviii 1892, qq.2079-80,2320,3773.
10 'Financial News', 15 February 1887; Stuart and Park,
    op.cit., pp.190-201;   Cheshire, op.cit., pp.98-105.
11 Cheshire, op.cit., p.87 quotes some salary figures,
    and G.H.McDermott, who introduced the notorious 'By
    Jingo' hit of the 1870s, provides some further details
    on the occasion of his bankruptcy, 'Era', 8, 29 August
    1885.
12 The brief careers of these unions are recorded in
    'Magnet' (Leeds), 17 August-28 December 1872;   'Era',
    7 September-21 December 1872. For militancy in the
    1880s, see 'Music Hall Artists' Association Gazette'.
    30 August-3 November 1886. A helpful source for
    details of wages, contracts, working conditions and
    various abuses within the business which artists were
    generally obliged to suffer is C.Coborn, 'The Man Who
    Broke The Bank: Memories of the Stage and Music
    Halls' (1928). A déclassé fugitive from the City,
    Coborn was a prominent unionist in the 1880s;   his
    autobiography is one of the readable few in what is
    generally a dismal genre. Theatrical reminiscence,
    warned Beerbohm, is the most awful weapon in the
    armoury of old age.
13 L.Blanc, 'Letters on England' 4 vols (1866-7), i, pp.
    61-2.
14 D.Cook, Coffee and comic songs, 'Time', May 1881;
    J.Hollingshead, Music hall history, 'Entr'acte Annual'
    (1886).
15 Holland was certainly as important a figure as Morton.
    A brilliant publicist, he managed or owned a suc-
    cession of London music halls, theatres and pleasure
    gardens before moving on to the new frontier of enter-
    tainment in Blackpool in the 1880s. 'Illustrated
    Sporting and Dramatic News', 9 January 1875;
    'Blackpool Gazette and News', 3 December 1895.
16 For cases brought by the society, formed in 1875, see
    'The Times', 10 June 1882.
17 A.Roberts, 'Fifty Years of Spoof' (1927), pp.28-9.
18 J.Burnley, 'Phases of Bradford Life' (Bradford, 1871),
    p.59;   D.J.Kirwan, 'Palace and Hovel, or Phases of
    London Life' (1963 reprint of 1870 US edn). The
    Victoria is a good example of a popular theatre which
    played music hall entertainment.
19 E.Jepson, 'Memories of a Victorian' (1933), pp.230-3.
    Perhaps this was the formidable Bessie Bellwood - ex-
    rabbit skinner turned star, see Vicinus, op.cit., pp.
    252-3.

20 Coborn, op.cit., pp.111,159; 'The Times', 29 December 1879; Mellor, op.cit., pp.30,142.
21 Fiske, op.cit., pp.133-4.
22 L.Senelick, Politics as entertainment: Victorian music-hall songs, 'Victorian Studies', xix (1975), pp.149-80. For a further consideration of the style and content of music hall entertainment, see C.M. MacInnes, 'Sweet Saturday Night' (1967), and G. Stedman Jones, Working-class culture and working-class politics in London, 1870-1900: notes on the remaking of a working class, 'Journal of Social History', vii (1974), pp.490-7.
23 W.Besant and J.Rice, 'Ready-Money Mortiboy: A Matter of Fact Story', 3 vols (1872), iii, p.19. I owe this reference to Anna Davin. Cf. for Birmingham and Bradford, SC on theatrical licences, 1866, q.7436, Burnley, op.cit., pp.55-63.
24 'The Times', 5 January 1865; 'Music Halls' Gazette', 8 August 1868.
25 (T.Wright), 'Some Habits and Customs of the Working Classes by a Journeyman Engineer' (1867), pp.198-9.
26 'Music Halls' Gazette', 23 May 1868. See also 'Musician and Music Hall Times', 28 May 1862, and 'Glowworm', 6 September 1865. These were some of the short-lived music hall papers of the 1860s; the staple professional papers were the 'Era', the licensed victuallers' paper, which overcame its initial distaste for the halls by the late 1850s, and the Leeds 'Magnet', which first appeared in 1866, but outlived the other newcomers.
27 J.Greenwood, Music hall morality, 'London Society', xiv (1868), pp.486-91.
28 'The Times', 15 October 1883; 'Judy', 2 September 1885.
29 Greenwood, loc.cit; Morton and Newton, op.cit., pp. 12-14. See also Hollingshead's evidence on the Alhambra, SC on theatrical licences, 1866, q.5263.
30 Coborn, op.cit., pp.102-4,129-30; G.Chirgwin, 'Chirgwin's Chirrups' (1912), p.25.
31 'Era', 19 September 1885. Bill Holland granted free use of his North Woolwich Pleasure Gardens to engineers and their families who held a benefit for striking Newcastle engineers, 'The Times', 4 October 1871.
32 J.Hole, 'The Working Classes of Leeds' (1863), p.116.
33 E.g. The drama in danger, 'SR', 7 January 1865; M. Browne, Theatres and music halls, 'Argosy', ii (1866), pp.117-28; Music halls and their effects, 'Meliora', x (1867), pp.246-56; J.Valentine, A plea for music in common life, 'Good Words', vii (1866), pp.473-6.

34   'Era', 26 October 1856; W.Lovett, 'The Life and
     Struggles of William Lovett' (1876), pp.288,372-5.
35   SC on public houses and places of public enter-
     tainment, 1852-3, q.870; SC on theatrical licences,
     1866, q.956, and qq.969,1124-5 for Sir Richard Mayne's
     assessment of London halls. Bolton's chief constable
     supported the Museum Music Hall against its critics,
     see 'BC', 1 February 1873.
36   M.Browne, Theatres and music halls, and 'Views and
     Opinions' (1866), pp.266-8, and Boucicault to SC on
     theatrical licences, 1866, qq.4237-8.
37   S.Headlam, The social work of the Church, 'Church
     Reformer', February 1882, and 'The Function of the
     stage' (1889). See also F.G.Bettany, 'Stewart
     Headlam: A Biography' (1926), pp.43-4; P.d'A.Jones,
     'The Christian Socialist Revival' (1968), p.102.
38   Headlam, report of speech at Newcastle, 'Church
     Reformer', 15 September 1884.
39   'House and Home', from the 1880s, exact reference
     mislaid. See also Social characteristics of London
     life, 'Beehive', 25 October 1865.
40   Besant and Rice, op.cit., ii, pp.159-66,260-74. A
     number of London caterers and a leading agent, H.J.
     Didcott, were Jewish. Morton's biographers were
     rather coy on this matter: he was, said Chance
     Newton, 'not altogether un-Hebraic', idem, 'Cues and
     Curtain Calls' (1927), p.270.
41   H.Shimmin, 'Liverpool Life' (Liverpool, 1856), pp.
     28-9; J.E.Ritchie, 'Days and Nights in London'
     (1880), pp.61-3; Our popular amusements, 'Dublin
     University Magazine', lxxxiv (1874), pp.233-44.
42   H.Mayhew, 'London Labour and the London Poor', 4 vols
     (Frank Cass edn, 1967), i, pp.40-2.
43   SC on theatrical licences, 1866, q.3607.
44   Music hall lyrics, 'SR', 20 September 1862. See also
     C.Mackay, Music hall literature, 'Social Notes', 1
     June 1878. For working-class writers, see G.J.
     Holyoake, 'The Social Means of Promoting Temperance'
     (1860), pp.18-19; J.M.Ludlow and L.Jones, 'The
     Progress of the Working Class, 1832-67' (1867), p.256;
     J.D.Burn, 'Autobiography of a Beggar Boy' (1882), p.
     605.
45   Ritchie, op.cit., pp.49-50.
46   Our music halls, 'Tinsley's Magazine', iv (1869), pp.
     216-33. See also H.Manton, 'Letters on the Theatres
     and Music Halls' (Birmingham, 1888), Birmingham
     Central Reference Library.
47   The quote is from H.Shimmin, 'Town Life' (Liverpool,
     1858), pp.152-4. There was undoubtedly some prosti-

tution in the halls, though the metropolitan police
gave them a clean bill of health before the 1866
committee, SC on theatrical licences, qq.916,1215.
But much of the easy sociability of the young audience
in the galleries, where a good deal of flirtation and
courting regularly took place, could well have been
construed as promiscuity or vice by the uninitiated
visitor.

48 SC on public houses and places of public enter-
tainment, 1852-3, qq.4013-30; Rev. E.Corderoy,
Popular amusements: lectures to the YMCA', pp.37-8;
SC on theatrical licences, 1866, q.583; M.Browne,
Theatres and music halls.

49 'BC', 18 January-22 February 1873, 29 January 1876.

50 For other campaigns against provincial halls and
singing saloons, see respective reports from Gosport,
Manchester, West Hartlepool and Bristol in 'Era', 5
October 1862; ibid., 12 September 1885; 'The Times',
14 November 1871; SC on intemperance, PP(HL) 1877,
xi, qq.5301-20.

51 The contest can be studied in G.Thorne, 'The Great
Acceptance: The Life of F.N.Charrington' (1912), pp.
104-34; The music halls and their enemies, 'SR', 7
March 1885; several reports and articles in 'Church
Reformer', notably Headlam, The battle of the music
halls, November 1889. For the role of the 'Methodist
Times' and the Social Purity movement, see D.P.Hughes,
'The Life of Hugh Price Hughes' (1904), pp.338-42.

52 Among the supporters of the company were Frederic
Harrison, Tom Hughes, Samuel Morley and Dean Stanley;
its history is recorded in C.Hamilton and L.Bayliss,
'The Old Vic' (1926), pp.176-88.

53 'Social Notes and Club News', 16 July 1881; J.
Hollingshead, 'My Lifetime', 2 vols (1895), ii, pp.
151-2; 'Coffee Public House News', 1 February 1881.
The charge of a trade boycott was made by William
Poel, the Victoria's manager, 'Church Reformer',
October 1884. See also R.Morton, 'The Adventures of
Arthur Roberts' (Bristol, 1895), pp.17-18.

54 'Coffee Public House News', 1 May 1884; 'Church
Reformer', October 1884.

55 J.Humphreys to 'The Times', 16 October 1883 and idem,
Up in the gallery, 'All The Year Round', 29 July 1882.

56 'Era', 29 August, 12 September 1852.

57 'A Journalist' (W.Mackay), 'Bohemian Days in Fleet
Street' (1913), p.23. There is a picture in Cheshire,
op.cit., p.22.

58 The proprietors' case is put in a pamphlet published
by their association, 'Regulation of Music Halls'

(1883), copy in the British Library of Political and Economic Science.

59 House rules of the early 1880s are reproduced in SC on theatres and places of entertainment, 1892, app. 3 and 4, pp.437-44.

60 Coborn, op.cit., p.232; W.Thorne, 'My Life's Battles' (1925), pp.28-9; G.Foster, 'The Spice of Life: Sixty Five Years in the Glamour World' (1939), p.135.

61 'Church Reformer', November 1889. Estimates of the relative revenues of refreshments and admissions are given in SC on theatrical licences, 1866, qq.1349-1758. See also Hollingshead to 'The Times', 17 October 1883.

62 SC on theatres and places of entertainment, 1892, qq. 1551-87.

63 Signs of status gratification show in several careers: Henry Holden, erstwhile Brummagem butcher, retired to a country estate at Malvern; Sam Lane of the Britannia in Hoxton became president of the Royal Thames Yacht Club; several London caterers - Morton, William Purkiss and Frederick Strange - took commissions in the Volunteers. The ultimate reward came in the 1900s with the creation of three music hall knights.

64 The sale of intoxicants was not, it should be noted, dispensed with - it was removed to the relative quarantine of ante-room bars. Proprietors of new purpose-built halls in London circumvented some of the hazards of the licensing procedure by taking out a theatre licence from the Lord Chamberlain's office, and obtaining permits for as many bars as they needed under a simple Excise licence; they were then covered for music and liquor but could not serve drink or allow smoking in the auditorium, thus destroying one of the characteristic features of the classic music hall. 'Entr'acte Annual' (1897), pp.11-13.

65 The apostle of the new conformity was Oswald (later Sir Oswald) Stoll who was soon to be found outside Charing Cross Station with a notebook, calculating the common denominator of a reformed popular taste, F.Barker, 'The House That Stoll Built: The Story of the Coliseum Theatre' (1957), p.11.

66 'Entr'acte Annual' (1900), p.13.

67 D.Farson, 'Marie Lloyd and Music Hall' (1972).

68 Stuart and Park, op.cit., pp.190-201; H.G.Hibbert, 'Fifty Years of a Londoner's Life' (1916), pp.40-2; W.R.Titterton, 'From Theatre to Music Hall' (1912), pp.120-3.

69 National Social Purity Crusade, 'The Nation's Morals:

Proceedings of the Public Morals Conference' (1910), pp.194-9.

CONCLUSIONS

1   J.Strutt, 'The Sports and Pastimes of the People of England' (1903 reprint of 1801 edn), p.15.
2   E.g. W.Hardwicke, Recreation of the working classes, 'Trans.NAPSS' (1867), pp.471-7,552-7; G.Turner, Amusements of the English people, 'Nineteenth Century', ii (1877), pp.820-30. See also Lord Brabazon, Great cities and social reform, 'Nineteenth Century', XIV (1883), pp.798-803.
3   H.Solly, 'These Eighty Years', 2 vols (1893), ii, p. 160. The title of Fuller's address is instructive - On our paramount duty to provide wholesome and pure recreations and amusements for the people, and the dire results and dangers which attend our neglect of it, 'Trans.NAPSS' (1874), pp.745-8.
4   C.Wilson, Economy and society in late-Victorian Britain, 'Economic History Review', XVIII (1965), pp. 183-98.
5   The speaker is Viscount Cranbrook, at the opening of his Bradford WMC, 'CIJ', 3 August 1883.
6   J.K.Cook, The labourer's leisure, 'Dublin University Magazine', XC (1877), pp.174-92.
7   S.A.Barnett, Hospitality, in J.M.Knapp, ed., 'The Universities and the Social Problem' (1895), pp.51-66. For an examination of this later phase which also overlaps the period covered in this book, see H.E. Meller, 'Leisure and the Changing City, 1870-1914' (1976), which gives particular attention to Bristol. This arrived too late for me to take full account of its findings.
8   M.Arnold, 'Culture and Anarchy' (Cambridge, 1966 reprint of 1869 edn), p.105; M.Browne, 'Views and Opinions' (1866), p.280; F.Freeman, Publicans and sinners, 'Weekly Dispatch', 11 February 1883.
9   S.W.Jevons, Methods of social reform: amusements of the people, 'Contemporary Review', xxxiii (1878), pp. 499-513; Our music halls, 'Tinsley's Magazine', iv (1869), pp.216-33; Social barriers, 'SR', 26 April 1873; 'The Times', 30 August 1860.
10 E.g. J.Lawson, 'Letters to the Young on Progress in Pudsey' (Stanninglen, 1887); W.E.Gladstone, Locksley Hall and the Jubilee, 'Nineteenth Century', xxi (1887), pp.1-18.
11 G.Gorer, 'Exploring English Character' (1955), p.13.

12   G.Best, 'Mid-Victorian Britain, 1815-75' (1971), pp.
     256-63; B.H.Harrison, 'Drink and the Victorians'
     (1971), pp.23-7. See also J.Myerscough, The recent
     history of the use of leisure time, in I.Appleton,
     ed., 'Leisure Research and Policy' (Edinburgh, 1974),
     p.16.

13   R.J.Morris, The history of self-help, 'New Society',
     3 December 1970, on the Woodhouse Temperance community
     in Leeds; L.L.Shiman, The Band of Hope movement,
     'Victorian Studies', viii (1973), p.65; idem, The
     Birstall Temperance Society, 'Yorkshire Archaeological
     Journal', xlvi (1974), pp.128-39.

14   Solly's address to the TUC in 1871 recorded in
     'Occasional Papers of the Working Men's Club and
     Institute Union', no.20, January 1872; W.Cowper, MP
     in 'The Times', 13 July 1863.

15   R.Q.Gray, Styles of life, the 'labour aristocracy' and
     class relations in later nineteenth century Edinburgh,
     'International Review of Social History', xviii
     (1973), pp.428-52; G.Crossick, The labour aristocracy
     and its values: a study of mid-Victorian Kentish
     London, 'Victorian Studies', xix (1976), pp.301-28.
     See also T.R.Tholfsen, The intellectual origins of
     mid-Victorian stability, 'Political Science
     Quarterly', lxxxvi (1971), pp.57-91. Relevant here
     too is a critical scrutiny of the general concept of
     the labour aristocracy by H.Pelling, 'Popular Politics
     and Society in Late Victorian Britain' (1968), pp.
     37-61.

16   H.H.Gerth and C.Wright Mills, 'Character and Social
     Structure' (New York, 1964 Harbinger edn), pp.10-11,
     120-4; R.Frankenberg, 'Communities in Britain:
     Social Life in Town and Country' (1966), pp.240-2.
     On observability, see the important article by R.K.
     Merton, The role-set: problems in sociological
     theory, 'British Journal of Sociology', viii (1957),
     pp.112-20.

17   G.Gissing, 'The Nether World' (John Murray reprint
     edn, 1903), p.69.

18   I have examined the themes raised here more fully in
     my unpublished paper, Working-class respectability in
     mid-Victorian England: ideology or role?, presented
     to the Canadian Historical Association conference
     held at Edmonton in June 1975. Useful conceptual
     insights are afforded by E.Goffman, Role distance, in
     'Encounters: Two Studies in the Sociology of Inter-
     action' (Penguin University edn, 1972), pp.75-134 and
     his The nature of deference and demeanour, in 'Inter-
     action Ritual' (Penguin University edn, 1972), p.58.

See also H.Newby, The deferential dialectic, 'Comparative Studies in Society and History, xvii (1975), pp. 139-64.

19 G. Stedman Jones, 'Outcast London' (Oxford, 1971).

20 Idem, Working-class culture and working-class politics in London, 1870-1900; notes on the remaking of a working class, 'Journal of Social History', vii (1974), pp.460-508. This article must be considered indispensable reading for all students of the period and its popular culture.

21 Report of factory inspectors, PP 1867, xvi, p.376.

22 P.N.Stearns, 'Lives of Lavour: Work in a Maturing Industrial Society' (1975), pp.269-99 and his Working-class women in Britain, 1890-1914, in M.Vicinus, ed., 'Suffer and Be Still: Women in the Victorian Age' (Bloomington, Ind., 1972), pp.100-20. See also S. Meacham, 'The sense of an impending clash': English working-class unrest before the First World War, 'American Historical Review', lxxvii (1972), pp. 1343-64.

23 For a stimulating analysis of this next stage, see S.Yeo's important study of the social history of Reading in the late nineteenth and early twentieth century 'Religion and Voluntary Organisations in Crisis' (1976), esp. ch.7.

Bibliography

General note: This listing does not offer a comprehensive
bibliography for the study of Victorian leisure, but
includes only those sources that were of substantial
importance for this particular study. It does not,
therefore, include all the materials consulted, nor all
of those referred to in the notes, though it does include
some previously uncited titles which relate directly to
general themes in the book. The newspapers and periodicals are those which were most extensively sampled for the
period though it has not been possible to itemise particular articles or reports. The majority of the printed
sources, unless specifically stated otherwise, are to be
found in the British Museum.

PRIMARY SOURCES

A Manuscript and other unpublished materials

Solly Collection, 17 vols, London, British Library of
Political and Economic Science (Misc. MSS 154).
Osborne Collection of newspaper cuttings, 1874-1907,
Birmingham, Central Public Library.
Place Collection of newspaper cuttings, BM.
Rye Collection of newspaper cuttings, London, Guildhall
Library.
Horringer and Ickworth Village Club minute and account
books, 1877-1902, in the possession of Mrs Z.Ward,
Horringer, Suffolk.
Newcastle upon Tyne Working Men's Club minute books,
1865-6, 1870-3, Newcastle, Central Public Library.
Star Music Hall account book, 1847-50, xerox copy from
the original in the possession of Mrs D.Scholefield,
Orpington, Kent BRL.

DYSON, S., 'Local Notes and Reminiscences of Farnworth',
Typescript 1894, Farnworth, Lancs, Central Public Library.
GREENHALGH, R., 'Sixty Years: Local Records and Remi-
niscences', MS 1908 BRL.
MACMILLAN, J., 'Description of Checks issued by Birmingham
Concert Halls, 1850-1920', MS 1924, Birmingham, Central
Public Library.

B Parliamentary materials

'Hansard's Parliamentary Debates'.
Annual reports of the factory inspectors.
Parliamentary Papers (Commons and Lords):
Select committee (SC) on the observation of the sabbath
(HC), 1831-2, vii.
SC on public walks (HC), 1833, xv.
SC on drunkenness (HC), 1834, viii.
SC on the education of the poorer classes (HC), 1838, vii.
Report of the commission on constabulary, 1839, xix.
SC on the operation of the Factory Act (HC), 1840, x.
First report of the commission on children's employment,
1842, xv.
Second report of the commission on children's employment,
1843, xiii, xiv.
SC on gaming (HC), 1844, vi.
SC on the laws governing gaming (HL), 1844, xii.
Report of the commission on the state of large towns,
1844, xvii.
Report of the commissioner on the state of mining
districts, 1844, xvi.
SC on the observation of the sabbath (HC), 1847, ix.
SC on public libraries (HC), 1849, xi.
Report of the commission on the state of the population
in mining districts, 1850, xxiii.
SC on the suppression of betting houses (HC), 1852-3, i.
SC on public houses and places of public entertainment
(HC), 1852-3, xxxvii.
SC further report on the licensing of places of public
entertainment (HC), 1854, xiv.
Lyon Playfair, Report on the London Mechanics' Insti-
tution, 1857-8, xlviii.
SC on public institutions (HC), 1860, xvi.
Report of the commission on popular education in England,
1861, xxi.
SC on theatrical licences and regulations (HC), 1866, xvi.
SC on bank holidays (HC), 1867-8, vii.
SC on the sale of liquors on Sunday (HC), 1867-8, xiv.
SC on intemperance (HL), 1877, xi.

SC on theatres and places of entertainment (HC), 1892,
xviii.
Third report of the commission on liquor licensing laws,
1898, xxxvi.

C Contemporary press (place of publication is London,
   unless otherwise stated)

i   Newspapers

'Beehive'; 'Bell's Life in London'; 'Bolton Chronicle';
'Bolton Evening News'; 'Bolton Free Press'; 'Bolton
Weekly Journal'; 'Bowtun Luminary' (Bolton); 'Daily
News'; 'Daily Telegraph'; 'Era'; 'Porcupine'
(Liverpool); 'The Times'; 'Weekly Dispatch'.

ii   Periodicals

'All The Year Round'; 'Argosy'; 'Bentley's Miscellany';
'Blackwood's Magazine'; 'Chambers's Edinburgh Journal';
'Colburn's Monthly Magazine'; 'Congregationalist';
'Contemporary Review'; 'Cornhill Magazine'; 'Dublin
Review'; 'Dublin University Magazine'; 'Edinburgh
Review'; 'Fortnightly Review'; 'Fraser's Magazine';
'Fun'; 'Good Words' (Edinburgh); 'Journal of the Society
of Arts'; 'London Society'; 'Nineteenth Century';
'Punch'; 'Quarterly Review'; 'St James Gazette';
'Saturday Review'; 'Time'; 'Tinsley's Magazine'.

iii Specialist, institutional and reforming press

'After Work: A Magazine for Workmen's Homes'; 'The All-
England Cricket and Football Journal and Athletic Review'
(Sheffield); 'Amateurs' Guide and Stage and Concert Hall
Reporter' (Birmingham); 'Athlete'; 'Athletic News'
(Manchester); 'Athletic Record and Monthly Journal of
Amateur Amusements'; 'Athletic Review and Journal of
Physical Education'; 'Baily's Magazine of Sports and
Pastimes'; 'Church Reformer'; 'Club and Institute Union
Journal'; 'Coffee Public House News'; 'Coffee Tavern
Gazette and Journal of Food Thrift'; 'Common Good';
'Dramatic and Musical Circular: An Epitome of Music Hall
Requirements'; 'Drury Lane Workmen's Hall Messenger';
'House and Home'; 'Illustrated Sporting and Dramatic
News'; 'Illustrated Sporting News'; 'Leisure Hour: A

Family Journal of Instruction and Recreation'; 'Licensed
Victuallers Gazette'; 'Magnet' (Leeds); 'Manager's Guide
and Artistes Advertiser' (Manchester); 'Midland Sporting
News' (Birmingham); 'Music Hall Artists Association
Gazette'; 'Music Halls' Gazette'; 'Musical Gazette';
'Musician and Music Hall Times'; 'People's Journal';
'Quarterly Messenger of the Young Men's Christian Associ-
ation'; 'Referee'; 'Refreshment News'; 'Rink'; 'Social
Notes and Club News'; 'Sporting Gazette'; 'Timethrift:
Or All Hours Turned to Good Account'; 'Tonic Sol-fa
Reporter'; 'Town'; 'Wheel World'; 'Working Men's
College Magazine'; 'Workman's Club Journal'; 'Workman's
Magazine'.

iv   Annual publications

'Dramatic, Equestrian and Musical Sick Fund Almanack';
'Dramatic, and Musical Directory of the United Kingdom';
'Entr'acte Annual'; 'Era Almanack'; 'Musical Artists,
Lecturers and Entertainers Guide, and Entrepreneurs
Directory'; 'Walters Theatrical and Sporting Directory'.

D Contemporary books, pamphlets, tracts and sermons
   (place of publication is London, unless otherwise
   stated)

ADAMS, J., 'A Letter to the Justices of the Peace of the
County of Middlesex, on the subject of Licences for Public
Music and Dancing' (1850).
ADAMS, W.E., 'Memoirs of a Social Atom', 2 vols (1903).
ANSTEY, F., 'Mr Punch's Model Music Hall Songs' (1892).
ARNOLD, M., 'Culture and Anarchy' (Cambridge, 1966 reprint
of 1869 edn).
ARNOLD, T., 'Thirteen Letters on our Social Condition'
(Sheffield, 1832).
AXON, W.E., 'The Black Knight of Ashton' (Manchester,
1870).
BAMFORD, S., 'Walks in South Lancashire' (Blackley, 1844).
BARCLAY, T., 'Memoirs and Medleys: The Autobiography of
a Bottle Washer' (Leicester, 1934).
BARLOW, R.G., 'Forty Seasons of First Class Cricket'
(Manchester, 1908).
BAYLY, M., 'Ragged Homes and How to Mend Them' (1860).
BELFORD, J., 'The Saturday Half-Holiday: Its Bearing on
the Due Observance of the Sabbath' (Glasgow, 1867).
BENNETT, A., 'Clayhanger' (Methuen reprint edn, 1947).
BENNETT, A.R., 'London and Londoners in the Eighteen
Fifties and Sixties' (1924).

BESANT, W. and RICE, J., 'Ready-Money Mortiboy: A Matter of Fact Story', 3 vols (1872).

BESANT, W., 'As We Are and As We May Be' (1903).

BEST, T., 'The Love of Pleasure' (Sheffield, 1862).

(BLACKBURN, C.F.), 'A Journeyman', 'A Continental Tour of Eight Days for Forty Shillings' (1878).

BLAIKIE, W.G., 'Better Days for Working People' (1863).

BLANC, L., 'Letters on England', 4 vols (1866-7).

(BLOUET, P.), 'Max O'Rell', 'John Bull and His Island' (1883).

BOARDMAN, W.H., 'Vaudeville Days' (1935).

BOX, C., 'The English Game of Cricket' (1877).

BOX, C., 'Musings for Athletes: Twelve Philosophical Essays' (1888).

BRASSEY, T., 'Lectures on the Labour Question' (1878).

BROWN, H.S., 'Lectures to Working Men' (1870).

BROWN, J.B., 'First Principles of Ecclesiastical Truth' (1871).

BROWN, J.B., 'The Gregarious Follies of Fashion: An Address to the Younger Generation' (1876).

BROWNE, M., 'Views and Opinions' (1866).

BUCKINGHAM, J.S., 'National Evils and Practical Remedies' (1849).

BULWER-LYTTON, E., 'England and the English', 2 vols (1833).

BURN, J.D., 'The Autobiography of a Beggar Boy' (1882).

BURNLEY, J., 'Phases of Bradford Life' (Bradford, 1871).

CHADWICK, E., 'Report on the Sanitary Condition of the Labouring Population of Great Britain' (1842, ed. M.W. Flinn, 1965).

CHANCELLOR, V.E., ed., 'Master and Artisan in Victorian England: The Diary of William Andrews and the Autobiography of Joseph Gutteridge' (1969).

CHESTER, G.J., 'The Young Man at Rest and at Play' (Sheffield, 1860).

CHESTER, G.J., 'The Temptations of Young Men in Towns' (Sheffield, 1862).

CLARKE, J.E., 'Plain Papers on the Social Economy of the People' (1858).

(CLAY, J.), 'Chaplain's Report on the Preston House of Correction' (Preston, 1841).

CLIFFORD-SMITH, J.L., 'The National Association and its Twenty Fifth Anniversary: A Manual and a Narrative' (1882).

COBORN, C., 'The Man Who Broke The Bank: Memories of the Stage and Music Halls' (1928).

COLLINS, W., 'Man and Wife', 3 vols (1870).

COOPER, T., 'The Life of Thomas Cooper' (1872).

COOPER, T., 'Thoughts at Fourscore' (1885).

CORDEROY, E., 'Popular Amusements: Lectures to the Young
Men's Christian Association' (1857).

COYNE, J.S., The barmaid, in A.Smith, ed., 'Sketches of
London Life and Character' (1859).

CUMMING, J., 'Labour, Rest and Recreation: Lectures to
the YMCA' (1855).

CURRIE, E.H., 'Appeal for a People's Palace' (1886).

DANA, R.H., 'Hospitable England in the Eighteen Seventies:
The Diary of a Young American, 1875-6' (1921).

DICKENS, C., 'Sketches by Boz', 2 vols (1836).

DICKENS, C., 'The Uncommercial Traveller' (1861).

DISRAELI, B., 'Sybil, or the Two Nations' (Brimley Johnson
reprint edn, 1904).

DODD, W., 'The Factory System Illustrated in a Series of
Letters to Lord Ashley' (1842).

DOWNER, A.R., 'Running Recollections and How to Train'
(1908).

DOYLE, R., 'The Foreign Tour of Messrs Brown, Jones, and
Robinson' (1854).

EARNSHAW, S., 'Upon the State of Education and the Working
Classes of Sheffield' (Sheffield, 1857).

EARNSHAW, S., 'The Tradition of the Elders' (Sheffield,
1860).

ELLIS, S.M., ed., 'Letters and Memoirs of Sir William
Hardman, A Mid-Victorian Pepys' (1923).

ENGELS, F., 'The Condition of the Working Class in
England' (Pan paperback reprint, 1969).

ESCOTT, T.H.S., 'England: Its People, Polity and
Pursuits' (1885).

(ESCOTT, T.H.S.), 'A Foreign Resident', 'Society in
London' (1886).

ESCOTT, T.H.S., 'Social Transformations of the Victorian
Age' (1897).

ESQUIROS, A., 'The English at Home', 4 vols (1861-3).

FAUCHER, L., 'Manchester in 1844: Its Present Condition
and Future Prospects' (Manchester, 1844).

'A Fellow Workman', 'The Races Defended as an Amusement'
(Newcastle upon Tyne, 1853).

FISKE, S., 'English Photographs by an American' (1869).

FITZGERALD, P., 'Music Hall Land' (1890).

FROST, T., 'The Old Showmen and the Old London Fairs'
(1874).

FROST, T., 'Forty Years' Recollections, Literary and
Political' (1880).

GALE, F., 'Modern English Sports: Their Use and Abuse'
(1885).

GALE, F., 'Sports and Recreations in Town and Country'
(1888).

GARDINER, F.J., 'The Eightieth Birthday of a Model

Institution: An Account of the Origin and Development of
Wisbech Workingmen's Club and Institute' (Wisbech, 1914).
GIBSON, A. and PICKFORD, W., 'Association Football and
the Men Who Made It', 4 vols (1905).
GISSING, G., 'The Nether World' (John Murray reprint edn,
1903).
GODWIN, G., 'Town Swamps and Social Bridges' (1859).
GREEN, S.G., 'The Working Classes of Great Britain:
Consideration of the Means for their Improvement and
Elevation' (Leeds, 1850).
GREG, S., 'Two Letters to Leonard Horner on the Capabili-
ties of the Factory System' (Manchester, 1840).
GUTHRIE, T., 'Popular Innocent Entertainments' (Glasgow,
1856).
HALL, B.T., 'Our Fifty Years: The Story of the Working
Men's Club and Institute Union' (1912).
HALL, E.H., 'Coffee Taverns, Cocoa Houses and Coffee
Palaces: Their Rise, Progress, and Prospects' (1878).
HARRISON, F., 'Sundays and Festivals: A Lecture' (1867).
HAWEIS, H.R., 'Thoughts for the Times' (1872).
HEADLAM, S.D., 'The Function of the Stage' (1889).
HEYWOOD, B., 'Addresses delivered at the Manchester
Mechanics' Institute' (1843).
HEYWOOD, T., 'A Memoir of Sir Benjamin Heywood'
(Manchester, 1863).
HODDER, E., 'The Junior Clerk: A Tale of City Life'
(1862).
HODDER, E., 'Life of Samuel Morley' (1887).
HOLE, J., 'The History and Management of Literary,
Scientific and Mechanics' Institutes' (1853).
HOLE, J., 'The Working Classes of Leeds' (1863).
HOLLINGSHEAD, J., 'Today: Essays and Miscellanies',
2 vols (1865).
HOLLINGSHEAD, J., 'My Lifetime', 2 vols (1895).
HOLYOAKE, G.J., 'The Rich Man's Six, and the Poor Man's
One Day: A Letter to Lord Palmerston' (1856).
HOLYOAKE, G.J., 'The Social Means of Promoting Temperance'
(1860).
HOPKINS, E., 'Work Amongst Working Men' (1879).
HOWITT, W., 'The Rural Life of England', 2 vols (1838).
HOWITT, W., 'The Country Year Book' (New York, 1850).
HUDSON, J.W., 'The History of Adult Education' (1851).
HUGHES, D.P., 'The Life of Hugh Price Hughes' (1904).
JACKSON, N.L., 'Sporting Days and Sporting Ways' (1932).
JERROLD, W.B., 'The Cockaynes in Paris, or Gone Abroad'
(1871).
JERROLD, W.B. and DORE, G., 'London: A Pilgrimage'
(1872).
JOHNS, E.F., ed., 'Words of Advice to Schoolboys by
Charles Kingsley' (1912).

JOHNSTON, J., 'Parks and Playgrounds for the People'
(1885).
JONES, H., 'Holiday Papers' (1864).
KAY, J., 'The Church and Popular Recreations' (1883).
KEMPE, J.E., ed., 'The Use and Abuse of the World', 3 vols
(1873-5).
KINGSLEY, C., 'Health and Education' (1874).
KINGSLEY, C., 'Sanitary and Social Essays' (1880).
KINGSLEY, F.E., ed., 'Charles Kingsley: His Letters and
Memories of his Life', 2 vols (1877).
KIRWAN, D.J., 'Palace and Hovel, or Phases of London Life'
(1963 reprint of 1870 US edn).
KNIGHT, C., 'Passages of a Working Life', 3 vols (1873).
LAWSON, J., 'Letters to the Young on Progress in Pudsey'
(Stanninglen, 1887).
LEVY, E.L., 'History of the Birmingham Athletic Club,
1866-98' (Birmingham, 1898).
LILWALL, J., 'The Half-Holiday Question Considered'
(1856).
LOVETT, W., 'The Life and Struggles of William Lovett'
(1876).
LUDLOW, J.M. and JONES, L., 'The Progress of the Working
Class, 1832-1867' (1867).
MANNERS, J., 'A Plea for National Holydays' (1843).
MANTON, H., 'Letters on the Theatres and Music Halls'
(Birmingham, 1888). Birmingham Central Reference Library.
MARRIOTT, W.T., 'Some Real Wants of the Working Classes'
(Manchester, 1860).
MAYHEW, H., 'London Labour and the London Poor', 4 vols
(Frank Cass reprint edn, 1967).
MAYHEW, H., The Cockaynes in Paris, in 'Shops and
Companies of London, and the Trades and Manufactories of
Great Britain' (1865).
MAYHEW, H., 'Report of the Trade and Hours of Closing at
Working Men's Clubs' (1871).
MERION, C., 'The Music Hall Stage and its Relationship
with the Church' (1884).
MILES, H.D., ed., 'Tom Sayers, His Life and Pugilistic
Career' (1866).
MILLER, D.P., 'The Life of a Showman' (1849).
(MILLER, W.H.), 'The Culture of Pleasure' (1872).
MORLEY, J., 'Studies in Conduct' (1867).
MORTON, R., 'The Adventures of Arthur Roberts' (Bristol,
1895).
MORTON, W.H. and NEWTON, H.C., 'Sixty Years' Stage
Service: The Life of Charles Morton' (1905).
NEALE, E.V., 'True Refinement: Address to the Rochdale
Working Men's Club' (Manchester, 1876).
NICHOLSON, R., 'Autobiography of a Fast Man' (1863).

'Occasional Papers of the Working Men's Club and Institute Union' (1863-72).
OKEY, T., 'A Basketful of Memories: An Autobiographical Sketch' (1930).
PHILPOTT, H.B., 'London at School: The Story of the School Board' (1904).
PLACE, F., 'The Improvement of the People' (1834).
PLACE, F., 'Autobiography' (ed. M.Thale, Cambridge, 1972).
'Practical Hints for the Management of Coffee Taverns' (1878).
PRATT, H., 'Notes of a Tour among Workmen's Clubs' (1870).
PRIMROSE, A., 'Address to the Middle Classes on Gymnastic Exercises' (1848).
RAE, W.F., 'The Business of Travel' (1891).
RATHBONE, W., 'The Increased Earnings of the Working Classes and Their Effect on Themselves and on the Future of England' (Liverpool, 1877).
'The Regulation of Music Halls: A Summary of the Attempts made by Music Hall Proprietors to obtain an Improvement of the Law' (1883).
RITCHIE, J.E., 'The Night Side of London' (1857).
RITCHIE, J.E., 'Days and Nights in London' (1880).
ROBERTS, A., 'Fifty Years of Spoof' (1927).
ROGERS, F., 'Labour, Life and Literature: Some Memories of Sixty Years' (1913).
ROTH, M., 'A Plea for the Compulsory Teaching of the Elements of Physical Education in our National Elementary Schools' (1870).
RYE, W., 'An Autobiography of an Ancient Athlete and Antiquarian' (Norwich, 1916).
SALA, G.A., 'Gaslight and Daylight, With Some London Scenes They Shine Upon' (1859).
SANGER, 'LORD' GEORGE, 'Seventy Years a Showman' (1910).
SARGANT, W.L., 'Economy of the Labouring Classes' (1857).
SHEARMAN, M., 'Athletics and Football' (1889).
SHIMMIN, H., 'Liverpool Life, its Pleasures, Practices and Pastimes' (Liverpool, 1856).
SHIMMIN, H., 'Town Life' (Liverpool, 1858).
SLANEY, R.A., 'A Plea for the Working Classes' (1847).
SMEE, W.R., 'National Holidays' (1871).
SMITH, C.M., 'The Working Man's Way in the World' (1853).
SMITH, J.S., 'Social Aspects' (1850).
SOLLY, H., 'How to Deal with the Unemployed Poor of London and with its Roughs and Criminal Classes?' (1868).
SOLLY, H., 'James Sandford, Carpenter and Chartist', 2 vols (1883).
SOLLY, H., 'These Eighty Years', 2 vols (1893).
SOLLY, H., 'Working Men's Social Clubs and Educational Institutes' (1904).

SPARKS, T. (C.DICKENS), 'Sunday Under Three Heads' (1836).
SPENCER, F.H., 'An Inspector's Testament' (1938).
SPENCER, H., 'Education, Intellectual, Moral and Physical' (1861).
STRUTT, J., 'The Sports and Pastimes of the People of England' (Methuen reprint edn, 1903).
STUART, C.D. and PARK, A.J., 'The Variety Stage: A History of the Music Halls from the Earliest Period to the Present Time' (1895).
SULLIVAN, J.F., 'The British Workingman by One Who Does Not Believe in Him' (1878).
TAINE, H., 'Notes on England' (1872).
TALBOT, C.J.C., ed., 'Meliora, Or Better Times to Come' (1852).
TAYLOR, W. Cooke, 'Notes of a Tour in the Manufacturing Districts of Lancashire' (Manchester, 1842).
THOMSON, C., 'The Autobiography of an Artisan' (1847).
THORNE, G., 'The Great Acceptance: The Life Story of F.N.Charrington' (1912).
THORNE, W., 'My Life's Battles' (1925).
TITTERTON, W.R., 'From Theatre to Music Hall' (1912).
'Transactions of the National Association for the Promotion of Social Science', 1857-86.
TROLLOPE, A., 'British Sports and Pastimes' (1868).
TROLLOPE, A., 'The New Zealander' (Oxford, 1972).
WALL, F., 'Fifty Years of Football' (1935).
WHITE, W., 'Illustrated Handbook of the Royal Alhambra Palace' (1869).
WHITTLE, P.A., 'Blackburn As It Is' (Preston, 1852).
WILKINSON, H.F., 'Modern Athletics' (1868).
WILLIAMS, J.E.H., 'Life of Sir George Williams' (1906).
WINGFIELD, W., 'The Game of Sphairistike' (1874).
(WRIGHT, T.), 'Some Habits and Customs of the Working Classes by a Journeyman Engineer' (1867).
WRIGHT, T., 'The Great Unwashed' (1868).
WRIGHT, T., 'Our New Masters' (1873).
WRIGHT, T., Bill Banks's day out, in A.Halliday, ed., 'The Savage Club Papers' (1868)

E   Contemporary books, etc. on Bolton and district (place of publication is Bolton, unless otherwise stated), BRL

Ancient Noble Order of United Oddfellows (Bolton Unity) Friendly Society, 'Grand Lodge Circular', 115 vols (1831-1959).
BAKER, F., 'The Moral Tone of the Factory System Defended' (1850).
BARLOW, W., 'Some Recollections of Ridgway Gates Sunday School' (1933).

BARTON, B.H., 'Historical Gleanings of Bolton and District' (1881).

BLACK, J., 'A Medico-Topographical, Geological and Statistical Sketch of Bolton and its Neighbourhood' (1837).

BRIMELOW, W., 'Political and Parliamentary History of Bolton' (1888).

CHAMBERLAIN, W., 'On the Causes that Public Worship is Neglected by the People' (1882).

CLEGG, J., 'A Chronicle History of Bolton' (1879).

CLEGG, J., ed., 'Autobiography of a Lancashire Lawyer' (1883).

CLEGG, J., 'Annals of Bolton' (1888).

ENTWHISTLE, E., 'Pastimes and Recreations', Essay read before Bolton Parish Church Mutual Improvement Society (1881).

ENTWHISTLE, J., 'Report on the Sanitary Condition of Bolton' (1848).

ENTWHISTLE, J., 'Light Upon Dark Places' (1884).

GRIMSHAW, T., 'The Cogitations of Thomas Grimshaw: Observations on the Customs, Manners, etc. of the People of Bolton' (1838).

GRIMSHAW, T., Autobiography, in 'Bolton Weekly Journal', 23 June-18 August 1877.

HAMPSON, T., 'Horwich: Its History, Legends and Church' (Wigan, 1883).

HILTON, J.D., 'Memoir of J.H.Raper' (1898).

HILTON, R.S., GRIMSHAW, T. and WITHERINGTON, W., 'Sunday Closing' (1853).

HOLDEN, J., 'Autobiography of Joseph Holden of Bolton' (1872).

JOHNSTON, J., 'Mawdsley Street Congregational Chapel, Bolton le Moors, 1808-1908: A Notable Record' (London, 1908).

MUSGRAVE, P., ed., 'Annals of the Pleiades Society, 1871-1911' (1911).

PEAPLES, F.W., 'History of the Greater and Little Bolton Co-operative Society, 1859-1909' (1910).

RICHARDSON, H.M., 'Reminiscences of Forty Years in Bolton' (1884).

ROTHWELL, S., 'Local Reminiscences' (1899).

SCHOLES, J.C., 'History of Bolton' (1892).

STATON, J.T., 'The Visit t' Paris Eggsibish' (1867).

WHITTLE, P.A., 'A History of Bolton' (1855).

SECONDARY SOURCES

A   Books (place of publication is London, unless otherwise
    stated)

ADDISON, W., 'English Fairs and Markets' (1952).
ALEXANDER, S., 'St Giles' Fair, 1830-1914: Popular
Culture and the Industrial Revolution in Nineteenth
Century Oxford' (Oxford, 1970).
ALTHAM, H.S., 'A History of Cricket', 2 vols (1962).
BANKS, J.A., 'Prosperity and Parenthood: A Study of
Family Planning among the Victorian Middle Classes'
(1954).
BARKER, F., 'The House That Stoll Built: The Story of the
Coliseum Theatre' (1957).
BEST, G., 'Mid-Victorian Britain, 1851-5' (1971).
BETTANY, F.G., 'Stewart Headlam: A Biography' (1926).
BIENEFELD, M.A., 'Working Hours in British Industry: An
Economic History' (1972).
BINFIELD, C., 'George Williams and the YMCA: A Study in
Victorian Social Attitudes' (1973).
BOWEN, R., 'Cricket: A History of its Growth and
Development throughout the World' (1970).
BOYSON, R., 'The Ashworth Cotton Enterprise: The Rise
and Fall of a Family Firm, 1818-80' (Oxford, 1970).
BRIGGS, A., 'Mass Entertainment: The Origins of a Modern
Industry' (Adelaide, 1960).
BROWN, W.E., 'Robert Heywood of Bolton' (Wakefield, 1970).
BURN, W.L., 'The Age of Equipoise: A Study of the Mid-
Victorian Generation' (1964).
CHAPMAN, G., 'Culture and Survival' (1940).
CHECKLAND, S.G., 'The Rise of an Industrial Society in
England, 1815-1885' (1964).
CHESHIRE, D.F., 'Music Hall in Britain' (Newton Abbot,
1974).
CHRISTIE, O.F., 'The Transition from Aristocracy, 1832-
1867' (1927).
CRAUFORD, A.L., 'Sam and Sallie: A Romance of the Stage'
(1933).
CUNNINGHAM, H., 'The Volunteer Force: A Social and
Political History, 1859-1908' (1975).
DARWIN, B., 'John Gully and His Times, 1783-1863' (1935).
DAVIDOFF, L., 'The Best Circles: Women and Society in
Victorian England' (Totowa, N.J., 1973).
DE GRAZIA, S., 'Of Time, Work and Leisure' (New York,
Anchor paperback edn, 1964).
DENT, J.J., 'Hodgson Pratt, Reformer: An Outline of His
Work' (1932).
DUMAZEDIER, J., 'Toward a Society of Leisure' (New York,
1967).

DUMAZEDIER, J., 'Sociology of Leisure' (Amsterdam, 1974).
DUNNING, E., ed., 'Sport: Readings from a Sociological
Perspective' (Toronto, 1972).
DYOS, H.J. and WOLFF, M., eds, 'The Victorian City',
2 vols (1973).
FARSON, D., 'Marie Lloyd and Music Hall' (1972).
FRANKENBERG, R., 'Communities in Britain: Social Life in
Town and Country' (1966).
GERTH, H.H. and MILLS, C.W., 'Character and Social
Structure' (New York, Harbinger paperback edn, 1964).
GIROUARD, M., 'Victorian Pubs' (1975).
GOFFMAN, E., 'Encounters: Two Studies in the Sociology
of Interaction' (Penguin University edn, 1972).
GOFFMAN, E., 'Interaction Ritual' (Penguin University edn,
1972).
GORER, G., 'Exploring English Character' (1955).
GORHAM, M. and DUNNETT, H.McG., 'Inside the Pub' (1950).
GOSDEN, P.H.J.H., 'The Friendly Societies in England,
1815-1875' (Manchester, 1961).
GREEN, G., WITTY, J.R. and USILL, H.V., 'The History of
the Football Association' (1953).
HAMER, H., 'Bolton, 1838-1938' (Bolton, 1938).
HAMILTON, C. and BAYLISS, L., 'The Old Vic' (1926).
HAMMOND, J.L., 'The Growth of Common Enjoyment' (Oxford,
1933).
HAMMOND, J.L. and HAMMOND, B., 'The Age of the Chartists,
1832-1854: A Study of Discontent' (1930).
HARRISON, B.H., 'Drink and the Victorians: The Temperance
Question in England, 1815-1872' (1971).
HARRISON, J.F.C., 'Learning and Living, 1790-1960: A
Study in the History of the English Adult Education
Movement' (1961).
HARRISON, J.F.C., 'The Early Victorians, 1832-1851'
(Panther edn, 1973).
HOBSBAWM, E.J., 'Industry and Empire' (1968).
HOGGART, R., 'The Uses of Literacy' (1957).
HOLE, C., 'English Sports and Pastimes' (1949).
HOUGHTON, W.E., 'The Victorian Frame of Mind, 1830-1870'
(New Haven, Conn., 1957).
HOWARD, D., 'London Theatres and Music Halls, 1850-1950'
(1970).
HOWKINS, A., 'Whitsun in Nineteenth Century Oxfordshire'
(Oxford, 1973).
INGLIS, K., 'The Churches and the Working Classes in
Victorian England' (1963).
JACKSON, B., 'Working Class Community' (1968).
JAMIESON, D.A., 'Powderhall and Pedestrianism: The
History of a Famous Sports Enclosure, 1870-1943'
(Edinburgh, 1943).

JONES, G.S., 'Outcast London: A Study in the Relationship Between Classes in Victorian Society' (Oxford, 1971).

JONES, P.d'A. 'The Christian Socialist Revival, 1877-1914: Religion, Class and Social Conscience in Late-Victorian England' (Princeton, N.J., 1968).

KITSON CLARK, G.S.R., 'The Making of Victorian England' (1962).

LOVESEY, P., 'Kings of Distance' (1968).

LOVESEY, P. and MCNAB, T., 'Guide to British Track and Field Literature, 1275-1968' (1969).

MACINNES, .C.M., 'Sweet Saturday Night' (1967).

MCINTOSH, P.C., 'Sport in Society' (1963).

MCINTOSH, P.C., 'Physical Education in England Since 1800' (second edn, 1968).

MACK, E.C., 'The Public Schools and British Opinion, 1780-1860' (1938).

MACK, E.C. and ARMYTAGE, W.H.G., 'Thomas Hughes' (1952).

MCKECHNIE, S., 'Popular Entertainments Through The Ages' (1931).

MACKERNESS, E.D., 'A Social History of English Music' (1964).

MALCOLMSON, R.W., 'Popular Recreations in English Society, 1700-1850' (Cambridge, 1973).

MANDER, R. and MITCHENSON, J., 'The British Music Hall' (1965).

MARPLES, M., 'A History of Football' (1954).

MARRUS, M.R., 'The Rise of Leisure in Industrial Society' (St Charles, Mo., 1974).

MARRUS, M.R., ed., 'The Emergence of Leisure' (New York, 1974).

MELLER, H.E., ed., 'Nottingham in the 1880s: A Study in Social Change' (Nottingham, 1971).

MELLER, H.E., 'Leisure and the Changing City, 1870-1914' (1976).

MELLOR, G.J., 'The Northern Music Hall: A Century of Popular Entertainment' (Newcastle upon Tyne, 1970).

MORRIS, P., 'Aston Villa' (1960).

MORRIS, P., 'West Bromwich Albion: Soccer in the Black Country' (1965).

MORTIMER, R., 'The Jockey Club' (1958).

MOTTRAM, R.H., 'Portrait of an Unknown Victorian' (1936).

MUNFORD, W.A., 'Penny Rate: Aspects of British Public Library History, 1850-1950' (1951).

NETTEL, R., 'Music in the Five Towns, 1840-1914: A Study in the Social Influence of Music in an Industrial District' (Oxford, 1944).

NEWSOME, D., 'Godliness and Good Learning: Four Studies on a Victorian Ideal' (1961).

PARKER, S., 'The Future of Work and Leisure' (1971).

PARKER, S., 'The Sociology of Leisure' (1976).
PELLING, H., 'Popular Politics and Society in Late Victorian Britain' (1968).
PERKIN, H., 'The Origins of Modern British Society, 1780-1880' (1969).
PIMLOTT, J.A.R., 'The Englishman's Holiday: A Social History' (1947).
PIMLOTT, J.A.R., 'Recreations' (1968).
POLLARD, S., 'A History of Labour in Sheffield' (Liverpool, 1959).
POLLARD, S., 'The Genesis of Modern Management' (1968).
PUDNEY, J.S., 'The Thomas Cook Story' (1953).
RAISTRICK, A., 'Two Centuries of Industrial Welfare' (1938).
REID, J.C., 'Bucks and Bruisers: Pierce Egan and Regency England' (1971).
SCOTT, H., 'The Early Doors: Origins of the Music Hall' (1946).
SHIPLEY, S., 'Club Life and Socialism in Mid-Victorian London' (Oxford, 1971).
SIMEY, M.B., 'Charitable Effort in Liverpool in the Nineteenth Century' (Liverpool, 1951).
SIMMONS, G.W., 'Tottenham Hotspur Football Club' (1947).
SIMON, B., 'Education and the Labour Movement, 1870-1918' (1965).
SMITH, M.A., PARKER, S. and SMITH, C.S., eds, 'Leisure and Society in Britain' (1973).
SOLLOWAY, R.A., 'Prelates and People: Ecclesiastical Social Thought in England, 1783-1852' (1969).
SPARKE, A., 'Bibliographia Boltoniensis' (Manchester, 1913).
SPILLER, B., 'Victorian Public Houses' (Newton Abbot, 1972).
STEARNS, P.N., 'Lives of Labour: Work in a Maturing Industrial Society' (1975).
SUTCLIFFE, C.E. and HARGREAVES, F., 'History of the Lancashire Football Association, 1878-1928' (Blackburn, 1928).
TAYLOR, J., 'From Self-Help to Glamour: The Working Man's Club, 1860-1972' (Oxford, 1972).
THOMPSON, E.P., 'The Making of the English Working Class' (New York, Vintage paperback edn, 1963).
TURNER, R.E., 'James Silk Buckingham, 1786-1855: A Social Biography' (1934).
TYLECOTE, M., 'Mechanics' Institutes of Lancashire and Yorkshire before 1851' (Manchester, 1957).
VAMPLEW, W., 'The Turf: A Social and Economic History of Horse Racing' (1976).
VICINUS, M., 'The Industrial Muse: A Study of Nineteenth Century British Working-Class Literature' (1974).

VICINUS, M., ed., 'Suffer and Be Still: Women in the
Victorian Age' (Bloomington, Ind., 1972).

WALVIN, J., 'The People's Game: A Social History of
British Football' (1975).

WICKHAM, E.R., 'Church and People in an Industrial City'
(Lutterworth, 1957).

WILKINSON, R., 'The Prefects: British Leadership and the
Public School Tradition' (Oxford, 1964).

WILLIAMS, R., 'Culture and Society, 1780-1850' (1961).

WROTH, W., 'Cremorne and the Later London Gardens' (1907).

WYMER, N., 'Sport in England' (1949).

YEO, S., 'Religion and Voluntary Organisations in Crisis'
(1976).

YOUNG, G.M., ed., 'Early Victorian England, 1830-65',
2 vols (Oxford, 1934).

YOUNG, P.M., 'The Wolves' (1959).

YOUNG, P.M., 'Bolton Wanderers' (1961).

YOUNG, P.M., 'Football in Sheffield' (1962).

YOUNG, P.M., 'Football on Merseyside' (1963).

YOUNG, P.M., 'A History of British Football' (1968).

B   Essays and journal articles

BAILEY, P.C., 'A mingled mass of perfectly legitimate
pleasures': the Victorian middle class and the problem
of leisure, 'Victorian Studies', xxi (1977).

BARKER, C., A theatre for the people, in K.Richards and
P.Thomson, eds, 'Essays on Nineteenth Century British
Theatre' (Manchester, 1971), pp.1-17.

BERGER, B.M., The sociology of leisure: some suggestions,
'Industrial Relations', i (1962), pp.31-45.

BURNS, T., Leisure in industrial society, in M.A.Smith et
al., eds, 'Leisure and Society in Britain' (1973), pp.
40-55.

CROSSICK, G., The labour aristocracy and its values: a
study of mid-Victorian Kentish London, 'Victorian
Studies', xix (1976), pp.301-28.

DINGLE, A.E., Drink and working-class living standards
in Britain, 1870-1914, 'Economic History Review', xxv
(1972), pp.608-22.

GRAY, R.Q., Styles of life, the 'labour aristocracy' and
class relations in later nineteenth century Edinburgh,
'International Review of Social History', xviii (1973),
pp.428-52.

HALEY, B.E., Sports and the Victorian world, 'Western
Humanities Review', xii (1968), pp.115-25.

HARRISON, B.H., The Sunday trading riots of 1855,
'Historical Journal', viii (1965), pp.219-45.

HARRISON, B.H., Drink and sobriety in England, 1815-1872, 'International Review of Social History', xii (1967), pp. 204-76.

HARRISON, B.H., Two roads to social reform: Francis Place and the 'Drunken Committee' of 1834, 'Historical Journal', xi (1968), pp.272-300.

HARRISON, B.H., Religion and recreation in nineteenth century England, 'Past and Present', 38 (1968), pp.98-125.

HARRISON, B.H., Pubs, in H.J.Dyos and M.Wolff, 'The Victorian City', 2 vols (1973), i, pp.161-90.

JOHNSON, R., Educational policy and social control in early Victorian England, 'Past and Present', 49 (1970), pp.96-119.

JONES, G.S., Working-class culture and working-class politics in London, 1870-1900: notes on the remaking of a working class, 'Journal of Social History', vii (1974), pp.460-508.

KENT, C., The Whittington Club: a bohemian experiment in middle-class social reform, 'Victorian Studies', xviii (1974), pp.31-55.

MCGREGOR, O.R., Social research and social policy in the nineteenth century, 'British Journal of Sociology', viii (1957), pp.146-57.

MANDLE, W.F., The professional cricketer in England in the nineteenth century, 'Labour History', xxiii (1972), pp.1-16.

MANDLE, W.F., Games people played: cricket and football in England and Victoria in the late nineteenth century, 'Historical Studies', xv (1973), pp.511-35.

MARRUS, M.R., Social drinking in the belle époque, 'Journal of Social History', vii (1974), pp.115-41.

MEACHAM, S., 'The sense of an impending clash': English working-class unrest before the First World War, 'American Historical Review', lxxvii (1972), pp.1343-64.

MERTON, R.K., The role-set: problems in sociological theory, 'British Journal of Sociology', viii (1957), pp. 112-20.

MORRIS, R.J., Leeds and the Crystal Palace, 'Victorian Studies', xiii (1970), pp.283-300.

MORRIS, R.J., The history of self-help, 'New Society', 3 December 1970.

MYERSCOUGH, J., The recent history of the use of leisure time, in I.Appleton, ed., 'Leisure Research and Policy' (Edinburgh, 1974), pp.3-16.

PLUMB, J.H., The public, literature and the arts in the eighteenth century, in P.Fritz and D.Williams, eds, 'The Triumph of Culture: Eighteenth Century Perspectives' (Toronto, 1972), pp.27-48.

PRICE, R.N., The working men's club movement and Victorian

social reform ideology, 'Victorian Studies', xv (1971), pp.117-47.

REID, D., The decline of Saint Monday, 1766-1876, 'Past and Present', 71 (1976), pp.76-101.

SCOTT, P., Cricket and the religious world in the Victorian period, 'Church Quarterly', iii (1970), pp. 134-44.

SENELICK, L., Politics as entertainment: Victorian music-hall songs, 'Victorian Studies', xix (1975), pp.149-80.

SHIMAN, L.L., The Band of Hope movement: respectable recreation for working-class children, 'Victorian Studies', xviii (1973), pp.49-74.

STORCH, R.D., The plague of blue locusts: police reform and popular resistance in northern England, 1840-57, 'International Review of Social History', xx (1975), pp. 61-90.

STORCH, R.D., The policeman as domestic missionary: urban discipline and popular culture in northern England, 1850-1880, 'Journal of Social History', ix (1976), pp.481-509.

TAYLOR, I.R., Soccer consciousness and soccer hooliganism, in S.Cohen, ed., 'Images of Deviance' (1971), pp.134-64.

THOMAS, K., Work and leisure in pre-industrial society, 'Past and Present', 29 (1964), pp.50-66.

THOMPSON, E.P., Time, work-discipline, and industrial capitalism, 'Past and Present', 38 (1967), pp.56-97.

THOMPSON, E.P., Patrician society, plebeian culture, 'Journal of Social History', vii (1974), pp.382-405.

WEBER, E., Gymnastics and sports in fin de siècle France: opium of the classes?, 'American Historical Review', lxxvi (1971), pp.70-97.

WILSON, C., Economy and society in late-Victorian Britain, 'Economic History Review', xviii (1965), pp.183-98.

Work and leisure in industrial society: conference report, 'Past and Present', 30 (1965), pp.96-103.

Working-class culture: conference report, 'Bull.SSLH', 9 (1964), pp.3-8.

The working class and leisure-class expression and/or social control: conference report, 'Bull.SSLH', 32 (1976), pp.5-18.

YEO, E., Robert Owen and radical culture, in S.Pollard and J.Salt, eds, 'Robert Owen: Prophet of the Poor' (Lewisburg, Pa, 1971), pp.84-114.

C Dissertations

ALLAN, K., 'Recreations and Amusements of the Industrial Working Class in the second quarter of the Nineteenth Century, with special reference to Lancashire', University of Manchester MA thesis, 1947.

DINGSDALE, A., 'Bolton: A Study in Urban Geography, 1793-1910', University of Durham BA Hons thesis, 1967.

ELSWORTH, M.H., 'The Provision for Physical Recreation in Bolton in the Nineteenth Century', University of Manchester Diploma in Advanced Study in Education dissertation, 1972.

FRANKLE, B.S., 'The Genteel Family: High-Victorian Conceptions of Domesticity and Good Behaviour', University of Wisconsin PhD thesis, 1969.

MOLYNEUX, D.D., 'The Development of Physical Education in the Birmingham District, 1871-1892', University of Birmingham MA thesis, 1957.

SMITH, M.B., 'The Growth and Development of Popular Entertainments and Pastimes in the Lancashire Cotton Towns, 1830-1870', University of Lancaster MLitt thesis, 1970.

Index

Acts of Parliament: Bank
    Holidays, 81; Beer-
    shops, 23,28; Cruelty
    to Animals, 18; Edu-
    cation (1870), 130;
    Enclosures, 38; Limited
    Liability, 149; Public
    Libraries, 39; Ten
    Hours, 13-14,49-50,56;
    Theatre, 149,193n73
Adams, W.E., 20
Agnew, Sir Andrew, 18
Airlie, James, 100
Amateur Athletic Associ-
    ation, 140
Amateur Athletic Club, 131
    134,140,199n12
Amateur Rowing Association,
    131
Aristocracy: conduct as
    leisure class, 40,64,
    73-4; patronage of
    traditional sports,
    22-5; recreational
    reform and, 40-1,92,
    111-12; see also
    Gentleman, the
Army officers, 75,156,
    194n10
Arnold, Matthew, 63,124,173
Arnold, Thomas, 127
Ashworth, Edmund and Henry,
    15,43,50,58,78,114-15
Aston Villa FC, 139

'Athletic News', 142,218n49
Athletics, 131,132-4,135,
    140; see also Pedestri-
    anism

Bainbridge, John, 108,109
Baker, Edward, 86
Baker, Robert, 81-2,180
Bamford, Samuel, 11,57,90
Barber's shop, as working-
    class rendezvous, 86
Barclay, Tom, 86
Barmaids, 16,148
Barnett, Canon, 172
Baths, public, 50,51,82
Beal, James, 120
'Beehive', 115
Beer, see Drink, alcoholic
Beershops, 28,107
Belle Vue, 15
'Bell's Life in London',
    28,87,133
Besant, Walter: 'Ready-
    Money Mortiboy', 154,
    159; other references,
    57,100,105,121
Best, Geoffrey, 175
Bicycle Union, 131,218n49
Bicycling, 77,131,218n49
Bill Banks's day out, see
    Wright, Thomas
Billiards, 60,69
Birmingham: football and

248

STUDIES IN SOCIAL HISTORY

Editor: *HAROLD PERKIN*

Professor of Social History, University of Lancaster

Assistant Editor: *ERIC J. EVANS*

Lecturer in History, University of Lancaster

◇◇